HOME REPAIR
WITHOUT DESPAIR

THE FAMILY
Handyman

HOME REPAIR

WITHOUT DESPAIR

08-12-2011

SMART IDEAS FOR SAVING THOU$ANDS

Reader's
Digest

The Reader's Digest Association, Inc.
Pleasantville, New York/Montreal

A READER'S DIGEST BOOK

Copyright © 2010 The Reader's Digest Association, Inc.

FOR THE FAMILY HANDYMAN
(See page 287 for a complete staff listing.)
Editor in Chief: Ken Collier
Project Editor: Mary Flanagan
Contributing Designers: Joel Anderson, Pamela Griffith, Teresa Marrone
Contributing Copy Editors: Donna Bierbach, Peggy Parker
Vice President, Publisher: Lora Gier

FOR READER'S DIGEST
U.S. Project Editor: Kim Casey
Project Production Coordinator: Wayne Morrison
Indexer: Andrea Chesman
Senior Art Director: George McKeon
Executive Editor, Trade Publishing: Dolores York
Manufacturing Manager: Elizabeth Dinda
Associate Publisher, Trade Publishing: Rosanne McManus
President and Publisher, Trade Publishing: Harold Clarke

Library of Congress Cataloging in Publication Data is available upon request.

ISBN 13: 978-1-60652-135-9

We are committed to both the quality of our products and the service we provide to our customers. We value your comments, so please feel free to contact us.

The Reader's Digest Association, Inc.
Adult Trade Publishing
Reader's Digest Road
Pleasantville, NY 10570-7000

For more Reader's Digest products and information, visit our website at www.rd.com.

For more information about *The Family Handyman* magazine, visit www.thefamilyhandyman.com.

Printed in China

1 3 5 7 9 10 8 6 4 2

WARNING: All do-it-yourself activities involve a degree of risk. Skills, materials, tools, and site conditions vary widely. Although the editors have made every effort to ensure accuracy, the reader remains responsible for the selection and use of tools, materials, and methods. Always obey local codes and laws, follow manufacturer's operating instructions, and observe safety precautions.

Contents

(continued on page 6)

Contents

Introduction

Since the 1950s, *The Family Handyman* magazine has been written for and by do-it-yourselfers. As a group, we DIYers relish the satisfaction of a job well done, and the pleasure of being able to pass along what we know to others. *Home Repair without Despair* brings you a collection of the best projects, techniques, hints and tips from our issues. Within, our editors share their knowledge, enthusiasm and real-life experience.

We hope you are inspired by this book. From the editors of *The Family Handyman*, best of luck with all of your DIY endeavors.

—The staff of *The Family Handyman* magazine

SAFETY FIRST–ALWAYS!

Tackling home improvement projects and repairs can be endlessly rewarding. But, as most of us know, with the rewards come risks. As you go about your home improvement projects and repairs, stay alert for these hazards:

Aluminum wiring Aluminum wiring, installed in about 7 million homes between 1965 and 1973, requires special techniques and materials to make safe connections. This wiring is dull gray, not the dull orange characteristic of copper. Hire a licensed electrician certified to work with it. For more information visit inspect-ny.com/aluminum.htm.

Asbestos Texture sprayed on ceilings before 1978, adhesives and tiles for vinyl and asphalt floors before 1980, and vermiculite insulation (with gray granules) all may contain asbestos. Other building materials, made between 1940 and 1980, could also contain asbestos. If you suspect that materials you're removing or working around contain asbestos, contact your health department or visit epa.gov/asbestos for information.

Smoke alarms According to statistics, this year fire will claim the lives of 30 of our readers and the homes of 500 others. Don't become part of this statistic. Well over 60 percent of house-fire fatalities occur in homes that are missing smoke alarms or have disabled alarms or alarms with dead batteries. Test your smoke alarms every month and replace units that are more than 10 years old.

Backdrafting As you make your home more energy-efficient and airtight, existing ducts and chimneys can't always successfully vent combustion gases, including potentially deadly carbon monoxide (CO). Install a UL-listed CO detector.

Buried utilities A few days before you dig in your yard, have your underground water, gas and electrical lines marked. Just dial 811 or go to call811.com.

Five-gallon buckets From 1984–2003, more than 200 children drowned in 5-gallon buckets. Store empty buckets upside down and store ones with liquids with the cover securely snapped.

Lead paint If your home was built before 1979, it may contain lead paint, which is a serious health hazard, especially for children six and under. Take precautions when you scrape or remove it. Contact your public health department for detailed safety information or call (800) 424-LEAD to receive an information pamphlet.

Spontaneous combustion Rags saturated with oil finishes like Danish oil and linseed oil, and oil-based paints and stains can spontaneously combust if left bunched up. Always dry them outdoors, spread out loosely. When the oil has thoroughly dried, you can safely throw them in the trash.

Mini-blind and other cords for window coverings

According to Parents for Window Blind Safety, more than 768 children have died from corded window treatments since 1973. Most accidents occur when infants in cribs near windows become entangled in looped cords or when toddlers looking out windows or climbing furniture lose their footing and becoming wrapped up in cords. Recalls, regulations, new products and new designs have lessened the dangers, but older existing window covering cords still pose a threat, and some experts maintain that no corded window treatment—old or new—is completely safe. In addition, some older vinyl blinds present a lead poisoning threat. For more information visit windowblindskillchildren.org or the Consumer Product Safety Commission at cpsc.gov or (800) 638-2772.

1 Interior Projects, Repairs & Remodeling

IN THIS CHAPTER

REPLACE YOUR WEATHER STRIP

COMPASS

SCRIBED LINE

OLD SWEEP

1 Scribe a line on the door 3/8 in. above the top of the threshold. Remove the door and carefully cut along the line with a circular saw.

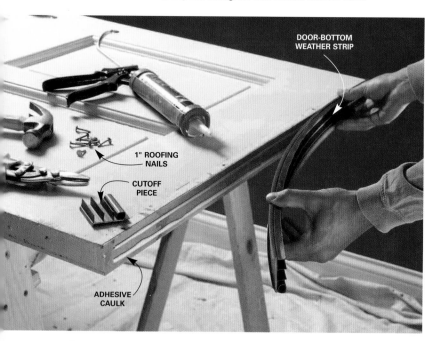

DOOR-BOTTOM WEATHER STRIP

1" ROOFING NAILS

CUTOFF PIECE

ADHESIVE CAULK

2 Cut the door bottom to length with tin snips or a utility knife. Apply two parallel beads of adhesive caulk the length of the door and nail the door bottom to the door.

Older wood doors usually rely on a non-adjustable threshold to keep the weather out. If your old door doesn't seal tight against the threshold, you're wasting energy. You could screw a surface-applied weather strip to the face of the door, but a door-bottom weather strip is a less obtrusive way to create a good seal.

The door bottom we're using is available at most home centers and hardware stores. If you can't find a door bottom that's smooth on one side, you can slice off the barbed flanges from bottoms designed for steel or fiberglass doors.

Cut the bottom of the door to allow enough (but not too much) clearance to install the new door bottom. The goal is to create an even 3/8-in. space between the top of the existing threshold and the bottom of the door. Close the door and measure the largest gap between the door and the threshold. If the gap is less than 3/8 in., calculate how much you'll have to cut off the bottom to equal 3/8 in. Mark this distance on the door at the point you measured. Then use a scribing tool to extend a mark across the bottom of the door (**Photo 1**).

Remove the hinge pins and move the door to a set of sawhorses. Mount a sharp blade in your circular saw and cut along the line. Protect the surface of the door with masking tape. If you have a veneered door, score along the line with a sharp utility knife before sawing to avoid chipping the veneer.

Cut the door-bottom weather strip about 1/8 in. shorter than the width of the door and tack it to the bottom of the door with a staple gun. Rehang the door to test the fit. If it's too snug, remove the weather strip and trim a bit more from the door. When the fit is perfect, remove the staples and mount the weather strip (**Photo 2**).

TWO JALOUSIE WINDOW FIXES

1 Replace broken glass

Putting in a new piece of jalousie window glass is an easy, straightforward fix. However, because the glass is thicker than standard glass and has polished edges, it usually has to be special-ordered ($20 to $25 per pane, from glass companies or hardware stores). Bring exact glass dimensions and a chunk of the broken glass to get the right thickness.

Remove the setscrews in the metal housing at each end of the glass, then take out the metal wedges that hold the glass (**Photo 1**). Hold on to the setscrews—they're tiny and disappear instantly if dropped. Carefully pull the broken glass out when the wedges are out.

Clean any dirt and corrosion out of the metal housing at the ends, then slide in the new glass (**Photo 2**).

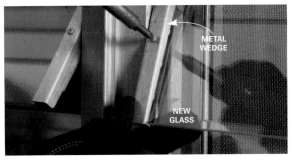

1 Hold the glass in place and carefully slide the metal wedge out of the way so the glass will slip out.

2 Set the new glass into place, push the wedges back in, then lock them into place with the setscrews.

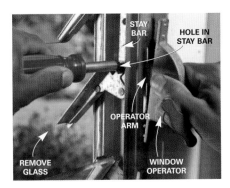

1 Push the stay bar pivot pin out of the operator arm by pushing a screwdriver through the hole in the stay bar.

2 Install a new window operator

Jalousie window operators can fail because of worn-out gears, corrosion or lack of lubrication. First try cleaning and applying silicone lubricant to all the moving parts. If that doesn't help, the only fix is to replace them. Jalousie windows and doors are no longer being made, but replacement hardware for most types is still available, either at hardware stores or on the Internet (see the Buyer's Guide).

For easier access, first take out the glass pane near the broken operator. Remove the screws that hold the operator in place, then disengage the stay bar (the bar that controls the window movement) and the operator arm (**Photo 1**).

Fit the new operator back into place, reattach it to the stay bar (**Photo 2**) and put the glass pane back in.

To keep the window working smoothly, periodically clean out dirt and debris from the track and pivots with compressed air or a vacuum and spray all moving parts with silicone lubricant.

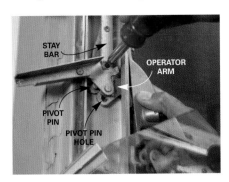

2 Guide the pivot pin back into the new operator arm, then screw the operator to the frame.

Buyer's Guide

Here are two sources for jalousie window parts:

■ BLAINE WINDOW: blainewindow.com. (800) 678-1919.
■ SWISCO INC.: swisco.com

FROM
GRUNGY...

TO GREAT!

UPGRADE YOUR LAUNDRY SINK

Replacing a grungy old laundry sink is a simple Saturday morning project that will dramatically improve the looks of your laundry room. And you can make your sink more functional too by upgrading from a typical laundry faucet to a kitchen sink faucet with a convenient sprayer and soap dispenser.

You'll find a selection of laundry sinks and kitchen faucets at home centers. Inspect your sink plumbing before you shop and make a list of the parts you'll need. If your old trap assembly is chrome plated, consider replacing it with plastic. Plastic traps are easier to install and maintain. Also, buy flexible braided stainless steel supply tubes. They simplify the task of connecting the faucet to the water supply. We spent $175 for the sink, faucet, and new supply tubes and drain parts.

Start by closing the water valves that lead to the faucet and disconnecting the supply tubes. Put a small pail under the trap to catch the water, then remove the trap by unscrewing the large slip nuts (**Photo 1**). Then, remove the screws that may secure the laundry sink to the wall

and remove the sink.

Your new laundry sink may have punch-outs for a laundry faucet, but if you'll be installing a kitchen faucet, don't use them. Drill holes instead. Check your new faucet to determine the hole locations and mark them on the sink. Drill the holes with a 1-1/2-in. hole saw (**Photo 2**). To enlarge an existing hole, clamp a scrap of wood to the bottom of the sink deck, under the existing hole. Then mark the center of the new hole on the wood and drill the hole with a hole saw as you normally would. The wood scrap will keep the hole saw centered.

Mount the faucet and soap dispenser on the sink according to the manufacturer's instructions (**Photo 3**). Then move the laundry sink into position (**Photo 4**). Hand-tighten the braided stainless supply tube nuts onto the valves and then tighten one more revolution to create a good seal. If you're using new plastic drain parts, use a hacksaw to cut the trap arm and tailpiece to fit. Secure the sink to the wall with adhesive caulk or screws.

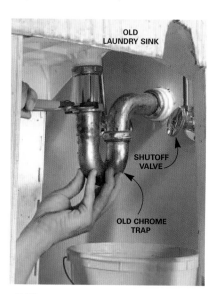

1 Disconnect the plumbing and remove the screws that hold the sink to the wall.

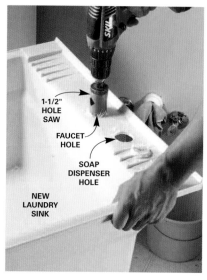

2 Drill holes in the sink for the new faucet and soap dispenser.

REMOVE OLD CAULK THE EASY WAY

Scraping out moldy caulk from around a bathtub is a tough, tedious job. And if you get too aggressive, you'll chip a tile or mar the tub finish. Make the job a lot easier by first softening the caulk with a caulk remover (less than $10 at hardware stores).

Application is simple. Just squeeze the remover onto the caulk, making sure it covers the edges (**Photo 1**). Let it sit for several hours (or as directed on the package). Then start scraping out the old caulk (**Photo 2**). The caulk remover works by destroying the bond between the caulk and the tub or tile, so that instead of chipping at the caulk with a razor blade, you just pull away big chunks of it with a putty knife. Most removers work on both silicone and acrylic latex caulks.

Clean off the residue with soap and water, let dry and then recaulk.

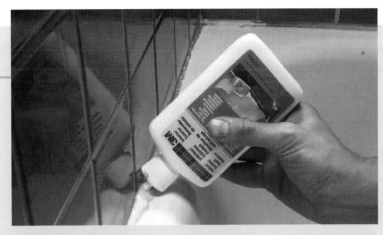

1 Spread a wide bead of caulk remover along the caulk line, covering it completely.

2 Remove the loosened caulk with a putty knife, pulling it out from the gap between the tile and the tub.

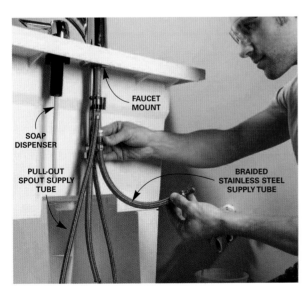

SOAP DISPENSER

FAUCET MOUNT

PULL-OUT SPOUT SUPPLY TUBE

BRAIDED STAINLESS STEEL SUPPLY TUBE

3 Mount the faucet and soap dispenser to the laundry sink according to the instructions with the faucet. Connect the braided supply tubes to the faucet.

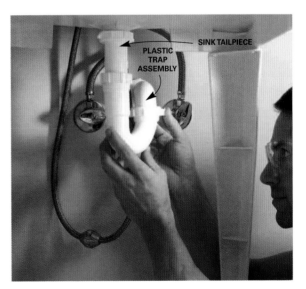

SINK TAILPIECE

PLASTIC TRAP ASSEMBLY

4 Connect the supply lines to the shutoff valves. Cut and install the new drain parts.

STORAGE SOLUTIONS

Clutter-busting strategies for every room in your home

The Family Handyman has hidden in a top-secret location the world's largest collection of storage ideas: everything from architectural plans to sketches on napkins and wrinkled old photos, plus thousands of clever suggestions sent in by our readers. We rounded up some professional storage gurus and together we dug into that enormous mess, argued about which tips were the best, and created this collection of our favorite storage tips and advice.

Maximize closet space

There's no such thing as a closet that's big enough. But you can store more stuff in the space you already have with a closet organizer system. For economy and quick installation, you can't beat wire-shelving systems; you can outfit a typical closet in an afternoon for less than $200. Home centers have everything you need. But before you go shopping, spend a few minutes online checking out options, accessories and installation steps. Two good sites to browse are closetmaid.com and rubbermaid.com.

If you want a more elegant look, be prepared to spend hundreds more—or build your own. We built this plywood version in a couple of weekends for about $300. Despite its furniture-grade appearance, it's a project any intermediate woodworker can handle. To see how to build a storage system in your closet, go to thefamilyhandyman.com and search for "closet system."

Boost bathroom storage

Many bathrooms have wall space, usually next to the door, that's perfect for an extra medicine cabinet—or even two. With "recessed" cabinets that fit between studs, you don't lose an inch of bathroom space. Medicine cabinets are available at home centers starting at about $35. To browse a broad range of styles, search online for "medicine cabinet." To see how to install one, go to thefamilyhandyman.com and search for "behind door medicine cabinet."

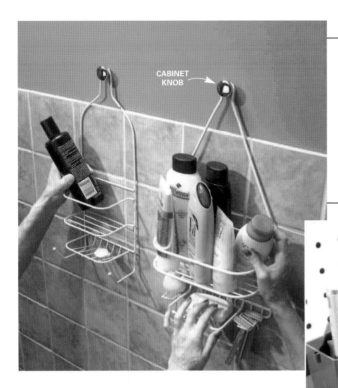

More shower shelves

The trouble with those shower caddies that hang from the showerhead pipe is that you have only one showerhead. To get more space for your bath potions, hang another caddy on a cabinet knob. With a No. 8-32 hanger screw, you can screw the knob into a stud. To fasten to drywall, use a screw-in drywall anchor along with the hanger screw.

Easy-mount mini bins

Electrical junction boxes can hold a lot more than wiring. You can nail or screw them to just about anything anywhere. In the shop, they're great for those tools that can't hang on hooks—tape measures, markers, chisels. Plastic boxes come in various sizes and shapes and cost 75¢ to $3 each.

Optimize cabinet space

Lower cabinets offer the biggest storage spaces in your kitchen. But the back half of cabinets is usually wasted—it's filled with forgotten stuff or left empty because it's out of sight and out of reach. Rollout shelves reclaim that space. You can buy rollouts or build your own. To see how we built these rollouts, which fit around plumbing under a sink, go to thefamilyhandyman.com and search for "sink roll out." To see another version, search for "cabinet roll out." To buy rollouts (starting at about $45 each), visit a home center or search online for "cabinet rollout."

Fill those cavities

An unfinished wall or ceiling isn't an eyesore; it's a storage opportunity. With 15 bucks' worth of shelf hardware and 1x4s, you can pack 8 ft. or more of storage into one wall stud cavity. For about $2 per ft., you can turn ceiling joist space into storage space with wire shelving, although we discovered that this is a bad place to store basketballs.

Giant twist ties

Don't toss out those leftover scraps of electrical cable. They let you bundle up and neatly store all kinds of stuff. To hang up or carry your bundle, twist a loop in the cable.

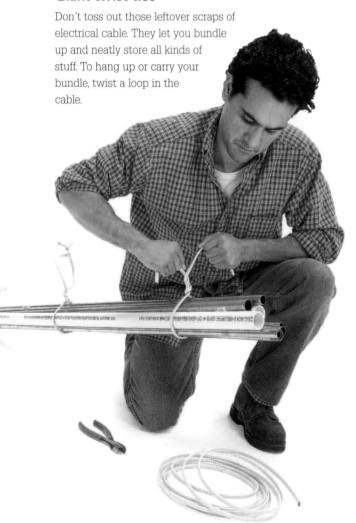

DIVIDER

Add slim spaces to cabinets

Every kitchen needs a slot for flat cookware like cookie sheets and pizza pans. The simplest way to create these slots is to add extra shelves spaced a few inches apart. Since most cabinets have adjustable shelves, you just have to pick up a bag of shelf supports at a home center ($3) and cut new shelves from plywood or particleboard. A vertical niche like the one shown here is a bit more convenient than shelves because the stored items aren't stacked up; you can pull out one sheet without removing the whole stack. To make it, just add a plywood divider, drill holes for shelf supports and shorten the existing adjustable shelf.

HandyHints®

EASIER GROUT HAZE CLEANUP

The thousands of microscopic fabric hooks on a microfiber cloth make it perfect to cut through the dried grout haze left after a tiling project. You'll still have to rinse and repeat, but the haze will clean up faster than it would with an ordinary rag.

SOLO DRYWALL HANGING

Hanging that top course of drywall is challenging when you're alone. Make the job easier by creating a simple bracket between 1 and 2 ft. from each end of the sheet with a couple of 16d nails. Just sink them into the studs 48-1/2 in. down from the ceiling and about 1 in. deep. Hoist the sheet and rest the bottom edge on the nails. Push the sheet up against the ceiling with one hand and tack it into place with the other with a few prestarted drywall nails.

NAIL

PHOTO POSITIONING

To hang a picture frame right where you want it, make a guide for your nail. Tape over the head of a thumbtack or stick the head on double-faced tape right under the picture's mounting bracket. Hold the picture in place and push on the frame until the tack's point pricks the wall. Now you have a tiny mark to show you where to place your hanging nail.

NO-HANGMAN ZONE

MARKER CLEANUP

When the permanent marker has ended up in the wrong hands, vegetable oil can clean it off lots of surfaces—even skin! Then just wipe up with a damp cloth and you're done.

MAKE **OLD** WINDOWS LIKE **NEW**

Don't replace casement windows— repair them

If you're thinking about replacing your casement windows because they're drafty, fogged up or just hard to open, consider this: You can fix most of the problems yourself for a fraction of the cost of new windows—and it won't take you more than an hour or two per window. In this story, we'll walk you through the fixes for the most common casement window problems. (Casement windows are the type that swing like doors.) You won't need any specialty tools, and the materials are available from most window manufacturers or online window supply companies (see the Buyer's Guide, p. 20).

Although your windows may look different from the ones shown here, the techniques for removing the sash and fixing problems are similar.

Fix a stripped crank handle

If you turn your window handle and nothing happens, the gears on your handle, crank operator shaft or both are probably stripped. Take off the handle and look for signs of wear. If the teeth are worn, replace the handle (prices start at $5; see the Buyer's Guide, p. 20). If the shaft is worn, you can replace the whole operator (see the next fix). But here's a home remedy to try first.

Start by backing out the setscrew to remove the handle (some newer handles don't have setscrews and simply pull off—and this fix won't work). If you have a folding handle, mark where the setscrew is on the operator shaft when the window is closed and the handle is folded up. Remove the handle and file the shaft so the setscrew can lock onto the shaft (**photo right**). The metal is tough; it'll take about 15 minutes to get a flat side. Or use a rotary tool with a grinder bit to speed up the job. Vacuum the shavings out of the operator so they won't harm the moving parts.

Reattach the handle with a longer setscrew (35¢ at hardware stores). If you open and close the window a lot, this fix may not hold up in the long run.

SETSCREW

OPERATOR SHAFT

File a flat spot on the operator shaft, then insert a longer setscrew into the handle. The flat side lets the setscrew lock onto the shaft.

1 Open the window until the crank arm bushing is aligned with the guide track notch. Push down on the arm to pop the bushing out of the track.

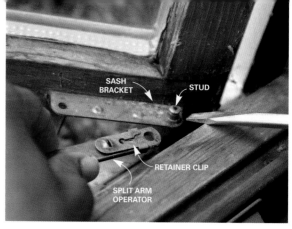

2 Slide back the retainer clip on the arm and pry the arm off the stud on the sash bracket with a screwdriver.

Replace a stubborn crank operator

If the splines on the crank operator shaft are worn or broken off, the gears don't turn easily or at all, then it's time to replace the crank operator (prices start at $20).

You don't need the make, model or serial number of the crank operator. You just need a picture. Snap a digital photo, email it to a hardware supply company (see the Buyer's Guide) and the company will sell you a new one. Or mail the company a print photo. You can also look at online catalogs at the Web sites listed on p. 20 to find an operator that matches yours.

To replace the operator, first take the crank arm off the sash. Most crank arms slip out of a notch on the guide track on the sash (**Photo 1**). Others are pried off with a flathead screwdriver, or a channel is unscrewed from along the bottom of the sash. If the operator also contains a split arm operator, unhook that, too (**Photo 2**).

Slide or pry off the operator cover. If you have a removable cover, cut along the casement cover with a utility knife to slice through any paint or stain that seals it on the window jamb. Remove the trim screws along the top of

3 Lift off the casement cover to expose the crank operator. Remove the screws, take out the crank operator and replace it.

the casement cover. Gently pry the cover loose (**Photo 3**). Be careful—the cover can easily break! Unscrew the crank operator. Set the new operator in place, aligning it with the existing screw holes, and screw it to the jamb. If the cover isn't removable, crank operator screws will be accessible on the exterior of the window.

Align the new hinge arm with the screw holes and fasten it into place. If the screw holes are stripped out, fill them with toothpicks dipped in wood glue, let the glue dry, then cut the toothpicks flush.

Replace a sagging hinge

Over time, hinge arms that support heavy windows can start to sag, causing the sash to hit the frame in the lower corner that's opposite the hinge. First make sure the window sash is square and centered in the window opening. If it's not, see the fix on p. 20. To eliminate drag in a window that fits squarely, replace the hinge arms at the top and the bottom of the window. You can buy the hinges at window hardware supply stores (see the Buyer's Guide, p. 20). Prices start at $16.

Remove the sash from the window. The hinge arms are located near a corner or in the middle of the window frame. Unscrew the hinge arms from the window, then install the new ones in the same locations (**photo left**).

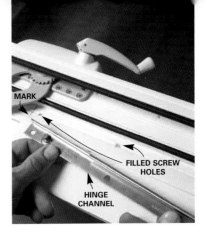

1 Open the sash and disconnect the crank arm. Pry the split arm operator off the top and the bottom of the sash with a screwdriver (the hinge arms easily pop off).

2 Slide the hinge shoes out of the hinge channels at the top and bottom of the window to remove the sash.

3 Set the hinge channel in place, slightly over from its former location. Drill new holes, then screw it to the jamb.

Fix a sticking window

If you have a window that drags against the frame when you open it, close the window and examine it from the outside. The sash should fit squarely and be centered in the frame. If not, you can adjust the position of the sash by slightly moving the hinge channel. (If the window is centered and square but still drags, see "Replace a sagging hinge" on p. 19.)

You can move the channel at the top or the bottom of the window, depending on where the sash is dragging (but don't move both channels). Start by taking out the sash (Photos 1 and 2). If the hinge arm is screwed to the sash, see Photo 1, p. 21.

Mark the hinge channel location on the frame, then unscrew the channel. Fill the screw holes with epoxy (for vinyl windows) or wood filler (for wood windows). Filling the holes keeps the screws from realigning with their old locations when you reinstall the channel. Scrape the filled holes smooth before the epoxy sets. Place the channel back on the jamb, about 1/8 in. over from the mark (move the channel away from the side of the sash that's dragging), drill 1/8-in. pilot holes and then reinstall the channel (Photo 3).

Figure A: Casement window operation

When you turn the handle, the operator moves the crank arm and the split arm operator. The split arm operator then opens the window sash. Casement window operators come in several styles. They may look complex, but they're easy to disconnect, remove and replace.

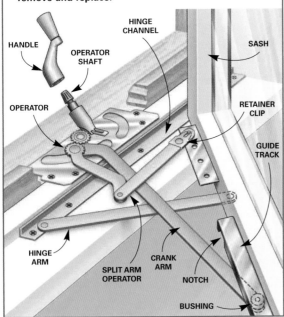

Is the window "glued" shut?

If the window is stuck shut, it's likely that the weather strip is sticking. After you muscle it open, spray silicone lubricant on a rag and wipe it on the weather stripping. Silicone lubricants, such as DuPont Teflon, start at $4 per can. Don't use oily lubricants; they attract dust.

Buyer's Guide

■ **BLAINE WINDOW HARDWARE:** Window hardware, including hard to find and obsolete hardware parts. Will find your replacement parts using your photos. (800) 678-1919. blainewindow.com

■ **GLASS DISTRIBUTORS:** Window hardware. (301) 779-2430. glassdistributorsinc.com

■ **PRIME-LINE PRODUCTS:** Replacement handles. Prime-line-products.com

■ **REPLACEMENT HARDWARE MFG:** Window hardware, including obsolete parts. Will find replacement parts using your photos. (800) 780-5051. replacementhardware.com

■ **TRUTH HARDWARE:** Window hardware. Refers homeowners to regional distributors, which can find parts using your photos. (800) 866-7884. truth.com

Seal a drafty window

Weather stripping often becomes loose, worn or distorted when the sash drags or when the strip gets sticky and attaches itself to the frame, then pulls loose when the sash is opened. Windows have weather strip on the sash, frame or both. Regardless of its location, the steps for removing and replacing it are the same. Weather stripping is available from your window manufacturer (prices start at $15). The window brand and glass manufacturer date are etched in the corner of the glass or in the aluminum spacer between the glass panes. You'll also need the height and width of your sash (take these measurements yourself).

If the weather strip is in good shape and loose in only a few places, like the corners, apply a dab of polyurethane sealant ($5 at hardware stores) to the groove and press the weather strip into place. Otherwise, replace the entire weather strip. First remove the sash and set it on a work surface so you can access all four sides. If the weather strip is one continuous piece, cut it apart at the corners with a utility knife.

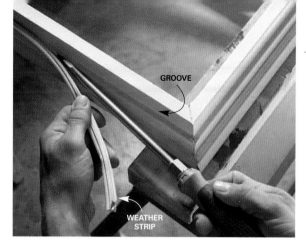

Work the old weather strip out of the groove gently to avoid tearing it and leaving the spline stuck in the groove.

Starting at a corner, pull the weather strip loose from the sash (**photo above**). If the spline tears off and remains stuck in the groove, make a hook from stiff wire to dig it out.

Work the new weather strip into the groove, starting at a corner. You'll hear it click as the strip slides into the groove.

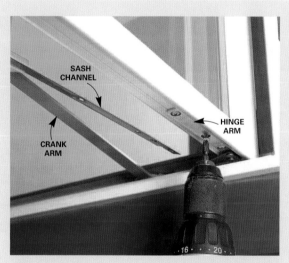

1 Take off the sash by removing the screws in the channel and the hinge arms. Then slide the sash off the hinge arms.

Replace a fogged sash

If you have broken glass or fogging (condensation between the glass panes), you'll have to replace the glass or the entire sash. If the sash is in good shape (not warped or cracked), you can sometimes replace just the glass. Call your window manufacturer to see whether glass replacement is an option and if a fogged window is covered under your warranty. You'll need the information that's etched into the corner of the glass and the sash dimensions.

2 Align the sash lip with the hinge arms, then slide the sash onto the hinges. Insert screws to fasten the sash in place.

Contact a glass repair specialist to have only the glass replaced. Prices start at $160 for a 17 x 36-in. window. Or you can replace the sash yourself. Order it through the manufacturer (prices start at $110).

To replace the sash, first remove the old one. You take this sash off by removing the hinge screws (**Photo 1**). For sashes that slide out, see **Photos 1 and 2**, p. 20. Remove any hardware from the damaged sash and install it on the new sash (this sash doesn't require any hardware).

Install the new sash by sliding it onto the hinge arms, then screw it to the hinges (**Photo 2**).

Do's&Don'ts

INSULATING WALLS

It's easy to insulate your walls with fiberglass insulation (at least when they're open!), but the job still requires attention to detail to get the maximum benefit. Every gap and compressed batt leaves a path for heat or cold to escape. Here are a few do's and don'ts to help you get the job done right.

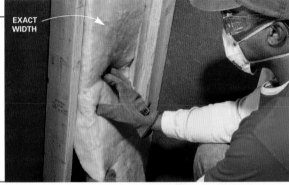

Do measure and cut the fiberglass batt for an **exact fit.** Add about 1/4 in. to the measurement to ensure a snug fit. Use a 4- to 6-in.-wide board or strip of plywood as a straightedge to guide your utility knife. Line up the edge of the board at the proper width, compress the insulation and cut it with a sharp utility knife. A scrap of plywood under the batt will protect finished floors and keep the blade from dulling on concrete.

EXACT WIDTH

Don't stuff full-width batts into spaces that are too narrow. Crumpling batts to fit narrow spaces creates uninsulated air pockets. And packed insulation has a lower R-value.

Don't buy paper-faced insulation for standard wall insulating jobs. The paper facing makes cutting the batts difficult. And it's hard to create a tight vapor retarder with paper-faced batts.

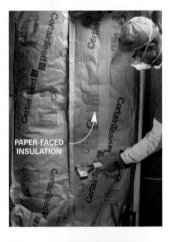

PAPER-FACED INSULATION

CRUMPLED BATT

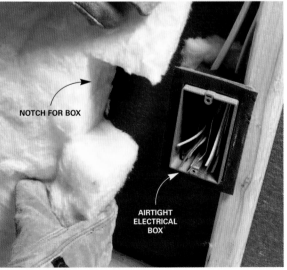

NOTCH FOR BOX

AIRTIGHT ELECTRICAL BOX

Do notch fiberglass batts around electrical **boxes.** Put the batt in place, and use a scissors to snip around the box. Tuck the snipped-out plug of insulation behind the box. Don't wrap fiberglass batts around electrical boxes or stuff full batts behind them. That creates gaps and air convection routes around the box.

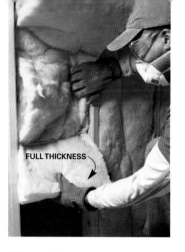

Don't tuck full-thickness batts behind pipes and cables. Compressing the fiberglass decreases its insulating value and creates voids between the insulation and the drywall.

Do split apart the batts to fit around wires and pipes to get the full value of the insulation.

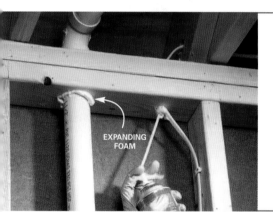

Do plug holes in the top and bottom plates with expanding spray foam. Even small holes can let a lot of air escape. Don't leave gaps around wires, pipes or ducts unplugged. These gaps create pathways for warm interior air to leak into the attic, wasting energy and causing attic condensation or even ice dams in cold climates.

Do buy unfaced friction-fit batts and seal the walls with a 4-mil poly vapor retarder. Seal the gap between the bottom plate of the wall and the floor with acoustical sealant or caulk. Press the poly into the sealant. Use special airtight electrical boxes (p. 22) or seal the poly to the electrical box with acoustical sealant. Tape the seams in the poly with sheathing tape.

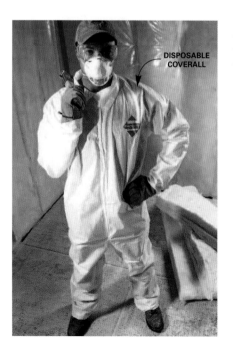

Do protect your skin, eyes and lungs when you're working with fiberglass. If you're installing a lot of it, consider wearing a disposable coverall ($6 to $10 at paint stores and home centers).

Do seal around window and door jambs with expanding spray foam. The main purpose of the spray foam is to seal the space around the window to prevent air infiltration. Use foam that's labeled for window and door insulating. This "minimal-expanding" type reduces the chance of warping the jamb. If there's still space around the window after the foam cures, lightly stuff the remaining space with strips of fiberglass insulation.

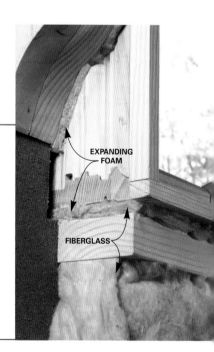

LAYING OUT TILE FOR TUBS & SHOWERS

Get started with the right layout and you can achieve a perfect tile job!

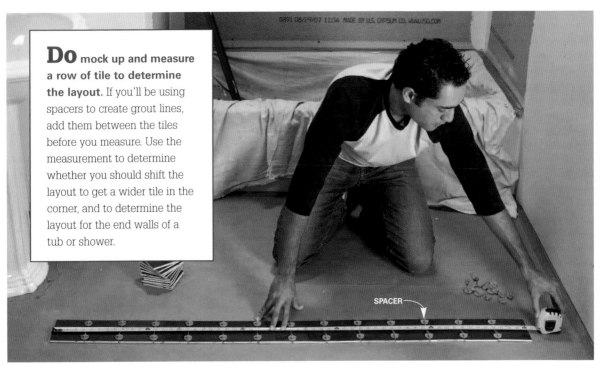

Do mock up and measure a row of tile to determine the layout. If you'll be using spacers to create grout lines, add them between the tiles before you measure. Use the measurement to determine whether you should shift the layout to get a wider tile in the corner, and to determine the layout for the end walls of a tub or shower.

SPACER

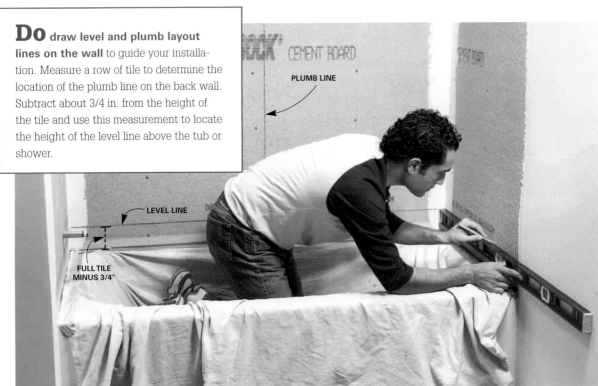

Do draw level and plumb layout lines on the wall to guide your installation. Measure a row of tile to determine the location of the plumb line on the back wall. Subtract about 3/4 in. from the height of the tile and use this measurement to locate the height of the level line above the tub or shower.

CEMENT BOARD

PLUMB LINE

LEVEL LINE

FULL TILE MINUS 3/4"

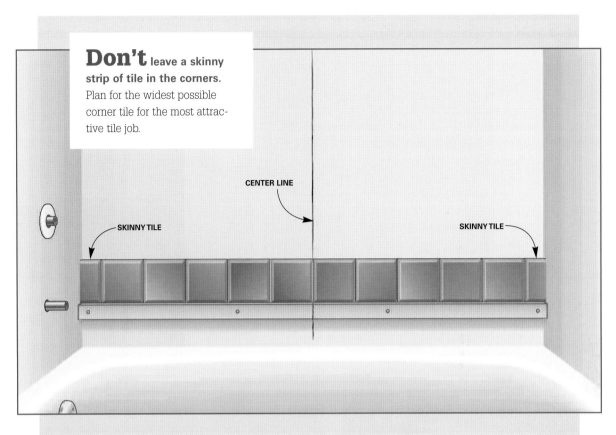

Don't leave a skinny strip of tile in the corners.

Plan for the widest possible corner tile for the most attractive tile job.

CENTER LINE

SKINNY TILE

SKINNY TILE

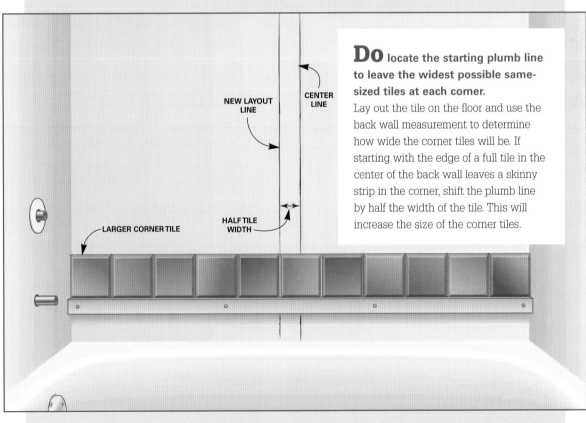

Do locate the starting plumb line to leave the widest possible same-sized tiles at each corner.

Lay out the tile on the floor and use the back wall measurement to determine how wide the corner tiles will be. If starting with the edge of a full tile in the center of the back wall leaves a skinny strip in the corner, shift the plumb line by half the width of the tile. This will increase the size of the corner tiles.

NEW LAYOUT LINE

CENTER LINE

HALF TILE WIDTH

LARGER CORNER TILE

Do's & Don'ts

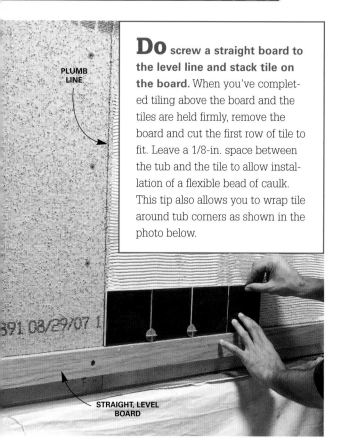

Do screw a straight board to the level line and stack tile on the board. When you've completed tiling above the board and the tiles are held firmly, remove the board and cut the first row of tile to fit. Leave a 1/8-in. space between the tub and the tile to allow installation of a flexible bead of caulk. This tip also allows you to wrap tile around tub corners as shown in the photo below.

PLUMB LINE

STRAIGHT, LEVEL BOARD

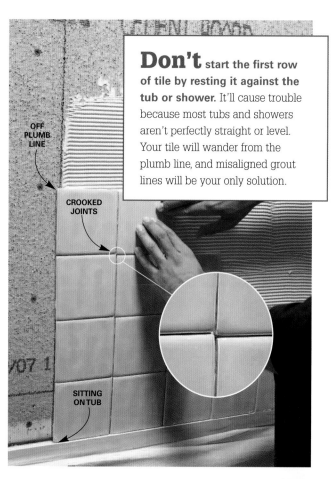

Don't start the first row of tile by resting it against the tub or shower. It'll cause trouble because most tubs and showers aren't perfectly straight or level. Your tile will wander from the plumb line, and misaligned grout lines will be your only solution.

OFF PLUMB LINE

CROOKED JOINTS

SITTING ON TUB

Do plan the tile layout so a column of tile extends past the end of the tub. Use the method shown in the top photo, p. 24, to determine how wide the corner tile needs to be in order to extend the tile beyond the tub. Plan to extend the tile 2 or 3 in. beyond the tub and to leave at least a half tile along the wall if possible.

NICE FIT

EXTEND PAST EDGE

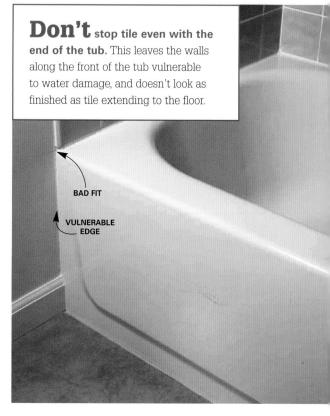

Don't stop tile even with the end of the tub. This leaves the walls along the front of the tub vulnerable to water damage, and doesn't look as finished as tile extending to the floor.

BAD FIT

VULNERABLE EDGE

DRYWALL **TAPING**

How to get better taping results with less hassle

Drywall taping is a skill that's easy to learn but tough to master. The good news is that by following the tips in this article, you can eliminate a lot of frustration. These tips will help you get off to a good start and prevent problems like bubbling tape, messed-up mud and cracked corners.

POTATO MASHER–TYPE MIXER

Do mix the compound. If you've just opened a bucket, remove about a quart of the joint compound to make room for water. Then add about two or three cups of water and start mixing the compound. Pros use a powerful 1/2-in. drill with a special mixing paddle. But a hand-powered giant "potato masher"–type mixer made for this purpose ($12) works great for the casual taper.

The best consistency for joint compound depends on its purpose. It should be pudding consistency for hand taping, and a little thicker for the final coats. For smaller jobs, transfer some of the joint compound to another pail before mixing so you can make custom batches for taping or finishing.

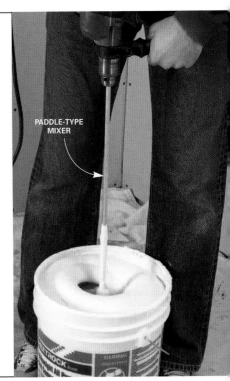

PADDLE-TYPE MIXER

Don't use compound right out of the pail. Joint compound straight from the pail is simply too thick to apply and spread evenly. So before you start taping, begin by thinning and mixing the joint compound.

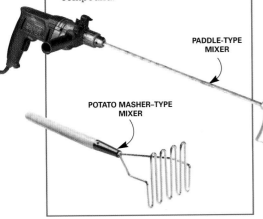

PADDLE-TYPE MIXER

POTATO MASHER–TYPE MIXER

Do prefill gaps with "setting" compound. Setting-type compound is perfect for prefilling because it hardens quickly and doesn't shrink as much as regular joint compound.

Start by breaking or cutting out areas of the drywall that are broken or crushed, then peel away any paper shreds left around the edges. Then mix up a small batch of setting-type compound (if you mix too much, it'll harden before you use it up). Mix it thick so it'll stick in the holes without sagging. When the compound sets to the hardness of soap, scrape off high spots and lumps with the edge of your taping knife. Also fill gaps between sheets with setting compound and let it harden before you apply joint compound and tape.

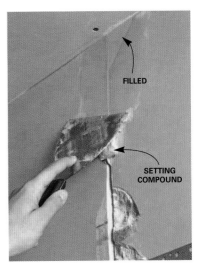

FILLED

SETTING COMPOUND

Do's & Don'ts

Do scrape ridges and bumps between coats.

Even experienced tapers leave little globs of joint compound and an occasional ridge. If you don't get rid of these after they dry, they'll cause you all kinds of grief. Chunks of dried compound can break off and get stuck under your taping knife and cause streaks in your fresh joint compound that you'll have to fill in later. Avoid the problem by scraping the joints between coats. All it takes is a quick once-over with a 6-in. taping knife to knock off ridges and bumps. Hold the knife at a low angle and push it across the taped joints.

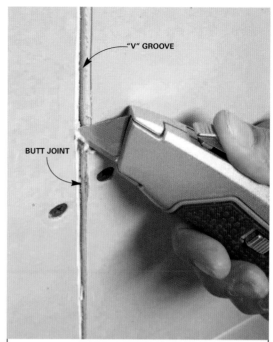

Do cut "V" grooves at butt joints.

The paper facing on drywall ends may show through the taped seam. Avoid this problem by carving a shallow "V" groove between the sheets after you hang them. Then fill the "V" with setting-type joint compound before you cover the seam with joint compound and tape. This will really help out with the toughest taping challenge—butt joints.

Do embed the tape completely.

You can avoid a lot of extra work later by making sure paper tape is thoroughly embedded in the joint compound. Start by laying a thick bed of joint compound down the center of the seam. Then smooth it down to a consistent thickness of about 1/8 in. with your 5- or 6-in. taping knife. Wet the tape and press it into the joint compound. Then, starting at the center and working toward the ends, press the tape into the joint compound with your knife. The key to success is making sure joint compound oozes out from under both sides of the tape as you embed it.

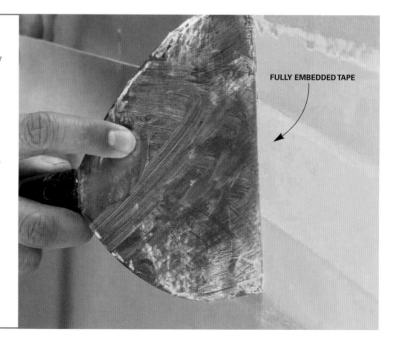

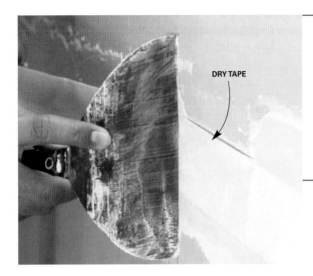

Don't leave dry tape. Paper tape that's not completely embedded in joint compound will bubble or fall off later when it dries. Keep a close eye on the tape as you embed it with the taping knife. If you see sections of the tape where one or both sides remain dry with no joint compound oozing out, pull off the tape and apply more joint compound under the dry areas. Then reapply the tape over the new joint compound.

Don't mud both sides of the corner at once. It's pretty easy to get a nearly flawless coat of joint compound on the first side of an inside corner. But if you start on the second side before the first is dry, things get tough. That's because it's impossible to avoid messing up the wet compound on the first side, and you won't be able to avoid making a groove in the corner.

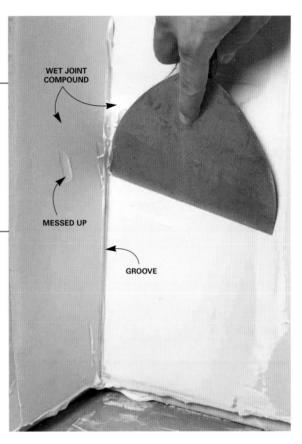

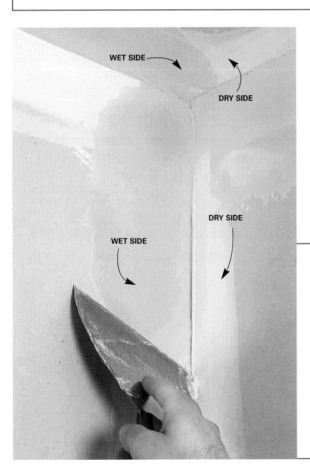

Do mud one side of the corner at a time. The trick is to coat one side of each corner and let it dry overnight before troweling joint compound on each adjacent side. Start by spreading about a 3-in. band of joint compound over the tape on one side of the corner. Then smooth it with a 5- or 6-in. taping knife. Press the outside edge of the knife against the drywall to create a feathered edge that won't require much sanding. Try to avoid leaving too much joint compound over the tape— a buildup at the corner will make it harder to fit baseboard or crown moldings tight to the wall.

Do's&Don'ts

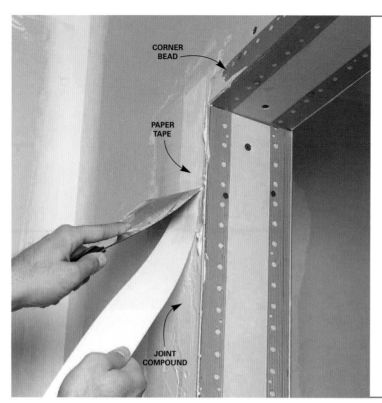

CORNER BEAD

PAPER TAPE

JOINT COMPOUND

Do tape over metal corner beads. Cracking along the edge of metal outside corner beads is a common problem. And usually it doesn't happen until after the wall is painted, so repairing the crack means repainting the wall again! There are a couple of solutions. One method that's become standard practice for professional tapers is to use special corner bead that is held on by joint compound rather than nails. No-Coat Ultratrim is one such product. For information on where to buy Ultratrim and other No-Coat products, go to no-coat.com.

If you don't want to go shopping for special corner bead, avoid future cracking by applying paper tape over the metal edge after you've nailed on the bead. Embed the tape just as you would on any joint. Then fill the corner as usual.

Do cut out bubbled or loose tape. Even if you're diligent about embedding the tape, you'll occasionally run into a section of tape that bubbles or comes loose. Don't try to bury the problem with more compound. It'll just reappear later. Instead, cut around the damaged area with a utility knife and remove the tape. Avoid a divot in this spot by filling the recess with setting compound and letting it harden before applying another coat of joint compound.

WET PAPER TAPE

Do wet the paper tape. Wetting the tape before you embed it in the joint compound can help eliminate troublesome bubbles that show up after the joint dries. Keep a bucket of water nearby and quickly run each piece of tape through it before applying the tape to the wall.

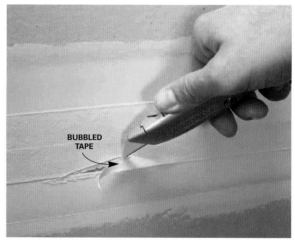

BUBBLED TAPE

TIPS FOR BETTER **GROUTING**

Grouting can be a rewarding task. It's the last step in a tile job, so you know you're almost done. And filling the joints with grout brings out the beauty of the tile. But if you've ever had grout turn rock hard before getting it off the tile, you know grouting can also be a nightmare. So to help you avoid problems and get the best results with the least effort, we've assembled these grouting tips.

Don't spread too much grout at once. Temperature and humidity affect how quickly grout starts to harden after you spread it on the wall. And once it does start to harden, you'll really have to hustle to get it cleaned off the tile and get the joints shaped before the grout turns rock hard. Avoid this problem by grouting small areas at a time. Start by spreading grout onto a 3 x 3-ft. area. Finish grouting, shaping the joints and cleaning each section before proceeding.

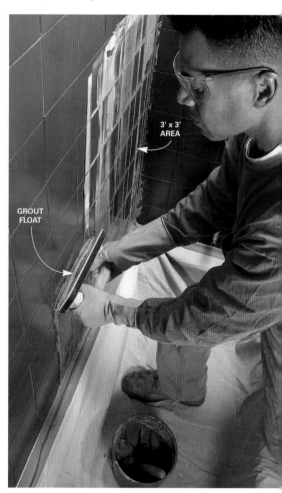

3' x 3' AREA

GROUT FLOAT

Scoop grout from the bucket with your grout float and apply it to the wall with upward strokes. Don't worry about getting it into the joints yet.

Do let the grout slake. It's tempting to skip this step, but it's important to let the grout set for 10 minutes after mixing. This step, called slaking, allows the water to completely moisten the dry ingredients. Remix the grout after the slaking period and adjust the mixture by adding a little more powder or water until you reach the viscosity of mayonnaise. Be careful, though—it doesn't take much of either to radically change the consistency.

GROUT

Remix the grout after letting it set for 10 or 15 minutes. Add a little water if the grout is too thick.

Do's&Don'ts

Fill the joints by pushing the grout at an angle to the joints with a grout float. Start in one corner and work methodically to fill all the joints.

Do tool the joints. Shape and compact the grout by dragging a tool across every joint. The tool can be anything from the rounded corner of the grout float to the rounded end of a toothbrush handle. Whatever is handy and has about the right radius to create a slightly concave joint will work. Don't use metal tools. They can damage the tile or leave marks.

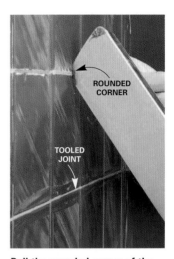

Pull the rounded corner of the grout float over every joint to shape them.

Do force grout into the joints. For a long-lasting grout job, make sure all the joints are completely filled with grout. To accomplish this, make several passes over the same area from different directions with the grout float. Hold the float with its face at an angle of about 45 degrees to the tile to force the grout into the joint. When the joints are filled, remove excess grout from the face of the tiles by holding the float at almost 90 degrees to the tile and scraping it off.

Do use a clean, damp sponge to remove grout. Start with a clean bucket of water. Wet your grouting sponge and wring it out until it's just damp. Then, starting along one side of the grouted area, position the sponge so that the corner of one long side of the sponge is in contact with the wall and drag the sponge in a continuous stroke up the wall. Now rotate the sponge to expose a clean corner and repeat the process alongside the first stroke. When you've used all four corners of the sponge, rinse it in clean water, wring it out, and continue the process until you've cleaned the entire area once. Clean the tiles two or three more times using the same process until they're free of grout residue. A thin film of grout may appear when the water evaporates. Buff this off with a soft cloth.

Remove grout from the face of the tile with the corner of a damp sponge. Swipe from bottom to top, using a clean corner of the sponge for each stroke.

Don't use a dripping wet sponge to clean grout from the tile. If water runs down, the sponge is too wet.

Don't scrub the grout or use too much water.

Let the grout harden slightly before you clean off the excess. Test the grout by pressing on it with your finger. When it's hard enough to resist denting, you can start cleaning the excess grout from the face of the tile and shaping the joints. Two common mistakes at this point are using too much water, and scrubbing the tile like you're washing a wall. Too much water will weaken the tile and cause the grout color to be uneven when it dries. And scrubbing doesn't remove grout efficiently; it just moves it around.

Do remove grout from corners before caulking.

Because it's flexible and can handle slight movement, caulk is used at corners instead of grout. For a good tile installation, apply a neat bead of matching caulk at vulnerable areas like along the tub or countertop and at inside corners. But to achieve a good-quality caulk joint, you'll first have to remove the grout from these areas. Most home centers and tile shops will have caulk to match the color of your grout.

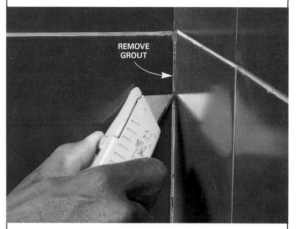

Remove grout from inside corners and along the tub to make room for caulk. Use a utility knife for narrow spaces or an old screwdriver or putty knife for wider joints.

Apply a thin coat of sealer to porous stone. Follow the application instructions on the label. Wipe up excess sealer with a cloth to avoid puddles. Then let the sealer dry before you grout.

Do seal porous tile before grouting.

If you don't seal porous tile and stone, grout will stick like glue and be nearly impossible to clean off. There are two different products that can make it easier to clean grout from porous stone and tile. If you're installing a matte finish tile or other tile with a rough or porous surface but don't want the sheen that a sealer would leave, apply a liquid grout release product. Grout release forms a thin film that prevents grout from sticking but washes off as you clean off the grout.

Use a sealer rather than grout release if you want to enhance the color of stone or leave a "wet" looking finish. You may have to apply another coat of sealer after grouting for maximum protection and to enhance the color of the stone.

Question&Answer

PLUG LEAKY DUCTS

I was recently building some shelving near my basement ceiling and felt all kinds of hot air leaking out of the exposed ductwork. Is this a big deal? After all, the escaped heat does stay in the house.

Whatever heat escapes in the basement isn't reaching your upper floors, and that's where your thermostat is located. So your furnace has to run longer (and use more fuel) just to maintain the set temperature.

Our heating expert confessed that he never thought duct leakage was a big issue until he saw a thermographic image showing just how much heat is lost at the duct joints. Today he's a believer in duct sealing.

Sealing duct joints is a DIY project. It's not only easy—it's cheap! Simply buy aluminum-colored silicone caulk and caulk every joint in rectangular ductwork (clean the joints first with a household spray cleaner and a rag to remove dust). Use the caulk to seal around the take-off boots to each branch run. Buy high-temperature UL181 aluminum foil tape ($15 per roll) in the duct section of a home center and use that to seal the joints of round ductwork.

Never use ordinary duct tape. Despite its name, it isn't approved for duct sealing and it doesn't hold up well over the long term.

1 Apply a bead of silicone caulk along both edges of the duct joint.

2 Seal round ducts with aluminum foil tape, not duct tape.

FINGER-SCAN ENTRY LOCKS

I read about a garage door opener that works by scanning your fingerprint. Is there anything like that for entry door locks?

Several companies offer biometric keyless locks for entry doors. One company is Kwikset. Its SmartScan locks are available at home centers for $200 (find retailers and more info at Kwikset.com). When you swipe your finger across a sensor, it reads your fingerprint and activates the battery-powered dead bolt. You don't need a key or a key code. Installation doesn't require hardwiring, and the batteries last about one year.

Also check out Artemis Solutions Group (the BioCert iQBioLock GuardianXLt costs $300; biometricdoorlock.com) and Bioaegis (the Biometric Fingerprint Door Lock LA9-3-A costs $200; visit bioaegis.com).

SPECIALTY CAULK FOR BETWEEN-FLOOR HOLES

Is it correct that any sealants used for plugging a hole in a wall are required by code to be fire retardant materials to prevent the spread of flames between floors and attics? Isn't ordinary expanding foam highly flammable and unacceptable for this application?

You're absolutely right. Any time you seal gaps between floors and attics, fire retardant sealants are mandatory.

Two companies that make fire retardant caulks and foam are DAP (800-543-3840; dap.com) and 3M (888-364-3577; 3m.com). The caulks and foam are available for $3 to $10 at home centers.

Fire retardant foam and sealants

INSULATION PANEL

FOAM ADHESIVE

Install insulation panels on bare foundation walls to save energy and enhance your home's curb appeal.

INSULATING FOUNDATION WALLS

My exterior foundation walls are exposed between the ground and where my siding starts. Any ideas on how I can insulate them and make them look nice?

Foundation insulation panels, such as the ones made by Styro Industries (888-702-9920; styro.net), are a good-looking option. The foam panels are available in 1-, 1-1/2- and 2-in. thicknesses, in different widths and lengths, and with either stucco or aggregate textures. We paid $14 for each 2 x 4-ft., 1-in.-thick panel. The panels attach to concrete, stone or block walls with rigid-foam adhesive and can be cut with a utility knife or a circular saw with a masonry blade. Detailed installation instructions and retailers are listed on the company's Web site.

Styro also has premixed, precolored brush-on or trowel-on acrylic coatings for exterior masonry walls that are already covered with foam insulation ($68 for a 5-gallon bucket that covers 80 sq. ft.).

According to Styro, an uninsulated foundation accounts for up to 22 percent of the energy loss in a home. So insulation panels will improve your home's energy efficiency—and its looks.

Question&Answer

PAINT VARNISHED DOORS

I have ugly stained and varnished doors and trim in my house. I'd like to just paint the whole works. What's the best way to get a good-looking result?

Start by sanding the surface with a random-orbital sander and 150-grit paper. Use a fine-grit sanding sponge to get into crevices. Don't try to sand off all the varnish. The goal is to remove any flaky varnish and to roughen the surface for a good primer bond. Wipe off the dust with a brush.

Then roll on a coat of BIN or KILZ (available at home centers for about $8 per quart). Have the home center or paint store tint the primer to a grayish color to help cover the underlying varnish. It also helps the finish paint cover with fewer coats. Apply the primer with a 6-in. high-density foam roller ($5 to $8 at home centers) to avoid brush marks.

If you want to keep the wood grain from showing through the paint, trowel a thin layer of spackling compound over the entire surface (Ready Patch is one brand, available at home centers for $6 for 1 qt.; zinsser.com). Use a 4- or 6-in. putty knife to work the compound into the wood grain pores and to fill holes. Wait for the compound to dry, then hand-sand with 220-grit sandpaper. Roll on a second coat of primer. Let it dry overnight, sand again with 220-grit sandpaper, then use a new foam roller to apply the paint.

CAUTION: If your home was built before 1979, check the paint for lead before you scrape or sand. For more information, go to hud.gov/offices/lead.

Painting steps:
1. Sand with 150-grit paper
2. Prime with stain-killing primer
3. Spread on spackling compound
4. Prime with tinted primer
5. Paint with acrylic latex

AVOID "PATTING" PAINTBRUSHES

I recently bought a paintbrush with a lifetime guarantee. One thing that could void the warranty is "sidewalk patting," which sounds like something you could get arrested for. So what is sidewalk patting?

We had to dig deep to find the answer. Even some of the paint experts we talked to had never heard the term before. Turns out that "patting" just means striking the brush against any hard surface, like a sidewalk, to get excess paint out of the bristles before cleaning, or the water out after washing. Patting can damage the ferrule, which is the metal band at the end of the handle that holds the bristles together. If the ferrule is damaged, the bristles will fall out, which is why patting voids a warranty.

New Tools&Gear

Bath cabinet hides an eyesore

Let's face it. Most toilet brushes aren't beautiful, and they take up valuable bathroom real estate. That's why the Brush-Away, an in-the-wall toilet brush cabinet, was invented. The door opens when you need the brush, then closes to conceal it when you're done. The door is removable to make cabinet cleaning easy.

It's designed to fit between the studs, so installation is just a matter of cutting a hole in the drywall and adhering the cabinet in place (it comes with a self-adhesive rim). You can install it in less than 30 minutes and paint it the same color as the wall to make it disappear. Buy it online for $40 plus $10 shipping (a toilet brush is included).

**Notech, (866) 275-8144.
brush-away.com**

Built-in shower lockers

If you're remodeling or adding a new shower, plan ahead for storage. Kohler's new shower lockers come in a couple of different sizes and colors for elegant storage right inside the shower wall. The built-in lockers offer quality and style—you won't find that with the slip-on bottle holders that fit over the showerhead arm (and usually fall off!).

The lockers mount on studs under cement boards and tile, so retrofitting an existing shower isn't an option. They're available in aluminum or acrylic with four removable shelves (makes cleaner easier!), so you can customize them for your shampoo bottles or soap. Prices start at $115. Find retailers on the company's Web site.

Kohler, (800) 456-4537. kohler.com

Apply a window decal, protect a bird

Most of the traditional strategies for preventing birds from flying into windows—hanging objects outside the windows, taping up balloons or tacking up netting—look terrible or block views. Duncraft's new removable UV Decals stick to the outside of the window to keep birds away.

The tinted decals are nearly transparent when viewed inside the house, but reflect ultraviolet sunlight outside that warns birds to change direction. Buy a set of six decals for $10 directly from the manufacturer.

Duncraft, (888) 879-5095. duncraft.com

New Tools & Gear

Rafter rollers add storage

There's a wealth of storage space above your attic and garage rafters, and the HomeTrak system lets you tap that area for storing boxes without having to crawl all over to reach them. Prop the back end of the track over a board

that you nail up, and place the front end in an aluminum hanger (included) that's installed over a board or rafter. Because the back is higher than the front, the boxes placed on the 12-in.-wide roller track slide forward—the same way beer cases slide in liquor store coolers—so you can easily reach them from the attic access or a single place in the garage. It's a great system for storing things like holiday decorations that you only use once a year.

The roller comes in two 4-ft. sections that you bolt together. It costs $100 and is available directly from the manufacturer.

HomeTrak, (864) 234-4848. home-trak.com

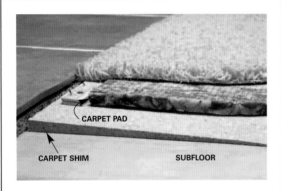

CARPET PAD

CARPET SHIM   SUBFLOOR

Ramped-up thresholds

Tile and wood floors are typically thicker than carpet, so where they abut a carpeted floor, you're stuck with a change in floor height. Even a slight floor height difference can pose a tripping (or stubbed toe!) hazard. But a new product called Carpet Shims eliminates that problem. It fits under the carpet to gradually raise the carpet's edge to match the higher level of an adjoining floor for a seamless transition between rooms. The incline is so subtle that you'll barely notice it as you walk across the transition.

The shims provide up to a 1/2-in. lift over an 8-in. or 12-in. ramp or up to a 1-in. lift over a 24-in. ramp (using the two-piece Super Shims). The shims are 32 in. or 48 in. long. Prices start at $6 per shim. Call the company to find a distributor in your area.

Carpet Shims, (877) 596-1591. carpetshims.com

Caulk for small jobs

Most of us never use an entire tube of caulk for a task. And since it's nearly impossible to reseal the unused portion, it hardens and eventually gets thrown out. GE has a solution to avoid the waste. Caulk Singles are designed for a single project—tear off the top, squeeze out the caulk (no caulk gun required!) and then throw away the empty package. Even if you've never caulked before, you'll be able to lay a nice, steady bead by squeezing the sides together.

One pack will handle small jobs like sink installations, and two will handle a bathtub or a window. Choose from white paintable acrylic, white silicone or clear waterproof silicone. The packs are available for $2 to $3.

GE, (877) 943-7325. caulksingles.com

3 QUICK CARPET FIXES

Get pro results—without the pro price

The carpet in your home is a big investment. So it's frustrating when a sputtering ember from the fireplace burns a hole in your beautiful rug or a spring storm floods the basement family room. But you don't have to call in a pro or just live with the damage until you replace the carpet. Solving these problems yourself isn't difficult, and you can increase the life of your carpet and save some real money.

We'll show you how to fix three common problems:

- Carpet that has pulled out of a metal threshold
- Small damaged spots such as holes, tears or burns
- Wet carpet from leaks or flooding

A carpet pro typically charges $125 to $150 for each of these repairs. If the repair involves a large area or the damage is more extensive, the cost can double. Doing the work yourself can cut the cost by two-thirds. The tools and materials you'll need are at home centers; most cost $15 or less.

CARPET CONSULTANT STEVE HOOVER

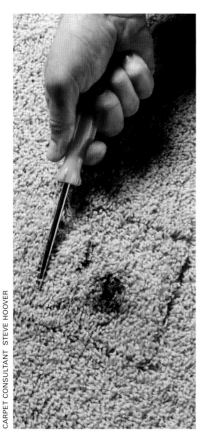

1 Patch a damaged spot

2 Rescue wet carpet

3 Reattach pulled-out carpet

1. PATCH A **DAMAGED SPOT**

You can patch a small hole, tear or burn using techniques that will make the repair virtually invisible. You'll need a small "plug" of carpet that matches the damaged piece. If you don't have a remnant, you can steal a piece from inside a closet or underneath a piece of furniture you never intend to move. (This may sound extreme, but it's a lot cheaper than replacing the entire carpet.)

If you have a "plush"-type carpet with a flat surface and no pattern, you can make a repair that's absolutely invisible. If your carpet has a color pattern, a textured surface design or looped yarn, you'll have to be fussier when you cut the plug, and the repair may be visible (but you're probably the only one who will notice it).

Before starting this repair, buy a carpet knife that has replaceable blades ($7). You'll also need a roll of one-sided carpet tape ($5). Be sure to choose heavy-duty tape reinforced with mesh, not the thin, flimsy version or the "hot-melt" type that requires a special iron to apply.

Cut out the damage and a matching plug

Be sure the area you're working in is well lit. To mark the area you'll cut out, part the carpet fibers around the damage as if you were parting your hair (**Photo 1**). Keep the part lines at

A carpet knife makes straighter, cleaner cuts than a utility knife.

1 Part the carpet fibers with a Phillips screwdriver. The parts mark your cutting lines and let you cut the backing without cutting or tearing the fibers.

least 1/2 in. from the damaged spot. Cut along the parts using a sharp, new blade in your carpet knife (**Photo 2**).

Next, cut a replacement plug, using the cutout as a template. To start, make a first cut in the replacement material, using a straightedge to guide your carpet knife. Then set the cutout on the replacement material with one edge aligned along that first cut. When you lay the cutout on top of the replacement material, make sure their naps are running in the same direction. You can tell which direction the nap is running by rubbing your hand over the carpeting and watching which way the fibers fall or stand up. Once you have the cutout lined up correctly, part the fibers around the three uncut sides just as you did before.

Cut along the parts and test-fit the plug in the cutout hole, making sure the nap of the plug matches the nap of the surrounding carpet. If the plug

2 Cut through the carpet backing. Make the cuts as straight as you can and avoid cutting completely through the carpet pad.

is a little too big, trim off a single row of fibers with sharp scissors (old, dull scissors will tear the fibers).

Prepare the hole for the new plug

Cut pieces of carpet tape and position them in the hole without removing the backing (**Photo 3**). Cut the ends of the tape diagonally so the pieces will frame the hole without overlapping. The tricky part is getting the tape positioned so it's halfway under the plug and halfway under the surrounding carpet. A helper makes this easier.

After marking their positions in the hole, remove the pieces from the hole and carefully (this is sticky stuff!) remove the protective backing from the tape. While pulling the carpeting up with one hand, slip the tape pieces back into the prepared hole one piece at a time (**Photo 4**). Be sure the edges of the tape line up with your markings.

CARPET TAPE

3 Test-fit all the pieces of carpet tape before you stick them in place permanently. Mark a square on the carpet pad to help align each piece later.

4 Peel off the tape's backing and set each piece in place, sticky side up. Don't let the super-sticky tape touch the carpet backing—or anything else—until it's in position.

Insert the plug

Now you're ready to fit the new plug into the hole. Pull the fibers of the surrounding carpet back from the edges. Push one side of the plug lightly onto the tape to make sure it's set exactly right—you really only have one shot at this (**Photo 5**). After you're sure the plug is placed correctly, use your fingers to work in the direction of the nap all the way around the hole as you press the plug down firmly onto each side of the tape.

A carpet tractor ($25) will do the best job of meshing the fibers, but a seam roller or even a rolling pin would work too. Place a telephone book on top of the plug overnight. Trim any fibers sticking up with a sharp scissors. You'll be surprised how "invisible" this repair is once you're finished. You can vacuum and clean your carpeting as you normally would, and this repair should last as long as your carpet does.

5 Set the plug tightly against one side of the hole. Then lower the other edges into place, holding back the surrounding fibers. Press the plug into the tape with your fingers, then with a carpet tractor.

A carpet tractor will mesh the fibers and make the repair invisible.

2. RESCUE **WET CARPET**

1 Dry out wet carpet right away. Fold back the carpet and start a fan. Cut around the soaked section of pad and scrape it up.

2 Lay replacement pad after the floor has dried. Duct-tape the seams where new pad meets old, and fasten the pad to the floor with adhesive or staples.

When carpet gets soaked, you have to act fast. The longer it stays soggy, the more likely it is to stretch out, discolor or get moldy. If a large area is waterlogged, complete replacement may be the best option. But if only a corner or a small room is soaked, you can save the carpet with just a couple of hours of work.

Tear out the soggy pad

First, go to the corner nearest the wet area, grab the carpet with pliers and pull the carpet off the tack strip. Continue pulling the carpet off the tack strip by hand until you can fold back the entire wet section. Run a fan or two to dry the carpet.

Wet carpet pad is like a big sponge. You have to get rid of it ASAP. Cut around the wet area with a utility knife. Make straight cuts so you have straight seams when you patch in the new pad. If the pad is glued to a concrete floor, scrape it up with a floor scraper ($10; **Photo 1**). If the pad is stapled to a wood subfloor, just pull up chunks of pad and pry or pull out the staples if you have just a few. For faster removal on a larger area, use a floor scraper. Have garbage bags handy to prevent drips on the carpeting. Wet pad is heavy. Don't fill the bags so full that you can't haul them out without wrecking your back!

Wipe up any water on the floor, then flop the wet carpet back into place. Drying it flat and in place helps the carpet retain its shape. Run fans until the floor and carpet are completely dry. This can take a couple of days.

Patch in the new pad

Measure the area of pad you need to replace and take a piece of the old pad to a flooring store or home center to find similar replacement pad. Pad costs about $4 per sq. yd. The color doesn't matter, but the new pad must be the same thickness and density as the old pad. Some stores will cut the pad to the size you need.

Fasten the pad to a concrete floor with carpet pad adhesive ($10 per gallon) and duct-tape the seams together (**Photo 2**). On a wood subfloor, all you need is a staple gun and 5/16-in. staples. Use a utility knife to trim off any pad covering the tack strip.

Reattach the carpet

As you refasten the carpet to the tack strip, you need to stretch it toward the wall. If you're dealing with a corner or a small area, you can use a knee kicker alone (see **Photo 3**, p. 44). Starting at one end of the loose carpet, set the head of the kicker about 2 in. from the tack strip and nudge the carpet tight against the wall. Force the carpet into the tack strip with a stiff putty knife. Also tuck the edge of the carpet into the space between the wall and the tack strip with a putty knife. Continue along the wall, moving the kicker over about a few inches each time.

If you're dealing with a larger area of carpet or if the carpet has stretched out of shape, bubbled or wrinkled after getting wet, you'll need to rent a power stretcher to restretch the carpet ($30 a day). For help with that job, search for "restretch carpet" at thefamilyhandyman.com.

A floor scraper is the best tool for removing old adhesive or staples.

3. REATTACH **PULLED-OUT CARPET**

If you have carpet that has pulled loose from a metal threshold, fix it now, before the exposed edge of the carpet begins to fray. If the damage extends more than an inch or so away from the threshold, you won't be able to make a good-looking repair. Aside from standard hand tools, you'll need a carpet knife ($7) and a knee kicker, which you can get at any rental center for about $15 per day. You'll also need a new metal threshold ($6 for 36 in.) and 1-1/2-in. ring-shank drywall nails.

Remove the old threshold

This repair is much easier if you first remove the door. You can do it with the door in place, but it'll take a little longer and you risk scratching the door. Carefully pry up the lip of the existing metal threshold along its entire length using a screwdriver or flat pry bar (**Photo 1**). Since you'll be replacing the threshold, you don't have to worry about wrecking it, but you want to work carefully so you don't damage the carpet edge even more. Once the threshold lip is bent up, use pliers to gently pull the carpeting up from the teeth inside the threshold. Roll the carpet back slightly to get it out of the way (you can leave the carpet pad in place).

Pry up the threshold slightly and pull the nails (**Photo 2**). To get an exact measurement for cutting the new threshold, don't measure the old threshold because it may be kinked. Instead, measure the opening and then cut the threshold with metal snips or a hacksaw.

Install the new threshold

If the carpet edge is in good shape, you can place the new threshold exactly where the old one was. If the edge is badly frayed, you'll need to trim off the damage using a carpet knife and a straightedge. Then position the new threshold farther into the carpeted room to compensate for the width you trimmed off. In most cases, you can place the new threshold about 1 in. from the original position, but not

THRESHOLD

1 Bend open the threshold's lip to release the carpet. Be careful not to snag the carpet as you push the screwdriver under the lip.

2 Pry up the threshold just enough to raise the nail heads. Then pull the nails and remove the threshold. Work from the carpeted side to avoid scratching the hard flooring. Nail down a new threshold.

more. If you've moved the threshold more than an inch, you may also need to trim the carpet pad so it doesn't cover the threshold pins.

If you're working on a wood sub-floor, nail down the replacement threshold with 1-1/2-in. ring-shank drywall nails. On a concrete floor, use heavy-duty construction adhesive to glue the threshold to the floor, and allow a day for it to dry before moving on to the next step.

Attach the carpet

Now you're ready to attach the carpet to the new threshold. Starting at one end of the threshold, set the head of the knee kicker about 2 in. from the threshold and kick with your knee to stretch the carpet toward the threshold (**Photo 3**). Kick firmly, but not with all your strength or you might rip the carpet. Force the carpet into the threshold teeth with a stiff putty knife. Then move the kicker over a few inches (the width of the kicker's head) and repeat the process until you reach the other end of the threshold. When you're done, tuck any loose carpet under nearby baseboards with a stiff putty knife. Finally, pound down the threshold lip with a rubber mallet (**Photo 4**).

You can rent a knee kicker for about $15 a day.

3 Nudge the carpet toward the threshold with a rented "knee kicker" and force the carpet into the threshold's teeth with a stiff putty knife.

KNEE KICKER

4 Drive down the lip, tapping gradually back and forth along its entire length. On the final pass, pound hard to lock the carpet into the threshold.

5 REASONS
TO TEAR OUT
YOUR OWN CARPET

Save $80 in an hour and fix floor problems before the installer shows up

Installing new carpet yourself usually isn't smart. When you consider the rental cost of special tools, your time and the risk of wrecking an expensive piece of carpet, it just doesn't make sense. But tearing out the old carpet does.

Save money

Depending on where you live, an installer will charge $3 to $5 per square yard for tear-out. By removing the carpet from a 12 x 15-ft. room, you'll save $60 to $100 for an hour's work. Talk to your installer to find out exactly what you'll save by doing it yourself.

Silence squeaks

With a bare floor, you can eliminate floor squeaks the easiest, most effective way: by driving screws into the floor joists. Existing nails or screws tell you where the joists are. Walk around the room, pencil in hand, and mark squeaky spots. Drive screws 6 in. apart and add more screws if needed until the squeak is gone. In most cases, 2-in. screws are best; for subfloors thicker than 3/4 in., use 2-1/2-in. screws. If you want to prevent squeaks from developing, add screws along all the floor joists. For more on stopping squeaks, go to thefamilyhandyman.com and search for "floor squeaks."

Seal stinky stains

Left untreated, pet urine stains can stink for years. To stop the stench, wet the area with a 50/50 mix of bleach and water. After five minutes, wipe up the bleach and let the floor dry completely. Then seal the stain with a stain-blocking primer, such as KILZ, BIN or 1-2-3. Be sure to choose a primer that's recommended for masonry if you have a concrete floor.

Hide wires

You can keep phone lines, speaker wire and coaxial cable out of sight and safe from the vacuum cleaner by installing them before the new carpet goes in. Just staple the wire every 3 to 4 ft. alongside the tack strip. Run it around the perimeter of the room, but not across doorways or other pathways where foot traffic will damage it. Most important, don't use this trick to hide extension cords or electrical wiring.

Replace rotten subfloor

If your subfloor has any rotten areas, it's best that you discover and fix them; the installer will charge you at least $75 and maybe much more. Rotten subflooring is common near exterior doors, especially patio doors. Set your circular saw depth to match subfloor thickness and cut around the damage. Cut along joists so the edges of the new patch can rest on them. Then pull out the damaged piece, cut a matching patch and screw it to the joists. To prevent additional damage, stop the water source. Caulking around the exterior trim and under the door sill may work, but the surest fix is proper sill flashing. For more information, search for "replace entry door" at thefamilyhandyman.com.

GreatGoofs®

Wallpaper remover, maple syrup style

We painted and wallpapered our kitchen just before selling our house and moving out of Vermont. But before we left the state, I thought it would be good for the kids to learn how real maple syrup is made. So we tapped a big maple in our yard and collected about 15 gallons of sap to boil down. (It takes a lot of sap to make a little syrup.) We put the sap in a couple of large pots on the kitchen stove and left the house for the several hours required for the boiling-down process.

When we returned, the sap had boiled down into a couple of quarts of sweet, dark maple syrup. The kids were genuinely impressed. Unfortunately, we didn't think to ventilate during the boiling process. The kitchen was damp with condensation and most of the new wallpaper had literally been steamed off or was hanging in loose, wet strips. Today, 25 years later, none of the kids remember making maple syrup; they remember rehanging wallpaper.

Getting soaked

After spending a frustrating four hours replacing a kitchen faucet, I finally got the new one to quit leaking. But when I turned on the water, none came out: hot or cold. Frustrated, I called a plumber. He arrived and listened as I described the problem. Promptly, he unscrewed the small aerator screen from the tip of the faucet and tapped out a small pile of flaky material. These hard water deposits were clogging the faucet. During the faucet replacement, this crud had been dislodged from the pipes. The bill for his 30-second remedy: $40.

Sushi hubby

While remodeling our kitchen, my husband decided to take the cabinets down by himself. I went on an errand and came home to find him sitting in a chair, pale and shaken, staring at a collection of very large knives and even a meat cleaver, spread before him on the table. It seems I forgot to tell him that I always store our large kitchen cutlery on the very top of one cabinet, "safely" away from the kids. Needless to say, he got a real shocker when he was removing that cabinet from the wall and knives rained down around him.

Bathroom bust-out

I take my painting prep very seriously. So before painting the bathroom door, I took off the door handle rather than taping around it. But when I closed the door and heard the lock click, I realized I had left the latch in the door. "No need to panic," I thought to myself.

I fit the handle back into the door—but the latch wouldn't catch. I then tried to manually pull back the latch—but it wouldn't budge. Then I used my nail punch and hammer to remove the hinges—a sure bet—but the door was so tight in the frame I couldn't budge it. There I was, trapped in my own bathroom.

I considered escaping through the window, but given the 9 in. of snow outside, my stocking feet and no key to get back into the house, I decided against it. Mild panic fueled a couple of karate kicks that split that hollow-core door into splinters. I think I'll paint the new door before I hang it.

Not so handy man

When my husband was just starting out in the handyman business, he took a job installing an over-the-range–type microwave. Holding up the unit while securing it to the cabinet was next to impossible. So being a resourceful guy, he grabbed the cushions from the couch and stacked them on the stove to support the microwave while he attached the unit to its bracket. This worked great—until he inadvertently twisted one of the stove burner knobs with his belt buckle. Of course, the cushions caught on fire. He was able to get the flaming cushions outside before they burned down the whole house.

But he learned that there isn't much money to be made in small jobs, once you buy your customer a new couch.

Duct-tape failure

I finally installed a programmable thermostat to cut energy costs. The job went well—or so I thought, until my wife started kicking me at 4 in the morning. The house was a nose-numbing 45 degrees. I removed the new thermostat and duct-taped the old one back in place; I'd figure out the problem after work. When I heard the heat turn on, I smiled and went back to bed.

When I walked into the house that afternoon, a blast of hot air hit me. During the day, the weight of the old thermostat had pulled the duct tape from the wall, leaving the thermostat set in the "on" position. The gauge read a toasty 110 degrees!

Painting

Avoid drips as you paint

Masking tape does a good job of protecting woodwork—if it's applied well.

Clean off all the dirt and grime along the edge of the trim with a damp rag. Hold the tape tight against the wall and roll it out so the tape covers the edge. Press the tape against the wood with a putty knife along the entire length. Use painter's tape that's at least twice as wide as the trim and leave it flared out to protect the face of the trim from drips. When you're done, either remove the tape immediately while the paint is still wet or wait until the next day when it's totally dry. If you pull it free when the paint is partially dry, you may peel off bits of fresh paint along with the tape.

Elevate—then paint

Ever paint a chair and have it stick to your newspaper or drop cloth? Paint hassle-free by driving drywall screws about 1/2 in. into the bottom of the chair legs. Raising the chair this way makes it easier to paint and even lets you coat the bottom of the legs. Works great with brush-on paint as well.

2" DRYWALL SCREWS

New Tools & Gear

Handy paint pail for up high

We've seen more than our share of gadgets for painting from a ladder—we get new ones to test every month. But the HANDy Ladder Pail made it past the skeptics here. A bracket secures the pail to most step or extension ladders, which frees up both of your hands. A magnet in the side of the bucket holds your paintbrush ferrule so the brush is easy to grab and stays out of the paint. And the angled side of the pail has a built-in grid that's great for getting excess paint off paint rollers.

The pail is also handy for holding tools and fasteners—and window-washing gear. It's available at home centers and paint and hardware stores for $20.

Bercom, (877) 464-1170. handypaintpail.com

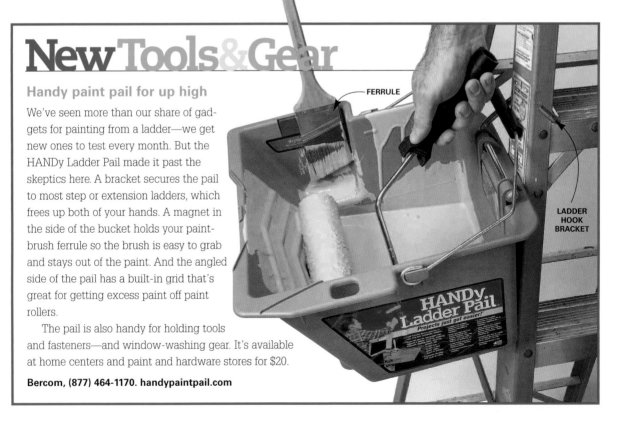

FERRULE

LADDER HOOK BRACKET

HANDy Ladder Pail
Projects just got easier!

PAINTING
PIZZAZZ

From dull to dramatic in one weekend

For less than $100, you can transform a room in a single weekend. All it takes is some paint, glaze and masking tape. We'll show you how to create three distinctly different decorative finish designs using simple tools and techniques. Even though the three finishes look unique, they're all created by masking off sections of the wall and applying a glaze finish.

The techniques for masking and glazing are easy to learn and don't require any special skills. However, you will need a good bit of patience since each finish entails multiple layers of glaze and careful applications of masking tape. You only need to paint one wall to achieve a dramatic effect. You could complete a wall in a day, but it's better to set aside a weekend to allow plenty of drying time between coats of glaze.

The first step in each finish is to paint the wall with the base coat color. For this you'll need typical painting supplies like a stepladder, drop cloth, paintbrush and roller. In addition, each of the designs requires slightly different tools and materials, and we'll tell you about these as we show you how to create each pattern.

Random rectangles p. 50

Weathered wainscot p. 54

Shimmery stripes p. 52

Painting

Recipe for rectangles shown here:

BASE COAT COLOR: Benjamin Moore Semolina 2155-40, eggshell.
FIRST SET OF RECTANGLES: One part Benjamin Moore Dash of Curry 2159-10 thinned with 3 parts Benjamin Moore Latex Glaze Extender Clear 408.
SECOND SET OF RECTANGLES: One part Modern Masters Tequila Gold ME661 thinned with two parts Glaze Extender.
THIRD SET OF RECTANGLES: One part Modern Masters Gold Rush ME658 thinned with two parts Glaze Extender.
FOURTH LAYER OF RECTANGLES: One part Modern Masters Flash Copper ME656 thinned with one part Glaze Extender.

RANDOM RECTANGLES

Four layers of glazed boxes overlap to create this contemporary design. We chose golden hues, but you could produce the same effect using different colors. In general, use a darker or more opaque color for the first layer of boxes, and lighten the color and increase the transparency for each of the three succeeding layers. Where layers overlap, new shades and colors will appear. That's why it's essential to create a sample board before you start.

We used latex paint thinned with glaze for the first layer and thinned semi-opaque metallic finishes for the next two layers. Before you commit to applying the finish to the wall, choose your colors and mix the glazes. Then make a sample board by painting a piece of drywall, hardboard or MDF (medium-density fiberboard) and applying the glaze. Overlap sections of glaze on the board to see the effect. Of course, if you like the way our wall looks, just copy our formula. When you're happy with the choice of colors, you can start on the wall.

Choosing the size and position of the boxes may seem daunting, but don't worry. The wall will look better with each layer you apply. Buy a watercolor pencil at an art supply store in a color that matches your color scheme and use it to mark the walls. The watercolor lines will disappear as you apply the glaze to the boxes. We drew square and rectangular boxes that ranged in size from a 34 x 14-in. rectangle to a 48-in. square. **Photos 1 – 3** show the process. Draw the fourth layer of boxes to enclose any base coat color that hasn't been covered by previous layers.

Tape off a series of boxes. Then, using the following steps, you'll spread a thin layer of glaze within the taped-off boxes to create a cloudy effect. Wet the sponges and wring them out before starting. Then use one sponge to spread a few 6-in.-long swaths of glaze on a small section of a box. "Pounce" the flat side of a second dampened sponge onto the glaze to spread it out. Rinse the pouncing sponge in clean water occasionally to get rid of built-up glaze. Work quickly across the box so that you never have to overlap onto an area of glaze that's already dry. Complete all the boxes with the first glaze color and let the glaze dry at least a couple of hours before starting on the next layer.

Draw another set of boxes on the wall that overlaps the first set and repeat the glazing process. Repeat these steps for the third layer. Complete the wall by covering any unglazed base coat with the fourth layer of glazed rectangles.

1 Mark rectangles on the wall using a level and a watercolor pencil. Then frame the rectangles with masking tape.

WATERCOLOR PENCIL

2 Spread random 6-in. swaths of glaze with the end of a sponge. Pounce with the second sponge to spread the glaze.

GLAZED RECTANGLE

APPLICATION SPONGE

POUNCING SPONGE

3 Add a second, third and fourth layer of overlapping boxes, using a lighter-colored glaze for each layer. Let the glaze dry at least two hours between layers.

SECOND LAYER OF GLAZE

Corner technique

Finishing right up to an inside corner with a sponge is difficult. You'll get uneven coverage or a buildup of glaze that looks bad. A better technique is to finish within a few inches of the corner with the sponge. Then, while the finish is still wet, use a dry brush in a pouncing motion to work the glaze into the corner.

Painting

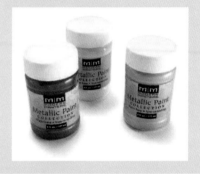

SHIMMERY STRIPES

Overlapping bands of glaze applied between torn strips of masking tape create this wavy striped wall. This pattern repeats every 15 in. and is made up of three layers of glaze. See **Figure A** (online at thefamilyhandyman.com) for the masking tape placement for each stripe. The recipe above right lists the paint and metallic glaze colors we used. You can choose your own colors to create a unique look or copy our recipe.

You'll need three rolls of masking tape for one 12-ft.-long wall. We used 2-in.-wide blue "long-mask" tape from 3M and liked the tearing characteristics, but you can experiment with other brands. **Photo 2** shows how to tear the tape.

Apply the glaze with the edge of one sponge and use it to spread a short swath of glaze onto the wall (**Photo 3**). Pounce a second dampened sponge over the glaze to spread it out in a thin layer (**Photo 4**). Twist the sponge as you pounce it to produce a random pattern. **Photo 5** shows how to mask off and apply glaze to the second and third stripes.

LAYOUT MARK

2"-WIDE TAPE

1 Stripe the wall with masking tape. Stick the tape to the top of the wall, then stretch out a section long enough to reach the bottom before you press it to the wall.

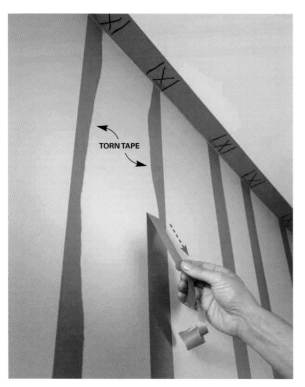

2 Tear one edge of each piece of tape to create a wavy edge. Wavy edges should face each other.

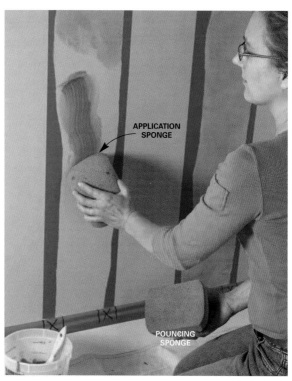

3 Wipe a swath of glaze onto the wall with the sponge. Start a few inches from the completed area.

4 Pounce the flat side of a second dampened sponge between the torn edges of the tape to spread the glaze. Remove the tape and let the glaze dry.

5 Apply masking tape for the next set of stripes. Tear the tape edges and apply the glaze using the same technique as you used for the first stripe. Remove the tape and let the glaze dry. Repeat the masking, tearing and glazing steps for the final stripe.

Painting

CHEESECLOTH

WEATHERED WAINSCOT

Create the look of mossy tiles with this simple masking and glaze technique. After marking off and masking around the diagonal squares (**Photos 1 and 2**), use cheesecloth to apply a cloudy layer of glaze (**Photo 3**). Then add a second uneven layer of glaze to produce a mottled effect. Pull off the tape and let the glaze dry. Then apply masking tape around the remaining triangles and apply two coats of glaze to them. Add a molding along the top to create an elegant wainscot.

Mix one part latex paint to three parts glaze to make the finish. Then cut a 30-in. piece of cheesecloth from the roll and unfold it. You'll find pads of cheesecloth at most full-service paint stores. Dampen the cheesecloth with water and lightly bunch it up to prepare it for use. **Photos 1 – 5** show how to mark and mask off the squares and how to apply the glaze. We used special Frog Tape, (see "New Tools & Gear," p. 57) which is designed to minimize the amount of paint that creeps under the edges. (You could also use blue masking tape.) Just lightly press down the edges of the Frog Tape with a plastic putty knife to seal them. Let the first layer of glaze dry. Then add a second layer in a random pattern to create darker and lighter areas. Remove the tape and let the glaze dry completely before masking around the remaining triangles and repeating the process.

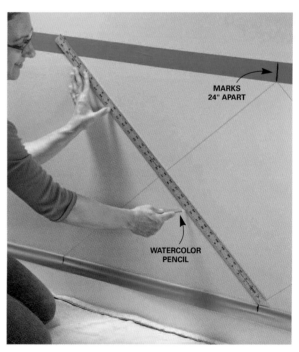

MARKS 24" APART

WATERCOLOR PENCIL

1 Draw a diamond pattern on the wall. First make marks 24 in. apart on the top and bottom pieces of masking tape. Then connect the marks with diagonal lines to form the pattern.

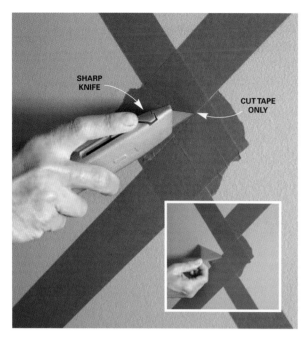

2 Create perfect corners where the squares meet. Mask around the squares, then slice off the excess tape. Use a sharp utility knife and light pressure to avoid cutting into the drywall.

3 Apply glaze with a small paintbrush. Quickly pounce over the glaze with bunched-up cheesecloth. Work in small sections until the square is covered.

There's a confusing variety of masking tape available. To choose the best type for any project, go to thefamilyhandyman.com and search for "masking tape."

4 Add a second layer of glaze in random patches after the first coat dries.

5 Complete the triangles by masking over the edges of the squares and applying glaze using the same recipe and techniques as before.

Painting

WORKING WITH GLAZE

Think of the thin, sugary layer on a glazed doughnut and you'll have a pretty good notion of what glaze is. In painting terms, it's a thin layer of oil or latex that varies from nearly transparent to nearly opaque, depending on the ratio of paint to glaze. Glaze is a liquid you mix with paint to get a translucent look, and is also the name of the thin layer you'll spread over the wall.

Mixing glaze

Mixing glaze isn't difficult. Use a measuring cup to get the right proportions, but don't worry about being too exact. You can add a little water to extend the working time and thin the glaze for easier workability. Just make sure it doesn't get so thin it runs down the wall. Each of our techniques requires applying from two to several coats of glaze on top of one another. To avoid problems, it's best to let each coat dry at least a few hours. It should be dry to the touch. Test by applying a piece of masking tape in an inconspicuous spot and removing it to make sure the tape won't pull partially dry glaze from the wall.

Application tips

In each of the decorative techniques we're showing, we've mixed either latex paint or special metallic finishes with latex glaze to create the finish. Both the "random rectangles" and the "shimmery stripes" techniques look better with even coats of glaze. There are several ways to avoid undesirable lap marks that can show up when you pounce over dried glaze. Starting out with a base coat layer of paint that has a little sheen helps because the glaze won't soak in and is easier to move around. We used latex paint with an eggshell sheen. For extra working time, buy "latex glaze extender" rather than plain latex glaze. When you

Mix glaze and paint or metallic finish according to the recipes to create the glaze mixture you'll apply to the wall.

apply the glaze, work from one side to the other. Work fast to avoid letting the leading edge dry out. It's also helpful to work in pairs, with one person dabbing on the glaze and the second person working it to achieve the desired finish. It's better to err on the side of applying too little glaze, since you can always add another coat.

Tools and techniques

The instructions for decorative painting often recommend sea sponges, but we found that the inexpensive "hump-backed" sponges available at paint stores work fine (top right photo on p. 50). They leave a soft, subtle texture that's desirable for the techniques we show here. Cheesecloth that's unfolded and lightly wadded is another good choice. In either case, the application technique is similar. You apply a little glaze to the wall with either a sponge or a brush, and then spread it out in a thin, even layer with a second sponge or a wad of cheesecloth. If you don't mind the extra work, simply practice on the wall. Then paint over it to prepare for the actual finish. Or you can practice on a painted piece of drywall, MDF or hardboard.

New Tools&Gear

Seep-proof painter's tape

The problem with most painter's tape is that it lets some paint seep behind it, even when it's properly applied. Frog Tape is different. Its special edge, called Paintblock, creates a micro barrier when it comes into contact with latex paint, keeping paint from running behind the tape. The photo shows our seat-of-the-pants test to see how it compares with other tapes. Conventional masking tape allowed a significant amount of paint bleed, blue painter's tape allowed minor bleeding, while the green Frog Tape produced crisp paint lines.

Frog Tape is especially good to use when you need crisp paint lines for decorative painting (we used miles of it for the "Painting Pizzazz" story on p. 49). But Frog Tape is more likely to lift off fresh paint, so be sure to pull it free immediately after painting or let the paint dry completely before removing it. We paid $7 for a roll of 1-in. tape.

Inspired Technologies, (877) 376-4827. frogtape.com

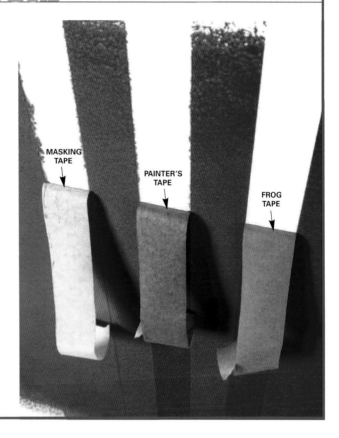

MASKING TAPE

PAINTER'S TAPE

FROG TAPE

Pizza box spray paint booth

Here's a tip that really delivers: Build a spray paint booth from large pizza boxes for small projects. Raise the lids, tape them together at the seam to create a corner and begin painting. Be sure to wear a paint vapor mask.

PRO **PAINTING** TIPS

We undoubtedly have more tips for painting than for any other type of home improvement project. Over the years, we've received hundreds of painting tips from readers and painting contractors. We combined them with our own and then worked with painting contractor Butch Zang to develop this list of the best painting tips of all time.

Dump the bumps

If you have a sprayed texture ceiling, drag a flat screwdriver along the edges of ceilings to scrape off a narrow strip of texture (you'll never notice it missing). This will ensure crisp paint lines when you cut in paint along the ceiling with a brush. Otherwise, you'll spend hours trying to paint around hundreds of texture bumps.

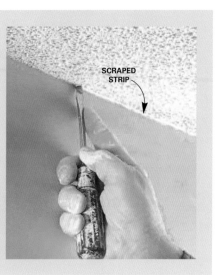

SCRAPED STRIP

" Roll the full length of walls from top to bottom and bottom to top, right to left. Keep the open side of the roller facing the side that's already painted. You'll put less pressure on that side, so you're less likely to leave roller marks. "

— **Butch Zang, painting contractor**

Paint out of a bucket

Forget about paint roller trays. They're inconvenient and easy to kick over or step in. Instead, pour all of the paint you need for the entire room into a 5-gallon bucket and stir the paint together. This ensures a consistent color throughout the room. If you switch gallons in the middle of a wall, the paint may look different—even if the color is mixed the same at the paint store. Hang a $2 roller screen in the bucket to use with your paint roller.

ROLLER SCREEN

PLASTIC

CANVAS DROP CLOTH

Clear the entire room before painting

If something is too big to take out, move it to the center of the room and cover it with plastic. Use canvas drop cloths. Unlike plastic, they stay put without tape and aren't slippery.

Use sanding sponges for trim

Sanding trim between coats of paint is the key to an ultra-smooth finish. But instead of reaching for sandpaper, use a sanding sponge. Sponges conform to the shape of the woodwork and get into the crevices where sandpaper can't go. They also apply even pressure to knock down rough spots over the entire surface.

FEATHERED EDGE

Painting ceilings

You can't keep a wet edge when painting ceilings—they're just too large—but you can minimize lap marks by feathering out the edges. Roll the nearly dry roller in different directions along the edge, feathering out the paint. Once you complete an entire length of the ceiling, move to the next section and paint over the feathered edge. If you need a second coat, apply the paint in the opposite direction.

Roll paint along trim and corners

As you cut in with a brush along trim or corners, roll the paint with a 3-in. roller so the texture will match the rest of the wall.

Painting

When it hits the fan

I was painting my living room one hot summer day and my good ol' dog, Hobbes, was looking for relief from the heat. He lay down in front of a box fan I had set up to dry the paint to grab some shut-eye.

As I was finishing the second coat, I stepped down off my ladder and right onto the back of my roller pan. It flew up, hit the back of the fan and sprayed paint all over the room—but especially on poor Hobbes. He slowly lifted his head, looked at his paint-covered body, stretched and went back to sleep.

While the dog didn't seem any the worse for the experience, I learned a hard lesson about paint pan placement.

New Tools & Gear

Miss-no-spots ceiling paint

It's not easy painting white over white, so Glidden's new EZ Track latex ceiling paint goes on pink, then turns to white in about 30 minutes. The bright color lets you easily see where you've painted so you can get nice, even coverage without missing any spots. EZ Track isn't the first paint to go on one color, then change to white, but it's the first that's widely available.

Glidden, (800) 454-3336. glidden.com

2 Electrical & High-Tech

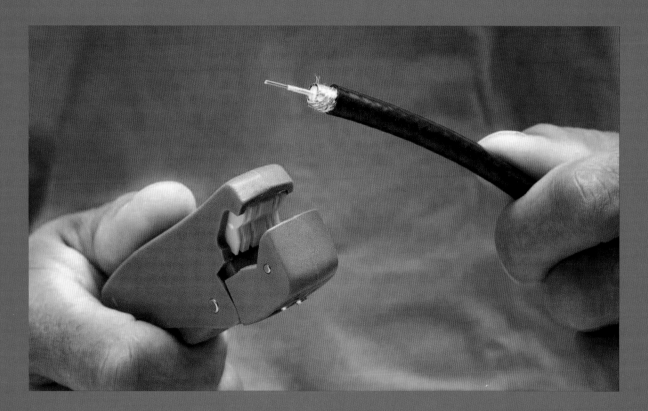

IN THIS CHAPTER

Question&Answer

LIGHT UP YOUR CLOSET

There are no light fixtures in any of the closets in my house. What's the best way to add a light?

The best lighting technique is to mount a pair of fluorescent fixtures as low as possible on the wall over the door. This lights your clothes and shelving well and casts light into those shadowy areas along the floor.

Linear fluorescents have several advantages over conventional lightbulbs. The long tubes cast light more evenly over the length of the closet. The slim profile lets you position them more easily in tight places, like over the door. The plastic cover on the "under-cabinet" or "closet" style shown protects them from bumps. They don't require an electrical box, so installation is easier. And the National Electrical Code allows more flexibility for their placement. NEC rules prohibit any fluorescent fixture mounted within 6 in. of the front edge of a shelf (measure from an invisible vertical line extended directly above the shelf lip). Incandescent fixtures must be at least 12 in. away. That much clearance isn't possible in most closets.

We recommend an under-cabinet–type fixture that uses a T-8 (1-in.-diameter) bulb. Buy the longest fixture that meets the electrical code and fits over the door. You can usually find the fixtures in 18-, 24- and 36-in. lengths at home centers ($20 to $40). For maximum light, simply join two fixtures end to end (**photo below**) or even stack them on top of each other if your space is especially narrow.

The best (and coolest!) way to control the light is with a motion detector mounted in the ceiling. The light will come on when you open the door or reach into the closet. And it will automatically switch off. Most under-cabinet fixtures have electronic ballasts, so buy a motion switch that works with electronic ballasts. They cost about $55 at electrical supply stores. (Leviton No. ODS10-ID is one example.)

Otherwise, you can mount a standard switch in a box on the wall outside the closet, or easier yet, mount a pull chain switch ($2 at hardware stores) on the fixture itself. To center a pull chain switch in the closet opening, join two fixtures with a short length of conduit when mounting them. You may have to drill a hole in the fixture to mount the switch. You can also order fixtures with pull chain switches online.

The biggest challenges are finding a power source and pulling a cable to the new fixture position. If you have an open area above the ceiling (attic shown here) or below the floor (basement, crawl space), you're in luck. You can generally find a nearby junction box with power and can run the new cable from there. Then either drill down through the top plates or up through the bottom plate and "fish" in the new cable. If you don't have open access from below or above, you'll probably have to cut open a wall to reach a junction box with power. If possible, make that cut inside the closet; say, opposite the junction box to an outlet in another room. Then run the cable, making as few wall cutouts as possible to get the cable to the switch and fixture. If you keep all cutouts inside the closet, you can more easily hide the wall repairs.

The rules for closet lights are stringent. Be sure to apply for an electrical permit so an inspector will check your plan and your work.

CABLE FROM
POWER SOURCE

SWITCH
BOX

CABLE TO
LIGHTS

24" FIXTURES

MOTION
SENSOR
SWITCH

CABLE
CLAMP

Tip
Look for a light fixture that has several "knock-outs" (prepunched holes) to give you more options for connecting the new cable.

BROKEN UNDERGROUND WIRE

I drove a steel fence post into the ground and severed an underground wire that feeds the lamppost. Now the light won't come on. What can I do?

Turn off power to the light at the circuit panel. Then dig 12 in. on each side of the post hole and gingerly work your way to the cable. You'll find the cable anywhere between 12 and 24 in. deep. When you locate the cable, use a noncontact voltage detector to ensure there's no power.

Use underground connectors to fix a severed cable.

Replace the whole section of cable that you dug up with the same gauge UF (underground feeder) cable. Cut the cable about 12 in. on either side of the break. Then strip back the sheathing 2 in. and the wire insulation 5/8 in. Use two special underground splice kits ($11 each at home centers) to connect the new cable section. Slide the heat shrink tube over one end of the cable, then connect the wires to the brass connector (**Photo 1**). Do this on both ends of the new cable. Once the damaged cable is replaced and the wires are joined with connectors, slide the heat-shrink tube over each connector (**Photo 2**). Heat the tube with a heat gun until it shrinks tight on the connector and sealant bubbles out the end.

If you have a broken underground line and no clue where the break is, hire an electrician with an underground open/short locator. For a service call that costs $200 or so, the electrician will be able to locate and mark the underground cable, determine how deep the cable is buried and pinpoint within a few inches where the problem exists.

1 Insert the wires into the connectors, making sure the colors match up, then tighten the screws.

2 Slide the heat-shrink tube over the connector. Use a heat gun to shrink it and seal the connection.

WHICH WAY IS UP?

When you show three-prong electrical outlets, the ground plug hole is always down. I was taught to install them with the ground plug up. What's the correct way?

Electricians endlessly debate this and vigorously exalt the virtues of installing it one way or the other, but we'll tell it to you straight—it just doesn't matter. Both ways are correct. The electrical code doesn't specify which direction the ground plug hole needs to face. One way isn't safer than the other—as long as the outlet is wired correctly.

It all comes down to aesthetics, so install them whatever way looks best to you. Incidentally, the ground plug is typically down in the United States, the opposite of how it's generally installed in Canada.

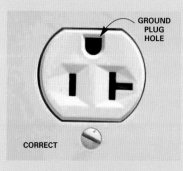

GROUND PLUG HOLE

CORRECT

STILL CORRECT

The electrical code allows outlets to be installed with the ground plug hole facing up, down or sideways. It's up to you.

Question&Answer

HALF-LIT LIGHTS

The fluorescent light in my garage only lights at the ends. Replacing the bulb didn't fix it. Any advice? The light fixture is about 20 years old.

The problem isn't the bulb—it's the starter. The starter is located on the lamp frame (there are typically two starters). When you turn on the light switch, the starter sends a jolt of electricity to the gas inside the fluorescent bulb. The ionized gas then conducts electricity and the bulb lights. When the starter stops working, the bulbs will either keep flickering without lighting or will only glow in the ends. (Flickering can also indicate the bulb needs replacing, but that didn't work for you.)

Replacing the starters is quick and easy—they simply twist in and out. Some starters are concealed under the bulbs, so they need to be removed first. A package of two starters costs $1.70. Bring the old one to the home center to be sure you buy the right replacement.

Most ballasts manufactured within the last 10 years or so don't need starters. Newer technology in electronic ballasts allows the lamps to light without them.

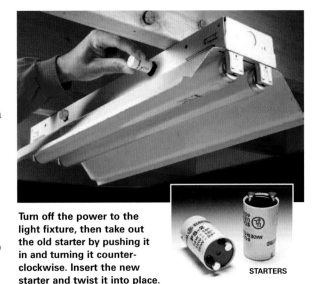

Turn off the power to the light fixture, then take out the old starter by pushing it in and turning it counter-clockwise. Insert the new starter and twist it into place.

STARTERS

CHOOSING THE RIGHT CFL

I want to put 100-watt CFL bulbs in fixtures rated for 60 watts. Could this possibly be a fire hazard?

As long as the CFL (compact fluorescent lamp) is a "100-watt incandescent equivalent" or "100-watt replacement" bulb, then everything is fine. When the label indicates that the CFL is

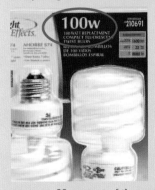

100-watt incandescent equivalent, it means the light output is roughly equal to that of a 100-watt conventional light-bulb. Their power consumption is not equivalent, however.

A 100-watt incandescent equivalent CFL will actually only draw about 27 watts. Some of those watts will be light; the rest will be heat. By contrast, 99 percent of the watts in a 100-watt incandescent bulb are given off as heat. CFLs only produce about one-third the heat of an incandescent bulb of an equal light output and are therefore a lot cooler and more efficient. So with the little bit of heat that's generated, there's absolutely no fire hazard with your plan.

GROUNDED OUTLETS REVISITED

I have been told that it is a mistake to replace a two-prong electrical outlet with a three-prong outlet that's not grounded. If it's an older house and doesn't have a ground, why is this unsafe?

Two-prong outlets are safe for two-prong lamps and appliances, but tools and appliances with three-prong plugs are designed to be plugged into grounded three-slot outlets to eliminate the possibility of electrical shocks. For example, if a window air conditioning unit with three prongs is plugged into a two-prong unground-ed outlet using an adapter and the air conditioner malfunctions, the metal case could become "hot" or electrified and become a shock hazard.

To tell if an outlet is grounded, remove the cover plate and touch one end of an electrical tester to a hot terminal and the other end to the metal box (if it's a plastic box, touch the metal threaded hole for the cover plate screw instead). If the tester lights up, then the outlet is grounded.

COAXIAL CABLE
MISTAKES

12 blunders that wreck TV reception and drag down Internet speed

R unning coaxial cable isn't like other wiring jobs; you have to follow a whole new set of rules. With coaxial cable, small mistakes lead to big problems: poor picture quality or slow Web cruising. So scan these simple rules before you run coax cable to your TV or computer.

1 Don't buy cheap cable

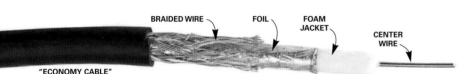

BRAIDED WIRE **FOIL** **FOAM JACKET** **CENTER WIRE**

"ECONOMY CABLE"

Shielding is what counts when it comes to cable quality. It blocks interference and keeps the signal clean. Skip the economy cable and go right for the "quad-shield" product. At about 30¢ per foot, quad-shield costs twice as much as cable labeled "dual" or "double-shield." But after spending big bucks on your TV or computer, skimping on coax just doesn't make sense.

High-quality cable has two layers of metal foil and two layers of braided wire to block interference. Economy cable has just one layer of each.

"QUAD-SHIELD CABLE"

2 Don't kink the cable

The wire at the center of coax cable is molded inside a foam jacket to keep it away from the shielding and to block interference. If you kink the cable or bend it around a sharp corner, you crush the foam. At that point, the damage is done and there's no way to undo it. Never bend cable around a radius smaller than 3 inches.

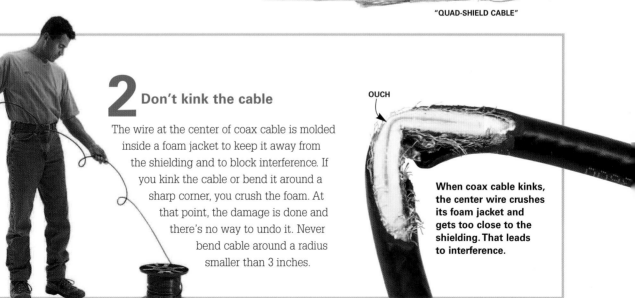

OUCH

When coax cable kinks, the center wire crushes its foam jacket and gets too close to the shielding. That leads to interference.

ELECTRICAL & HIGH-TECH

3 Don't pull too hard

Kinking and crushing aren't the only ways to damage the foam jacket surrounding the center wire. Pulling coax cable too hard tightens the braided wire shielding and compresses the foam (the way Chinese handcuffs tighten around your finger). That harms signal quality. The maximum pulling force for RG-6 cable is 35 pounds.

Make several short pulls through walls and ceilings instead of a long tug-of-war pull.

4 Don't run coax too close to electrical wiring

Electrical lines can cause nasty interference in coaxial cable. So keep coax cables as least 6 in. away from electrical cable, even if the cables are separated by wood or other building materials. To reduce any chance of trouble from phone lines, install "twisted pair" or shielded phone wiring.

Keep coax and electrical cables at least 6 in. apart. If the coax must cross over an electrical line, create a 90-degree intersection.

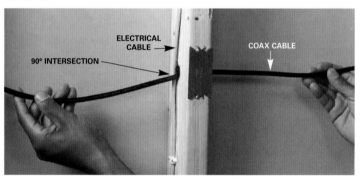

ELECTRICAL CABLE →

90° INTERSECTION →

COAX CABLE ↓

5 Don't crush the cable

There are a few kinds of staples made for coax, and all of them work well—as long as you don't drive them in too far. Forced too tightly over the cable, they'll crush the foam jacket inside, causing the same trouble as a kink. If you're running lots of coax, buy a special cable stapler ($40), which won't crush the cable. They're available at some home centers or online (search for "cable stapler"). When using a hammer, don't pound too hard. The staple shouldn't bite into the cable; a loose hold is better than a tight hold.

For kinder, gentler (and faster) cable stapling, use a stapler designed for the job. If you drive staples with a hammer, don't pound too hard.

CABLE STAPLER →

6 Don't space staples evenly

When it comes to attaching coaxial cable, neatness is bad. And here's why: Any type of fastener squashes the cable slightly. When coax cable is deformed, it reflects portions of the signal toward the source. If the deformed portions are evenly spaced, the reflections become rhythmic, causing double imaging. On Internet and satellite cable applications, these reflections can disrupt service. Uneven spacing between fasteners eliminates rhythmic reflections. So how far apart should you place staples? As far as possible. Use only as many staples as needed to hold the cable in place. Running up the side of a stud, for example, you typically need just three: one top, one bottom, one in between. Just make sure that the "between" staple isn't exactly halfway between the other two.

7 Don't let the shield show

The best cable-routing job can get fouled up if you aren't careful when you attach the end connector. Always fold back the foil and braided shield carefully before you attach the connector. A single strand of braid protruding into the connector area can ruin the signal. Double-check your work before you crimp or compress the connector.

A single strand of shielding exposed at the connector can degrade the signal. A sloppy connection like this one ruins the signal completely.

8 Don't nick the center wire

The signal carried by the center wire actually travels along the outside of the wire, not through the inside. So a tiny nick in the wire can cause a big obstacle for the signal. That's why a special coax stripper ($12 at home centers) is the only tool you should use to prepare the ends of the cable for connectors. Never use standard wire strippers or a knife.

A coax cable stripper cleanly cuts the outer jacket, the shielding and the foam jacket in one step—without harming the center wire.

COAX
STRIPPER

9 Don't use screw-on connectors

Solid connections at the ends of coax cable provide a clear path for the signal to follow. Loose connections weaken the signal. End connectors that screw on over the outer jacket of cable can loosen up over time and even fall off. Instead, use crimp-ring style connectors and a special crimping tool ($8 at home centers), or better yet, compression-style connectors. The compression tool costs about $17 at home centers.

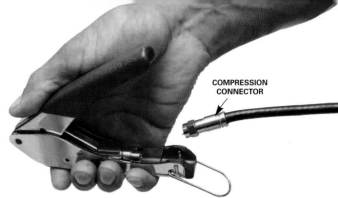

COMPRESSION CONNECTOR

Compression-type connectors grip cable firmly, without crushing the inner foam jacket as crimp-style connectors sometimes do.

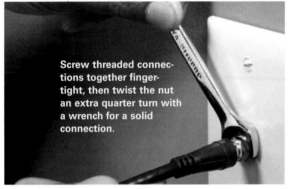

Screw threaded connections together finger-tight, then twist the nut an extra quarter turn with a wrench for a solid connection.

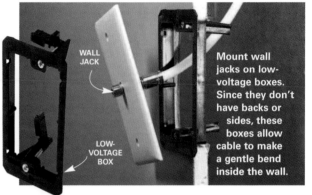

WALL JACK

LOW-VOLTAGE BOX

Mount wall jacks on low-voltage boxes. Since they don't have backs or sides, these boxes allow cable to make a gentle bend inside the wall.

10 Don't just finger-tighten connectors

As with end connectors, the threaded connectors on wall jacks, computers and TVs must provide a solid path for the signal. Most people finger-tighten these connections, but that just isn't good enough. Instead, use a 7/16-in. wrench to snug up the connection.

11 Don't use standard electrical boxes

The sides and back on a standard electrical box force you to bend the cable sharply inside the box. And you already know why that's bad (see Mistake No. 2). Low-voltage boxes let you make a gentle bend because they aren't really boxes at all, just frames that mount on drywall. These boxes cost about $2 each at home centers and can also be used for phone, speaker and other low-voltage wiring.

12 Don't use a cheap splitter

Every time you split a TV signal, it gets weaker. But you have to split the signal if you want to add a TV. Still, you can avoid poor picture quality. First, buy a splitter ($8 at home centers) that can handle the bandwidth needed for high-definition television and high-speed Internet. If you get poor picture quality after installing a splitter, call your cable provider for advice (they may increase your signal strength). You can also install an amplifier to boost the signal coming from your antenna, satellite or cable service. Amplifiers sell for as little as $20 at home centers, electronics stores and online (search for "TV amplifier"). But plan to spend $50 or more to get better results. And keep your receipt so you can return the amplifier if it doesn't help.

Judge a splitter by the numbers. If you have cable service, buy one labeled "5-1450 MHz." For satellite TV, look for a high end of at least 2200 MHz.

New Tools&Gear

NO-WIRE LED READING LIGHT

Reading in bed at night without disturbing your partner can be a challenge. Hard-wired lamps are a solution, but they require running wires in walls. An easier way is to install First Street's Overbed Dual LED Lamp. The lights run on four "D" batteries, so there's no wiring involved. The company says the batteries will last six to eight months, if the lamp is used for one to two hours a day. The fixture mounts to the wall with just a few screws driven through the housing. Each lamp slides along a track and is adjustable, so you can focus the light on your book or magazine.

The light isn't terribly bright, but it's enough to let you comfortably read at night—about like reading in bed by flashlight. Each lamp has its own on/off switch and is dimmable. The lamp fixture is available on the company's Web site for $60.

First Street, (800) 704-1209. firststreetonline.com

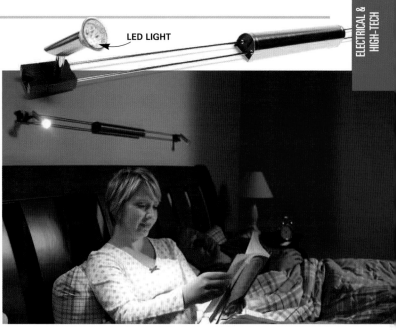

LED LIGHT

SOLAR PANEL

PORTABLE SOLAR POWER

Xantrex's portable power pack uses solar power to run your electronic devices, like your laptop, DVD player or small TV, so you can use them outside without hassling with extension cords. It's great when you want tunes or a movie on the beach or want to hear the ballgame while working in the garden.

The XPower Powerpack Solar ($170) runs 120-volt AC electronics or 12-volt DC devices (like cell phones). The detachable 5-watt solar panel recharges the 10-amp battery (or you can recharge it by plugging it into a standard wall outlet). Don't expect it to run your electronics all day, though. The company says the power pack extends the running time of battery-powered devices by 25 percent.

Xantrex, (408) 987-6030. xantrex.com

TODDLER-PROOF YOUR ELECTRICAL OUTLETS

You know those plastic plugs that people use to protect outlets from kids armed with butter knives? Well, they look awful and they're a pain to pull out when you need to use the outlet. CoverPlug offers a better solution. It fits into the ground hole openings, covers the entire outlet and can be painted to match the surrounding wall, making it hardly noticeable. It's also easy for an adult to remove. CoverPlug costs $17.50 for a two-pack. Retailers are listed on the company's Web site.

coverPlug Inc., (720) 529-1414. coverplug.com

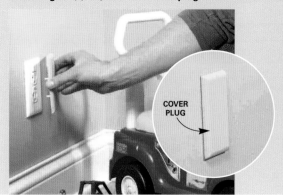

COVER PLUG

New Tools & Gear

SOLAR-POWERED LIGHTS FOR SHADY SPOTS

Floodlights that run on solar power aren't new, but Malibu's High Intensity Flood Light (LZ605) has some features that are. It has a 20-ft.-long cord, so you can place the solar panel in the sun, then put the light anywhere you want, including in the shade. The solar panel charges the batteries, which then power the light for up to 10 hours at a time, depending on the brightness setting.

Twelve power-sipping LED bulbs provide a bright, white light and stay lit much longer than conventional battery-powered bulbs. The solar flood light ($50) is available at home centers.

Malibu, (815) 675-7000. Malibulights.com

LIGHT IN SHADY SPOT

SOLAR PANEL IN SUNNY SPOT

MONITOR ELECTRIC USAGE

I watch the real-time miles-per-gallon readout in my hybrid vehicle while driving, and it has changed the way I drive. No more fast accelerations or driving with a lead foot (I'm now squeezing out an extra three or four miles per gallon). Blue Line Innovations' PowerCost Monitor ($150) does the same thing for home electrical use. It gives me a real-time readout of my energy usage and cost (based on my local rates) so I can adjust my habits to save money.

The six 60-watt bulbs in my recessed lights cost 3¢ an hour, and my air conditioner adds 21¢ an hour. Turning off lights and televisions when we leave rooms saves about a dime a day.

The PowerCost system consists of a sensor unit that's attached to the outside meter and a wireless display monitor that gives the readout. By tracking your usage over a 24-hour period, you can determine how much money you'll save by adjusting the thermostat setting of your air conditioner or heat pump a couple of degrees.

SENSOR UNIT

REAL-TIME COST PER HOUR

RUNNING COST

Blue Line Innovations, (866) 607-2583, save-electricity.ca

QUICK-CHECK POOL WATER TESTER

If testing your pool or spa water involves deciphering colors to figure out your pH balance, step into the digital age with the AquaChek Tru Test Digital Test Strip Reader. Just dip a test strip into the water, then stick it in the Reader for easy-to-read digital results in seconds for Free Chlorine/Bromine, pH and Total Alkalinity. Two "AA" batteries will power the Reader for the summer.

Find retailers on the company's Web site. The Reader costs $50 and comes with 25 test strips. Additional strips cost $10 for a pack of 50.

Hach Co., (888) 278-2243. aquachek.com

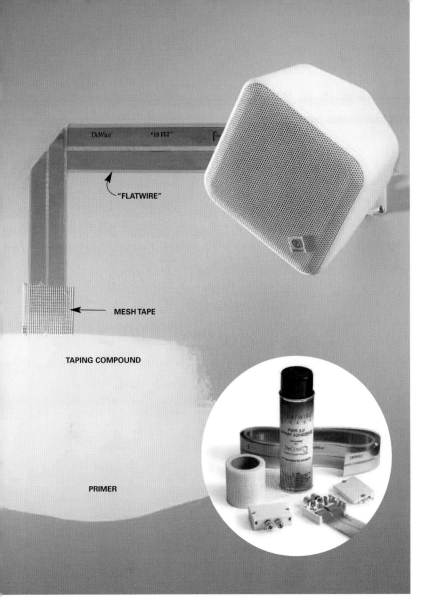

"FLATWIRE"

MESH TAPE

TAPING COMPOUND

PRIMER

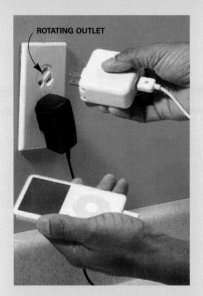

ROTATING OUTLET

FULL-CIRCLE ELECTRICAL OUTLET

Bulky plugs and night lights can hog electrical outlets so there's no room for a second plug—unless you're using 360 Electrical's rotating outlet ($10). Each socket rotates 360 degrees (in either direction) so you can turn them any way you need to make room for a second plug.

Instead of using wires, which would get twisted as the socket rotates, the outlet uses copper bands that encircle a receptacle drum to provide power. The outlets (15-amp rated) fit in a standard electrical box, but they aren't GFCI protected and can't be used with aluminum wiring.

360 Electrical, (801) 364-4900. 360electrical.com

HIDDEN WIRING SYSTEM THAT'S SUPER EASY TO INSTALL

Want to install a home theater system but dread the hassle of running all those low-voltage cables inside walls? Well, forget about all the drilling and cable fishing, and get out your taping tools. FlatWire is flat (thinner than a credit card) and runs on wall surfaces. Then it gets taped over, covered with joint compound, sanded, primed and painted. It blends right into the wall so no one even knows it's there.

FlatWire is available for audio, video, cable modems, Cat 5, or special low-voltage light fixtures (lights start at $50). The company expects to have its 120-volt wire cable approved for sale soon—if FlatWire can pull that off, it will be a truly impressive product! Prices range from $37.25 for 25 ft. of speaker wire to $250 for connecting five speakers to one receiver (the kit includes 100 ft. of speaker wire and 10 pairs of pin connectors). FlatWire's spray adhesive ($12), for adhering the wire to walls, and self-adhesive mesh tape ($5), for covering the wire, are extra. Detailed installation instructions are available on the company's Web site. It's definitely worth checking out.

FlatWire Technologies, (888) 352-8947. flatwirestore.com

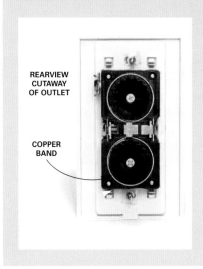

REARVIEW CUTAWAY OF OUTLET

COPPER BAND

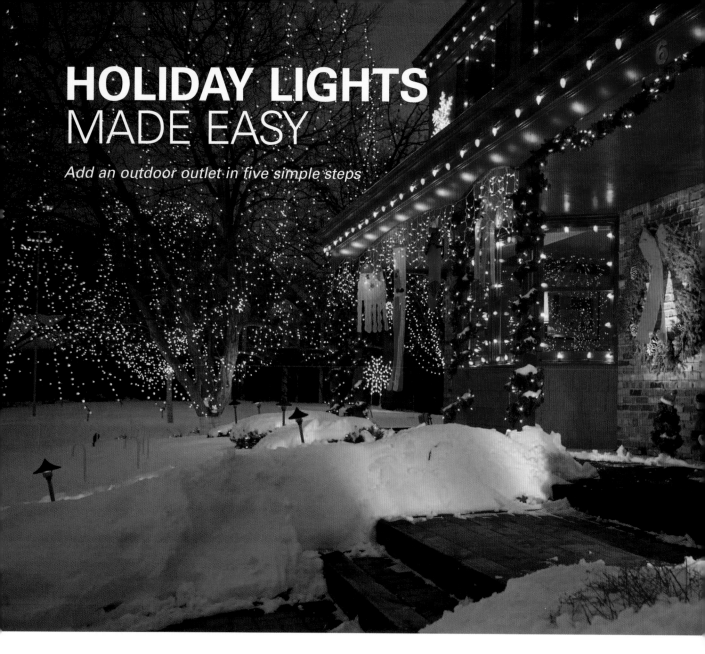

HOLIDAY LIGHTS
MADE EASY

Add an outdoor outlet in five simple steps

Most homes have only two exterior outlets—one in the front and one in the back. That may be OK most of the year, but it's a real hassle when you're hanging holiday lights. It can be dangerous, too: Overloading cords or outlets poses a fire hazard, while crisscrossing your driveway and sidewalk with cords creates tripping hazards.

In just a few hours, you can solve these problems forever by adding an outlet or two. In this story, we'll show you how to do just that. We've made adding an outlet as easy as possible—simply connect new wire to an existing interior outlet and install your new outlet on the opposite side of the wall. This eliminates the arduous task of fishing wires through finished rooms. To bypass the hassles of cutting a box-size hole in the exterior wall, mount the new outlet right to the siding.

Even if you've never worked with electricity before,

you can do this. Our Web site covers all of the basic skills you need to complete this project safely (visit thefamilyhandyman.com). Everything you need is available at home centers for less than $60 (see the Buyer's Guide, p. 76). Call your local inspections department to apply for a permit before you start.

Choose and mark the outlet location

To keep this project simple, place the new outlet in the same stud cavity as an existing indoor outlet. Start by choosing the interior outlet you want to use. Building codes prohibit tapping into circuits in the kitchen, bathroom, laundry room or into those dedicated to a large appliance, like a refrigerator. You can use living room, bedroom and basement circuits, but don't tap into a circuit that's already overloaded and trips the circuit breaker. To place the outlet somewhere other than opposite the interior outlet, see

Running cable from other power sources

If you don't want your exterior outlet location limited to where you have interior outlets, you'll have to tap into another electrical circuit. If you have an unfinished basement, you can tap into a junction box in the basement and run the cable out through the rim joist. This is even easier than tapping into a main floor outlet. Plus, it allows you to put your new outlet anywhere, not just opposite an interior outlet. Simply drill a hole through the rim joist and siding, then run a cable from a basement light fixture to the outlet location (Figure A).

A second option is to run wires inside 1/2-in. metal conduit from an existing exterior outlet to the new location (Figure B). The conduit can wrap around corners with a service ell, but don't run it in front of doors. Plant flowers or shrubs in front to cover it.

Figure A: Run a cable from the basement

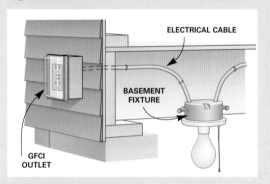

ELECTRICAL CABLE

BASEMENT FIXTURE

GFCI OUTLET

Figure B: Run wires inside conduit

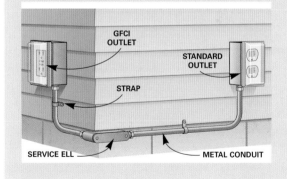

GFCI OUTLET

STANDARD OUTLET

STRAP

SERVICE ELL

METAL CONDUIT

"Running Cable from Other Power Sources," right.

Turn off the circuit breaker controlling the outlet. Use a noncontact voltage tester ($15) to be sure the power is off. Then unscrew and pull the receptacle out of the electrical box. Hold the voltage tester over the terminals to double-check that the power is off. Next, unscrew the wires from the outlet.

Make sure the junction box is large enough to hold an added set of wires. (An overstuffed box is a fire hazard.) If the box is plastic, shine a flashlight inside and look for a volume listing, such as 21 cu. in. (cubic inches). Then go to thefamilyhandyman.com and type

WARNING: Turn off the power at the main panel, remove the cover plate and outlet, and use a noncontact voltage tester to ensure the power is off.

"19473" into the search box to see a chart showing how to determine the minimum box size that's needed. If your box is metal, we recommend that you replace it (see "Replace an Electrical Box," p. 74). Most metal boxes are too small to hold additional wires.

Use a stud sensor to determine which side of the electrical box the stud is on. Place a 1/4- x 18-in.-long drill bit ($11) along the outside of the electrical box on the side

Replace an electrical box

If your existing electrical box isn't large enough to hold more wires, you'll have to replace it. Remove the old box before cutting a large opening for the new one. This allows you to see if anything is behind the wall before you make the cut.

To swap out boxes, cut the nails that hold the box in place (Photo 1). Then remove the box. Replace it with a plastic "remodeling" box ($2 at home centers). These boxes have wings that flip up and attach to the back side of the drywall or plaster. Hold the box over the wall opening and trace around it. Then enlarge the opening with a drywall saw. Don't overcut; you want a snug fit.

Feed the new cable from the outlet being added into the box before installing it (Photo 2). Wrap the cable with electrical tape where the sheathing meets the exposed wires so the sheathing will slide into the box easier.

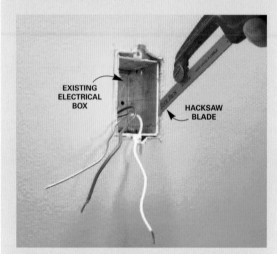

EXISTING ELECTRICAL BOX

HACKSAW BLADE

1 Cut the nails that fasten the box to the stud with a hacksaw blade. Pull out the box and loosen the clamps that hold the wire.

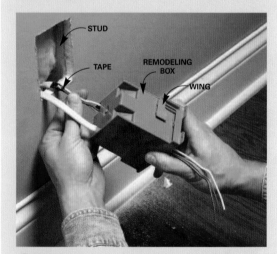

STUD

TAPE

REMODELING BOX

WING

2 Enlarge the wall opening for a remodeling box. Feed in the new and old cables, then mount the box. Caulk any gaps between the box and the wall.

CAUTION: If you have aluminum wiring, call in a licensed electrician who is certified to work with it. This wiring is dull gray, not the dull orange that is characteristic of copper wire.

away from the stud. Squeeze the bit between the box and the drywall. But don't worry if you make a small hole in the drywall. You can hide it later with the outlet cover plate. Drill through the wall and through the siding to mark the location for the new outlet (**Photo 1**). We tilted the drill bit downward to lower the outlet location (if it's near the ground you can hide it behind shrubs), but you can place it anywhere on the wall.

Find the marker hole outside and place the exterior junction box over it on the siding. If that's not where you want it located, move it straight up or down (staying in the same stud cavity) and mark the position of the box hole on the siding. Then drill a 1-in. hole over the smaller hole or the mark on the siding to make room for the cable.

If drilling through stucco, you'll probably wreck the bit, but you'll get through the siding. For brick, use a masonry drill bit with a hammer drill. Then drill a series of small-diameter holes around the marker hole and knock out the center with a hammer and chisel.

Run cable between the outlets

The new wire must be the same gauge (thickness) as the wire already in the box, which is most likely 14 gauge but could be 12. To check, use the labeled notches on wire-stripper pliers.

Run cable from the interior box to the hole in the exterior. Start by removing a knockout in the box by hitting it with a screwdriver. Then strip about 2 ft. of sheathing off the end of the cable and cut off two of the three wires. Tape the end of the remaining wire to the end of the sheathing, forming a loop. Feed the loop through the knockout into the wall cavity.

Bend the end of a wire coat hanger to form a hook. Insert it through the hole in the exterior, grab the wire loop in the wall and pull it back through the hole (**Photo 2**). Pull through at least 12 in. of cable to give yourself plenty to work with.

Wire the interior outlet

At the interior box, cut the cable so there's 12 in. sticking out, then remove the sheathing to expose the wires. Cut 6-in. pieces of wires from the coil and strip 3/4 in. of insulation off the ends. Screw these short pieces to the outlet: The bare copper goes to the ground screw (green), the white to either of the silver terminals, and the black to either of the brass screws on the other side. Hook the wires clockwise over the screws so they stay in place as you tighten the screws.

1 Drill a 1/4-in. hole alongside an existing electrical box to mark the location of the new outlet. Go outside and drill a 3/4-in. hole in the siding over or near the smaller hole.

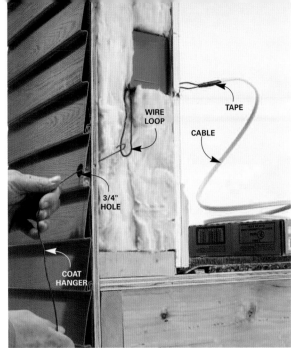

2 Cut off 2 ft. of sheathing and two wires from the cable. Tape the remaining wire to the sheathing, then feed the loop through a knockout in the interior box. Fish for the cable from the exterior hole using a hook made from wire. Pull the cable through the hole.

To wire the interior outlet, connect all of the hot wires (black and any other color except green or white), all the neutral wires (white), and all of the ground wires (green or bare copper as shown in **Photo 3**).

Gently fold the wires into the box, then reattach the outlet and cover plate. If you damaged the wall around the box, use an oversize cover plate to hide the problem.

Mount and wire the new outlet

We used a $20 TayMac weatherproof receptacle kit (see Buyer's Guide) for our exterior outlet. It came with a standard three-prong outlet, but since outside outlets must be GFCI protected, we replaced the kit outlet with a GFCI outlet.

Attach the two mounting lugs to the back of the metal electrical box, putting them in opposite corners. Fasten a clamp to the hole in the back of the box, then feed the cable through the clamp. Apply a heavy bead of silicone caulk around the clamp and place the box on the wall, inserting the clamp into the hole in the siding. The caulk makes the hole watertight. We placed our box horizontally on the lap siding so it could lie flat.

If you have lap siding (wood, hardboard, fiber cement) or plywood sheathing, mount the junction box to the house, using exterior-grade fasteners. Simply drive galvanized deck screws through the mounting lugs. For brick or stucco siding, mount the box with masonry anchors. For vinyl siding over composition board, use hollow wall anchors.

Fasten plugs into the openings on both ends of the box.

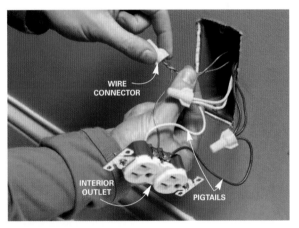

3 Strip 12 in. of sheathing from the cable in the interior box. Strip 3/4 in. of insulation off the ends of the wires. Fasten the pigtail wires to the outlet, then join the wires with wire connectors.

Use a file to scrape a small notch or "weep hole" in the bottom edge of the box. This allows any water that gets into the box to drain.

Next, strip insulation off the wire ends. Attach the ground wire to the green screw in the box and to the green screw on the GFCI outlet. Make sure to identify the line, hot and white terminals (they'll be labeled "line," "hot" and "white." Attach the black wire to the brass screw or adjacent push-in hole (labeled "line") and the white wire to the silver screw or push-in (**Photo 4**). Clip the ears off the outlet, fold the wires into the box and set the outlet in place.

You'll need to remove the middle of the plastic base so it'll fit over the GFCI outlet (don't worry, it's designed to

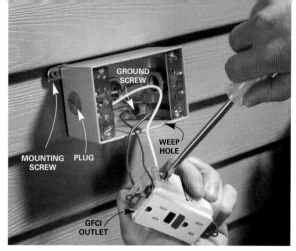

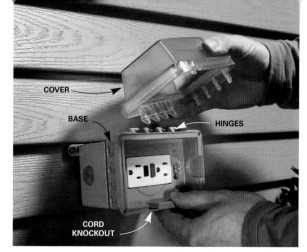

4 Attach a clamp to the box, feed the cable through it into the box, then caulk around the clamp. Mount the exterior outlet box to the house. Wire the outlet and set it in the box.

5 Screw the base to the box. Attach the plastic cover to the base, sliding it over the hinges until it snaps.

come out by twisting it with pliers). Set the base on the box, over the outlet. Make sure the hinges are at the top so the plastic cover will close over the outlet. Fasten the base to the box with the screws that came with the kit.

Attach the cover to the base (**Photo 5**). Push the hinge receptacles sideways over the hinges until they snap in place. Remove the cord knockouts in the base where the electrical cords will run. Turn the power on and plug in your miles of holiday lights!

Control lights with a timer

You don't want to have to step outside every night, especially in the middle of a winter deep freeze, to plug in or unplug your outlets. That's where timers come into play. Walk down a home center's electrical aisle and you'll see plenty of them. Be sure to buy one that's rated for outdoor use.

The most common timers plug into the outlet, then cords plug into the timer. Most don't need to be mounted. They just hang from the outlet. The least expensive models ($10) have a dial setting to run the lights for a specific period of time, such as two hours, six hours, or dusk to dawn (see 1, below). Slightly more expensive models ($20) have digital controls for programming (2).

If you don't want to fuss with setting the timer, buy a remote outdoor switch ($20; not shown). You can turn the lights off and on from inside the house, just like you open and close your garage door with a remote control from your vehicle. Look for one at home centers or search online for "remote outdoor switch."

If you need additional outlets in the yard, install an outlet strip rated for exterior use (3). They plug into your outlet, stake into the ground and offer multiple outlets. Look for them at home centers, starting at $12. You can only install one strip per outlet.

Or buy an outlet with a built-in timer. Hubbell Electrical Products makes one that we really like ($50; see 4 and the Buyer's Guide). It has four outlets, GFCI protection, a built-in junction box and a rocker switch so you can put two outlets on the timer and let the other two run continually. You can install this unit as your new exterior outlet, or if you already have an outlet, replace it with this.

1. TIMER WITH DIAL

2. TIMER WITH DIGITAL CONTROLS

3. OUTLET STRIP

4. OUTLET WITH BUILT-IN TIMER

FIX A LAMP CORD—THE RIGHT WAY!

Damaged plugs and nicked, frayed cords are a safety hazard and need to be replaced. Putting a new plug on is straightforward, but there are a few basic rules.

To prevent shocks from the metal parts of a light, lamp cords and two-wire extension cords are always polarized. This means the plug has a small blade for the hot wire and a wide blade for the neutral wire, and the wires feeding those blades should not be reversed when you put a new plug on. Always use a polarized plug for a lamp, extension cord or any other cord that's polarized to begin with. Don't ever use a nonpolarized replacement plug with same-size blades to replace a polarized plug. (Nonpolarized plugs are often found on double-insulated tools and some appliances.)

You can identify the neutral side of the wire just by looking for markings on one of the wires. The most common identifier is ribbing in the rubber insulation all along one edge, but it can also be a white wire or a white stripe (**photo right**).

To prepare the cut end for a new plug, cut or pull the two sides apart, then strip off about 3/4 in. of insulation (**Photo 1**). Lamp and extension cords are usually 18 gauge, but if you're not sure, strip the wire through the 14- or 16-gauge slot first. If it doesn't strip cleanly, try the next gauge. Note: Stranded ("STRD") wire gauges are marked on the left; solid gauges are marked on the right.

Twist the strands of wire tight, then fasten them into the replacement plug with the neutral on the wide-blade side (**Photo 2**). Then snap or screw the plug back together.

To identify the neutral wire, look for these markings:

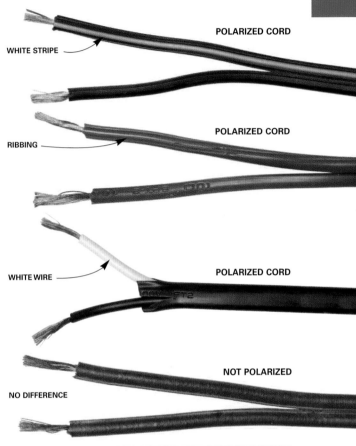

WHITE STRIPE — POLARIZED CORD

RIBBING — POLARIZED CORD

WHITE WIRE — POLARIZED CORD

NO DIFFERENCE — NOT POLARIZED

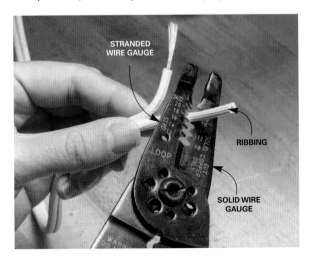

STRANDED WIRE GAUGE

RIBBING

SOLID WIRE GAUGE

1 Strip the insulation off the wire by cutting and pulling the wire through the wire stripper.

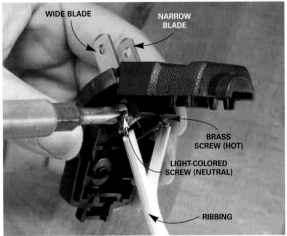

WIDE BLADE   NARROW BLADE

BRASS SCREW (HOT)

LIGHT-COLORED SCREW (NEUTRAL)

RIBBING

2 Wrap each wire around the correct screw in a clockwise direction, then screw it tight.

Home Care & Repair

UPGRADE YOUR RECESSED LIGHTS

Dissatisfied with the look of your recessed lights? You can change them in a few minutes just by changing the trim.

Remove the existing trim and bulb and look up inside the metal housing for a sticker with the brand name, the model number and compatible trim styles. If you can't find the information, or the brand isn't available, take the old trim to a lighting store and look for matches. Most manufacturers have several different types and sizes of housing that will accept a variety of trim styles.

Changing old, yellowed trim for new trim is simple—just pull out the old trim and attach the new trim in the same hooks. You can also replace standard trim with an eyeball-style trim ($20) that can be aimed in different directions, but it takes an extra step.

First, turn off the switch and circuit breaker and remove the bulb. Unscrew the wing nut that holds the base of the light in place and remove the socket (**Photo 1**). Then snap the socket into the top of the eyeball shroud and push the eyeball trim up into the can (**Photo 2**). Be sure to use the type of bulb recommended on the label in the housing.

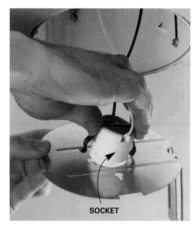

SOCKET

1 Remove the metal base from the housing, then pinch the spring clamps that hold the ceramic light socket in place.

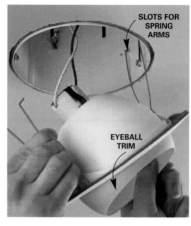

SLOTS FOR SPRING ARMS

EYEBALL TRIM

2 Slide the spring-loaded metal arms up into the slots in the housing, then push the trim up against the ceiling and put the lightbulb in.

SIMPLE SOLUTION FOR A TROUBLESOME LIGHT FIXTURE

Do you have bulbs that burn out quickly, lights that flicker, or a light fixture that simply doesn't work even though there's power to it? Try this 60-second fix before you call an electrician.

Turn off the power to the fixture and use a noncontact voltage tester to make sure the power is off. Then reach into the bulb socket with a flat-blade screwdriver and gently pry up on the tab that's centered at the bottom to restore good contact with the bulb.

TAB

DON'T BE LEFT IN THE DARK

Choose a backup power system before the next blackout

With the American power grid becoming less reliable every year, power outages are bound to occur more frequently and last longer. That means you could end up sitting in the dark, sweating without an air conditioner, and eating canned meals while $300 worth of food spoils in your freezer. Meanwhile, your basement could flood since the sump pump is now worthless—and your kids could go crazy without a TV or computer.

Power grid problems aside, we all lose electricity occasionally. But when outages become routine, leaving you without electricity for days on end, it's time to take action by getting a generator. Smaller, portable generators are great for powering the essentials, like the refrigerator and microwave, while large standby generators can power everything in your house.

We'll walk you through both types of generators (portable and standby) and both ways to deliver backup power (extension cords and subpanels). We'll cover the pros and cons of each system and give you an idea of prices.

TWO TYPES OF GENERATORS, TWO VERY DIFFERENT COSTS

Portable

When the power goes out, you have to start up a gas-powered portable generator and plug it into your appliances or a subpanel. Portable generators cost $500 to $1,500 depending on power output.

Standby

These generators are powered by natural gas or propane and start automatically during power outages. Prices start at $5,000 for a 7,000-watt unit, including installation.

Determine which generator you need

Your first step in adding backup power is deciding what you need (or want) to keep running when the electricity goes out. This determines the size (wattage) of the generator you'll need.

Walk through the house and make a list of everything you want to power during an outage. Look for a label on each appliance (they have to have one) that contains information such as wattage, model number and the year it was made (**photo right**). Some labels are right inside the door on appliances; others are on the back, so you have to pull the appliance away from the wall. Write down the item and how much wattage it uses. Be sure to include essential items, like refrigerators, freezers, a well pump if you have one, and a sump pump if your basement could flood. You can go a few hours or even days without an oven (use the microwave instead) and an air conditioner—they use a lot of power and would require you to buy a much bigger generator.

Add together the items' wattages, then multiply that number by 1.5 (appliances need the extra power to start up). That's the minimum wattage needed for your generator.

Estimate your power needs before you shop for a generator. Look for a label on each appliance that you want to power during an electrical outage. Add up the watts to determine the generator size you need.

WATTAGE REQUIREMENTS	
Microwave:	600 to 1,200 watts
Refrigerator:	700 to 1,200 watts
Freezer:	500 to 1,200 watts
Washing machine:	1,200 watts
1/3-hp sump pump:	800 watts
Television:	300 watts
Laptop computer:	250 watts
10,000-Btu air conditioner:	1,500 watts

Plug-in generators are the simplest solution

The most basic method of supplying backup power is running a portable generator in your yard, then plugging in extension cords that plug into your appliances. It's also the least expensive solution since you don't need to hire an electrician to install a subpanel. The downside is you have to run extension cords everywhere you want power, and you're limited to how many things you can plug in at once (most generators have either two or four outlets). You also have to start and maintain the generator.

When the power goes out, place the generator on a flat surface outside, at least 10 ft. from the house. Don't set it under awnings, canopies or carports, or inside the house or garage. It's absolutely critical that you keep the generator away from your house and especially away from doors and windows—your life could depend on it!

> Caution: Plug in a carbon monoxide detector when using a portable generator. It'll alert you if generator exhaust reaches a dangerous level inside the house.

Extension cords must be at least 14 gauge to carry adequate power. Follow the cord's maximum wattage rating (listed on the cord's label). Start up the generator, then plug in the extension cords (**photo below**). Be careful not to overload the generator by plugging in high-wattage appliances that you didn't plan for. It'll trip the breaker or blow a fuse on the generator, or damage the appliance motors.

Portable generators range in price from $500 for a 3,250-watt unit to $1,500 for a 10,000-watt unit. Options include wheels (get them—generators are very heavy to lift) and electric (key) starts rather than pull-starts. Consider how long the generator can run on a tank of gas. Some run just a few hours, so you'll have to get up in the middle of the night to add fuel. Others have 16-gallon fuel tanks that can run up to 10 hours. See the Buyer's Guide on p. 82 for buying information.

A portable generator with extension cords is the simplest and least expensive backup power system. Keep the generator at least 10 ft. from your house to avoid carbon monoxide poisoning.

A manual transfer switch subpanel makes portable power more convenient

To use a portable generator without the hassle of running extension cords, hire an electrician to install a manual transfer switch subpanel off your main circuit panel and install a dedicated inlet to power the subpanel (installing the subpanel is complex; not a DIY project). This setup gives you the advantage of powering entire circuits in the house, not just individual appliances. The drawback is you still have to start and maintain the gas-powered generator. And unless you buy a large generator (they're available with more than 15,000 watts), you're still limited in what you can power.

Before calling an electrician to add the subpanel, choose what you want to power during an outage. It's worth including a circuit that'll let you run your TV, computer and a lamp, especially if you lose power for days at a time, so you can keep everyone entertained. Plus, these electronic devices don't require a lot of wattage. The circuits you want powered will be moved from your main circuit panel to your subpanel, so they'll run when you have normal power and when you lose electricity and hook up the generator. Expect to pay $200 for materials and at least $500 for an electrician to install the subpanel and special inlet.

During a power outage, run a cord from the generator to the inlet, flip a manual transfer switch on the subpanel, and all the designated circuits will have power. Choose a heavy-duty extension cord (photo, p. 82) with twist-lock ends (generators have receptacles for these ends) that stay in place once they're plugged into the generator and inlet.

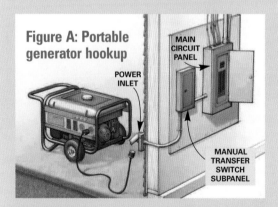

Figure A: Portable generator hookup

POWER INLET

MAIN CIRCUIT PANEL

MANUAL TRANSFER SWITCH SUBPANEL

A subpanel lets you connect a generator to your home's existing wiring. Run an extension cord from the generator to a special power inlet that's connected to a subpanel. Flip a manual transfer switch inside the subpanel to power selected circuits. Be sure to keep the generator at least 10 ft. from the house.

Standby generators are effortless

Standby generators automatically turn on when the power goes out—you don't have to do a thing. This is the best option if you frequently lose electricity and want to keep all or most of your appliances running. Most standby generators are powerful enough to run a central air conditioner, kitchen appliances and other large items—simultaneously. They're also quieter than portable generators and you don't need to worry about running cords or storing gasoline. The drawback is the price. You'll need to have the generator, transfer switch and subpanel professionally installed.

A transfer switch constantly monitors power. If you lose electricity, it starts the generator automatically—even if you're not home. When power is restored, the transfer switch shuts off the generator.

Standby generators connect to your home's fuel supply (natural gas or propane). If you don't already have one of these fuel lines coming into the house, you can install a propane tank.

Standby generators range from $5,000 for a 7,000-watt unit to more than $15,000 for a 30,000-watt unit (installation included). Home centers carry a limited selection of portable generators (but usually no standby units). Larger sizes and standby units are usually available through special order or from the manufacturer. See the Buyer's Guide below.

Figure B: Standby generator system

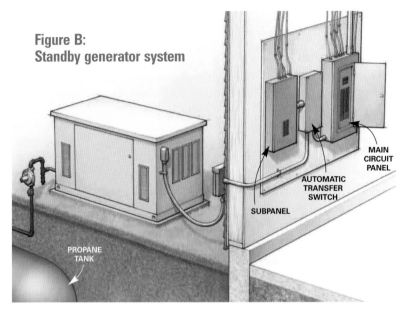

PROPANE TANK

SUBPANEL

AUTOMATIC TRANSFER SWITCH

MAIN CIRCUIT PANEL

Standby generators run off your home's natural gas supply or a propane tank, which can be underground. The transfer switch automatically starts the generator, which powers the circuits in the subpanel.

Use a heavy-duty, twist-lock extension cord to plug into the inlet that's connected to your subpanel. The special ends keep the cord from pulling loose. Some generators come with a twist-lock cord.

Buyer's Guide

- **BRIGGS & STRATTON: Portable and standby generators. (800) 743-4115 for portable generators, and (800) 732-2989 for standby generators. briggsandstratton.com**
- **CENTURION: Portable and standby generators. centuriongenerators.com**
- **GENERAC: Standby generators. (888) 436-3722; generac.com**
- **HONDA: Portable generators. hondapowerequipment.com**
- **KOHLER: Standby generators. (800) 544-2444; kohlersmartpower.com**

CAUTION: DON'T KILL A UTILITY WORKER
Don't attach a second male end to a power cord, then run it from the generator to a wall outlet to power a circuit (yes, people have done this). This may seem like a clever way to run power through your home's wiring system, but the electricity will run back through the circuit breaker panel and out to the utility lines, which can kill service personnel working on the lines, even if they're miles away.

HandyHints®

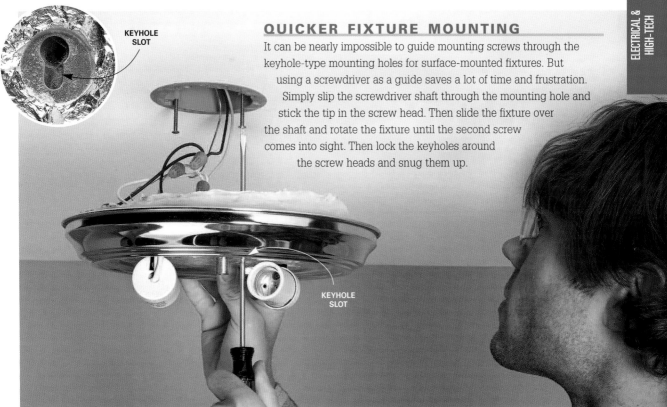

KEYHOLE SLOT

KEYHOLE SLOT

QUICKER FIXTURE MOUNTING

It can be nearly impossible to guide mounting screws through the keyhole-type mounting holes for surface-mounted fixtures. But using a screwdriver as a guide saves a lot of time and frustration. Simply slip the screwdriver shaft through the mounting hole and stick the tip in the screw head. Then slide the fixture over the shaft and rotate the fixture until the second screw comes into sight. Then lock the keyholes around the screw heads and snug them up.

EASY-READ PANEL

Make the circuit numbers stamped onto your electrical panel box easy to read by marking over each one with a black permanent marker. Lightly wipe away any excess ink with a rag dipped in a solvent like denatured alcohol.

CIRCUIT NUMBERS

CHARGER HIDEAWAY

Nothing clutters up a space more than the spaghetti heap of cords and plugs needed to recharge all those cell phones and other electronic toys. Create a discreet charging station with a small bread box and place a power strip inside. Drill a hole in the back to run the cord to the receptacle. Plug in your power-hungry devices and close the door for an orderly desktop or kitchen counter.

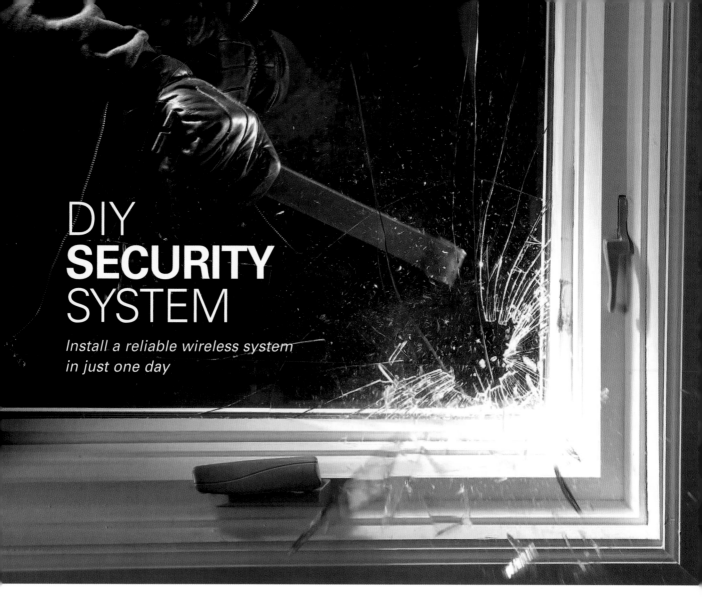

DIY
SECURITY
SYSTEM

Install a reliable wireless system in just one day

The wireless security systems of 20 years ago were notoriously unreliable. They produced so many false alarms that many homeowners stopped using them. That's all changed. Today you can buy professional-grade wireless security equipment that's extremely reliable, easy to install and affordable. A basic system starts at about $225 and tops out at $800 or so. If you add wireless smoke/heat detectors, plan to spend about $1,300. That's about half of what a professional alarm company would charge. Monitoring service, which notifies the police or fire department, can cost $40 or more per month. But if you shop around, you can get it for about $10 per month.

We'll show you how to plan your system so you can get it up and running in a single day. Plus, we'll show you how you can save money on equipment and neaten up the installation at the same time. Installation is easy. You just mount the transmitters at doors and windows and connect a control panel to phone lines and a power supply. All you'll need are basic tools—a drill, screwdrivers, wire stripper and a small pry bar.

Plan your system

Some alarm installers recommend eliminating window transmitters and installing motion sensors instead. These sensors are similar to the motion detectors that turn on outdoor floodlights. That approach can cut costs, but we don't recommend it. Motion sensors cause the majority of false alarms. Worse, they detect burglars only *after* they've entered your home. That can create a dangerous situation

Don't forget the permit

Most cities require permits for alarm systems (about $25 per year). Contact your city licensing department to get one, then stick it to a window in or near the front door. If you don't, your first false alarm may get you a fine plus a stern lecture from the police.

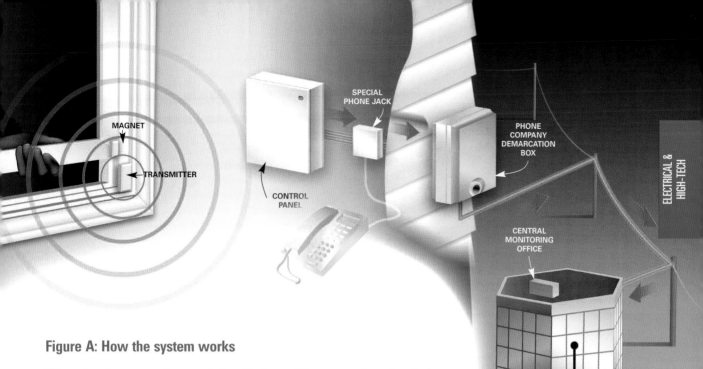

Figure A: How the system works

When a burglar opens a door or window, the transmitter senses a loss of contact with the magnet and sends a signal to the panel. The panel places a call to the monitoring service, which then contacts the police or fire department. The monitoring service can also call you or anyone else you've listed as "first contacts."

where you come face to face with a burglar in your hallway. Door and window transmitters are the only way to detect break-ins immediately. Don't let anyone convince you that motion detectors alone are a substitute for them. Glass-breakage sensors are available too, but are optional. Most burglars only break glass in order to unlock a door or window. Then, when they open the door or window, a standard transmitter will detect the entry.

To figure out how many transmitters you need, start by sketching all of the doors and windows on the ground level of your home. Number each opening, beginning with the front door and moving in a clockwise direction. Be sure to include the garage service door if you have an attached garage. Then count only the upper level openings that can be reached *without* a ladder (burglars rarely use ladders). Don't forget to count the patio door on an elevated deck.

Fire poses a greater danger to your family than burglary. So you may want to add wireless smoke detectors (about $90 each) to your system. That way, the alarm panel will notify your monitoring service of a fire condition and the service will call the fire department. You'll need a minimum of one wireless smoke detector on each floor. Add a smoke detector in each hallway leading to a bedroom, and one in each bedroom. If you have a gas furnace, water heater or clothes dryer, install one rate-of-rise (ROR) heat detector ($14) over each of these appliances and wire them into a transmitter.

Next, decide what kind of control panel you want. There are two types: A

> **Tip**
>
> Use the system for about a month before you officially connect to your monitoring service. That way, your "training" false alarms won't lead to police calls.

Save hundreds now— and $30 every month

Installing a wireless security system can be as easy as mounting transmitters on doors and windows and connecting a control panel to your phone line. You'll save $300 to $600 in parts and labor costs. Better yet, you'll avoid an expensive long-term monitoring contract with a security company. Instead, you can shop around and choose any monitoring service you like. That will save you about $30 every month—forever.

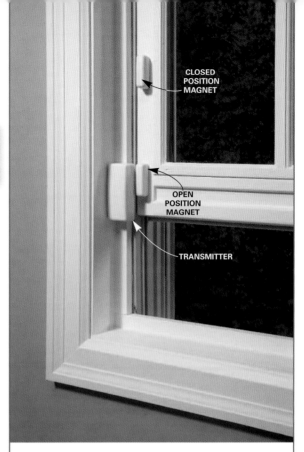

CLOSED POSITION MAGNET

OPEN POSITION MAGNET

TRANSMITTER

Get fresh air—and security

If you have double-hung windows, mount the transmitter and a magnet 6 in. above the sill. Then mount a second magnet near the bottom of the sash. That way, you can leave the window open a few inches and still turn on the security system. If a burglar opens the window farther, the alarm will activate.

"cabinet-style" panel consists of a keyboard that mounts near the door and a circuit board that mounts near your phone interface. A "self-contained" panel is a single unit that mounts near the door. This one-part panel is easier to install but has one weakness. An intruder entering through the door can tear it off the wall before the panel finishes notifying the monitoring service. With a two-part panel, the circuit board keeps working even if the keypad is disconnected. With either type of panel, you'll need a special phone jack (called an "RJ31X") to connect the panel to your phone lines.

Shop online

You won't find professional-quality alarm equipment at a local electronics retailer. Instead, fire up your computer and search for "security alarms" or "security systems" (two sources are listed in the Buyer's Guide, below). Look for suppliers that carry multiple brands and models so you don't get locked into equipment that's not right for you. In addition to good selection, look for a supplier that offers free system programming and technical support. Make sure the supplier doesn't require a high-cost, long-term monitoring contract. Before you place an order, call the supplier and discuss your plan. The staff will help you develop a materials list and program the alarm panel appropriately. Ask to have the components labeled for each zone.

Select a monitoring service

Your system doesn't have to be connected to a monitoring service that calls the police. It can simply trigger an alarm siren. But don't dismiss the importance of alarm monitoring. Crime statistics show that burglars aren't scared away by sirens. They know it will take at least three to five minutes for neighbors to call the police and just as long for police to respond to the call. A monitoring service can contact the authorities much faster. Insurance companies understand the importance of faster police/fire notification, and many offer discounts to offset some of the monitoring costs. So check with your insurer.

Alarm installation companies typically charge you $40 per month with a three-year minimum contract for alarm

monitoring. By installing your own system and dealing directly with a monitoring service, you can save at least $360 per year. Simply search the Internet for "alarm monitoring." Make sure the company is UL (Underwriter's Laboratory) listed.

If you've switched to digital phone service or Voice Over Internet Protocol (VoIP), make sure the monitoring company is equipped to handle those types of calls. If not, it may provide other means of transmitting an alarm signal, such as Internet, cellular, satellite or radio communicators. Ask how much the additional equipment costs and if there are any additional service fees.

Buyer's Guide

There are lots of online suppliers of security system equipment. Here are two that carry a large equipment selection and offer programming and monitoring services:

■ homesecuritystore.com
■ alarmsystemstore.com

Get a cleaner look with these installation tips

Surface-mounted transmitters and magnets (as shown on p. 86) are the easiest way to protect doors and windows. But there are approaches that add convenience, provide a neater installation and even save you a few bucks.

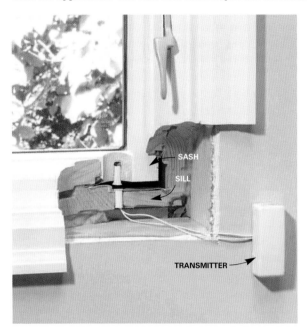

SASH

SILL

TRANSMITTER

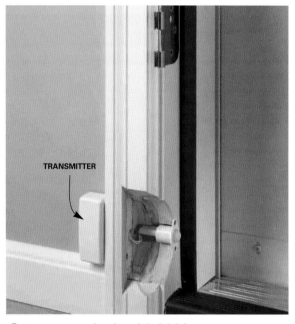

TRANSMITTER

Use hidden magnets in casement windows

Plunger contacts can make casement windows harder to open or close. Instead, use "recessed" magnetic contacts ($4). Just drill a hole in the sill near the side of the window that opens. Mark the location on the sash and drill another hole for the magnet. Then drill an angled hole at the edge of the side trim. Use a bent coat hanger to hook and "fish" the wires out toward the transmitter.

MAGNET

MAGNET CONTACT

Get a neater look with hidden contacts

If you don't like the look of transmitters and magnets, use "plunger" contacts ($4) on doors, double-hung windows and sliding patio doors. The plunger is a simple mechanical switch that triggers when pressure against it is released. When a door or window opens, the plunger triggers a separate transmitter ($40), which then sends a signal to the control panel. To install a plunger, drill a hole for the plunger and another hole in the drywall for the wires. If you paint it to match the wall, the transmitter will be barely noticeable.

PLUNGER CONTACT

CONTACTS

TRANSMITTER

Use one transmitter for multiple windows

If you have banks of windows, you can connect all the contacts (whether they're the plunger or magnetic type) to a single transmitter. On a bank of three windows, that saves you about $60. Plus, you get a neater look. The catch is that you have to remove the bottom piece of trim so you can run wires under the sill.

Question&Answer

CFLs FOR OUTDOOR PHOTOCELLS

Save energy and still use dimmers with these flood, spot and decorative CFLs.

Labels in image: OUTDOOR CFL FLOOD, DIMMABLE CFL FLOOD, DIMMABLE MINI SPOT, DECORATIVE CFL

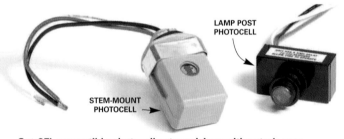

Get CFL-compatible photocells at precisionmulticontrols.com.

Labels in image: LAMP POST PHOTOCELL, STEM-MOUNT PHOTOCELL

I want to swap out some outdoor incandescent floodlights for compact fluorescent bulbs (CFLs), but there's one problem. The lights are controlled by a photocell, a feature we really like. We can't find any CFL bulbs that work with a photocell. Does such a thing even exist?

The problem is with the photocell, not the bulb. The circuitry in older photocells often isn't compatible with the ballasts in CFLs. But that doesn't mean you have to throw out the old fixture—just retrofit it. We found a manufacturer that guarantees its photocells will work with all CFLs on the market. Precision Multicontrols sells several styles of photocells and you can buy them at its Web site, precisionmulticontrols.com. Buy a weatherproof electrical box or a three-hole floodlight mounting plate and attach a stem-mounted photocell in one of the openings. Then connect the new photocell in place of the old one. If you have a lamppost, you can convert it with the "button"-style photocell shown.

Read the package label before you buy any outdoor CFL floodlight, especially if you live in Siberia—or even worse, Minnesota (like we do). Most have a cold-start temperature rating of only zero degrees F. But a company called 1000Bulbs.com sells outdoor CFL floodlights that are rated down to minus 20° F. It also stocks a wide variety of dimmable CFL bulbs for track lights and chandeliers.

PROTECT YOUR EXPENSIVE ELECTRONIC DEVICES

I just purchased a 50-in. plasma TV. Should I buy a surge protector for it just like I have for my computer?

Yes. Any device with a computer chip, whether it's a $20 digital clock or a $5,000 home theater system, is vulnerable to sudden voltage spikes that routinely travel through your electrical wiring. If the spike has enough energy, it'll punch through the chip and ruin it, forcing you to either junk your TV or spend hundreds of dollars for repairs. Lightning during storms causes most damaging surges, but smaller surges, many generated within your home (by vacuum cleaner motors, refrigerator compressors, and so on), also gradually degrade and destroy computer chips. Homes with long lines from the utility pole (rural and "outer ring" suburban homes) and in regions with lots of thunderstorms are especially vulnerable. For an expensive TV and any other electronic item you value highly, we recommend two-stage surge protection.

WHEN TO REPLACE FLUORESCENT BULBS

Some of the bulbs in my garage are turning black on the end. Is it hard on the ballast to keep using them until they go completely dead?

No. Bulbs with black ends can run for a long time and they won't damage your ballast at all. But you should have replacement bulbs on hand for the day when they begin flickering, take a long time to fire up or finally give up completely. That's because running a fluorescent fixture with a burned-out bulb will damage the ballast.

Bulbs with black ends don't require immediate replacement. But you should have new bulbs on hand so you can replace them promptly when they do burn out.

UPGRADE FLUORESCENT FIXTURES AND SAVE ENERGY

I've heard that the bulb manufacturers are going to phase out the T-12 fluorescent bulbs my shop lights use. I tried two of the energy-saving T-8 bulbs and they fit the sockets of my old fixture. Is it OK to use them in place of the old T-12s?

No. The bulbs may fit and light up, but if you don't update the ballast, the new bulbs will burn out in no time. To get the expected life and light output from the new bulbs, you'll have to install a ballast that's right for your fixture and the bulb. Ballasts are rated by the type and number of bulbs the fixture holds. The light output is determined by the "ballast factor." (This information is on the ballast label.) A high ballast factor means more lumens, but also more energy con-

Buy a new ballast based on the type and number of bulbs your fixture holds, as well as on the ballast factor and the sound rating.

sumption and shorter bulb life. Ballasts also come in magnetic and electronic versions. We recommend an electronic ballast with a ballast factor of 79 percent or less and an "A" noise rating ($22). That combination will give you adequate light output, low noise (hum), and long bulb life with a minimum of bulb "flicker."

The downside to updating your ballast is that a ballast costs almost as much as a new fixture. If your fixtures are high-quality ones you want to keep or they're mounted to the ceiling and wired in conduit, you'll save time by installing a new ballast. But if yours are hung by chains and plugged into a receptacle, buying a new fixture may be your best option.

Find electronic ballasts in the lighting department at most home centers.

CAUTION: Environmental Warning: Old ballasts may contain polychlorinated biphenyls (PCBs), a toxic substance that must be disposed of properly. Bring old ballasts to your local recycling center for disposal.

AUTOMATED LIGHTING FROM YOUR CAR

Are there any home lighting systems that will let me turn on the lights inside my house from my car? Timers aren't an option because I come home at different times, and I like to walk into a well-lit house.

One system is from Lutron (888-588-7661; lutron.com). Called AuroRa, it uses dimmers (which replace your existing switches), a tabletop master control that's plugged into a standard wall outlet, a wireless control and an antenna to control the lights. You just press a button to turn on or off the lights or dim them from your car, bedside or anywhere else you take the controller.

You install the dimmers in five areas of the home and control them with the wireless control. You can add controllers and dimmers at any time.

This system is ready to use right out of the box—no programming required. You only have to replace five conventional switches with the new dimmers.

The dimmers let you adjust the light levels in each room. When you turn on the lights with the controller, the lights turn on to the level currently set on the dimmer. Double-click the button and the light will turn on to 100 percent, regardless of where the dimmer slider is set, so you can overrule the setting if you want.

But home automation isn't cheap. This system starts at $800. Find retailers on the company's Web site.

Save Electricity & Water

ENERGY VAMPIRES

Save $100 a year or more by finding and fixing these watt wasters

According to the U.S. Department of Energy, you're paying $100 per year for nothing. The culprits are your "energy vampires," those electrical appliances that continuously draw power even after you've hit the "off" button. Admittedly, some items, like your refrigerator and heating system, need to run 24/7, but many others, like your computer, DVD player or coffeemaker, don't. The problem is that these appliances possess "smart" features—miscellaneous chips and/or electronic controls that prevent them from ever shutting down. Most energy vampires only suck a few watts apiece (see Figure A), but considering that the average home contains 20 of these watt wasters, the cost adds up. By some estimates, energy vampires now make up 11 percent of your utility bill and will cost you even more in the future. The good news is that you can search out and stake these vampires in the heart with a simple strategy and a few cool tools. You'll also learn how to keep the least efficient appliances out of your home in the first place.

The EPA estimates that energy vampires consume

$4 billion

worth of power per year. That's equal to the amount of electricity generated by 12 power plants!

Figure A: Where are the watts going?

Some appliances use more power than others even when doing nothing. Until recently, manufacturers didn't worry about standby power because consumers didn't consider the cost.

	WATTS CONSUMED	YEARLY COST @ 8¢ PER KW
Portable stereo	1 – 8	70¢ – $5.60
Component system	1 – 16	70¢ – $11.12
DVD player	1 – 13	70¢ – $9.10
5 battery chargers	1 each	$3.50
Printer	4 – 6	$2.80 – $4.20
Cable box	5 – 25	$3.50 – $17.50
Modem	4 – 20	$2.80 – $14.00
Satellite system	10 – 20	$7.00 – $14.00
Television	up to 23	up to $16.10
VCR	1 – 14	70¢ – $9.80
Computer (sleep mode)	1 – 6	70¢ – $4.20
Monitor (sleep mode)	up to 15	up to $10.50
Total		up to $120.00

New Tools & Gear

Water-use monitor

The WaterWatch Garden and Outdoor Meter is an easy, inexpensive ($10) way to monitor your outside water usage. Simply attach it to the end of your garden hose and it'll tell you how much water you're using (and paying for) to water the garden, wash the car or run the sprinklers. You can use the information to give each section of your yard the same amount of water and avoid waste. Or use it to precisely measure water when mixing concrete. The meter monitors water usage up to 100 gallons. When you turn off the water, the gauge starts over at zero. Buy it online from the manufacturer.

H2O Watch, (866) 426-9282. h2owatch.net

Check your computer

Some PCs draw as much as 250 watts, almost as much as an energy-efficient refrigerator. To rein in your power-hungry processor, set your machine to go into "sleep" or "hibernate" mode when left unused for more than 30 minutes. For more savings, turn off the processor, monitor, printer and speakers if they won't be used for more than two hours. Despite the myth, cycling your computer on and off will not damage the system.

Ways to stop the drain

Here are a few simple solutions that can help you stop unwanted energy vampires.

- **Pull the plug.** If an appliance has an indicator light, touch screen or feels the least bit warm to the touch, it's using power. You can't unplug everything, but pulling the plug on a few items, such as the coffeemaker, battery chargers and VCR, can save as much as turning off a light.

- **Strip stop.** Surge protectors enable you to turn off multiple devices with one switch. The Smart Strip (see Buyer's Guide) is handy when you can't easily reach the strip. This surge protector automatically shuts off peripherals when the main unit, such as your computer or TV, is turned off. The strip has "always on" receptacles for satellite boxes, modems and wireless routers.

- **Read the fine print.** Manufacturers don't usually include standby power info on the box. A plug-in meter is your best bet, but another way to decrease wasted electricity is by choosing appliances with fewer bells and whistles. Looking for the Energy Star logo can also help.

Meter readers and plug-in watt watchers

Unplugging your refrigerator, then manually reading the still-spinning meter, will show that you've got a problem, but because you're calculating a single moment, it's not terribly accurate. To find and fix the drain, you'll need either a digital meter reader or a plug-in meter. Both devices show real-time usage. More important, they track longer trends so you can see how much an appliance is costing you when it's on and off. Using one or both can help you pinpoint energy vampires. From there, you can decide to pull the plug or shop for an energy-efficient replacement.

Plug-in meters measure single devices. Simply plug the unit into the wall, then connect the appliance to the meter. P3 International's Kill A Watt EZ (model No. 4460) will tell you the operating cost of any household appliance per day, week, month or year. A meter can show you how much money you can save by upgrading older appliances. Replacing a 10-year-old refrigerator with an Energy Star model can save over $100 a year. Digital meter readers measure whole-house electricity use. They attach to your meter or panel box to provide real time and average usage/cost information. To find out how much all your energy vampires are costing you, turn off all the lights, unplug the refrigerator, then check the screen.

A meter reader displays real-time usage and records consumption info so that you can watch your watts over a longer time frame.

Buyer's Guide

- **The Energy Detective: (800) 959-5833. theenergydetective.com. The T.E.D. monitor shown costs $145.**

- **smart home systems: (888) 843-9103. smarthomeusa.com. The SmartStrip costs $31.**

SaveElectricity&Water

DUAL-FUEL HEAT PUMPS

This double-duty unit cools and helps heat your home... for less.
Replace your old A/C and save $500 each year!

Conventional heat pumps have been heating and cooling homes for decades. In fact, about one in three homes in the United States already uses one. However, there aren't many north of the Mason-Dixon Line because they don't work efficiently in subfreezing temperatures. These heat pumps are great at pumping heat in or out of a house in moderate temperature swings like those found in the Sun Belt. But they're notoriously inefficient and expensive to run in cold Northern winters.

"Dual-fuel" heat pumps are different. Attached to your existing furnace, this system looks (and works, during the summer) like a high-efficiency central air conditioner. However, in those mild spring and

fall months in the snowbelt, they provide cheap heat just as well as they do in the South. As the temperatures drop, the pump shuts off and tells your furnace to take over.

A dual-fuel heat pump, such as Lennox's XP-14, will cost about 20 to 25 percent more (including installation) than an A/C. Depending on your region and fuel costs, however, it can pay for itself in five or six years.

Heating with a dual-fuel heat pump

As long as the temperature is above 35° F or so, a heat pump can pull heat from the outside air for less than it costs to fire up the furnace. The furnace kicks in for only the coldest months.

Heat pumps save energy because transferring heat is easier than making it. Surprisingly, even when it feels cold outside, there is still a decent amount of heat waiting to be pumped. Under ideal conditions, a heat pump can transfer 300 percent more energy than it consumes. In contrast, a high-efficiency gas furnace is about 90 percent efficient.

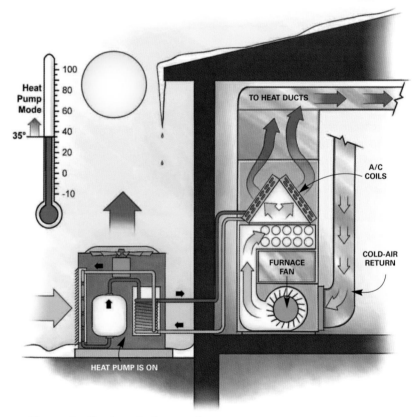

Figure A: Cool-period operation

During cooler seasons like fall and spring, the heat pump handles the heating duties. The dual-fuel system still incorporates the furnace, but without using any burners, just its air distribution features. The heat pump sends hot "refrigerant" through the air conditioning coil within the furnace. The furnace fan draws air from the home's cold-air returns and blows that air over the warm coil and then sends the warmed air throughout the house. In the summer, the heat pump reverses the refrigerant flow so cold liquid flows over the coil and cools your home just like a conventional air conditioner.

Pumping cheap heat out of thin air

As shown in **Figure A**, an air-source heat pump is basically a hybrid air conditioner. Both have a compressor (a high-pressure pump) that circulates refrigerant (a volatile gas) through indoor and outdoor coils, a network of tubes designed to facilitate the capture and release of heat. But while an air conditioner can move refrigerant in only one direction, a heat pump can force refrigerant in either direction, for heating one way and cooling the other. The pump does this by means of an extra diverting device called a switchover valve.

Run the numbers

To figure out whether a heat pump is practical for your home, you'll need to contact a heating contractor and ask a few questions:

Start with a Heating and Cooling Load Analysis. Don't trust the label on the old furnace; ask your installer to show you the math. According to some reports, there's a good chance that your system may not have been sized correctly in the first place. Even if it was sized properly originally, subsequent home improvement projects (new insulation, new windows or an addition) can change your heating and cooling needs.

Check the numbers. Manufacturers use different technologies, but one number can provide an apples-to-apples comparison. For cooling efficiency, check the Seasonal Efficiency Ratio (SEER). The higher the SEER, the more efficient the unit is. Of course, units with higher ratios cost more, but every two points can reduce cooling costs by about 15 percent. (Energy Star–rated pumps are at least 8 percent more efficient than standard models.)

Conduct a comparative cost analysis. If you live in an area with lower-priced natural gas and sky-high electrical rates, a heat pump will not pay itself off as quickly. Your installer can factor in local energy rates (including peak and off-peak electrical rates) to calculate your potential savings and payback.

Ask about compatibility. Dual-fuel heat pumps are designed to work as a straightforward A/C replacement, but older furnaces probably won't work with a new switch-hitting system. You'll probably have to upgrade to a brand new furnace to have this system—adding a sizable chunk to the cost of the project.

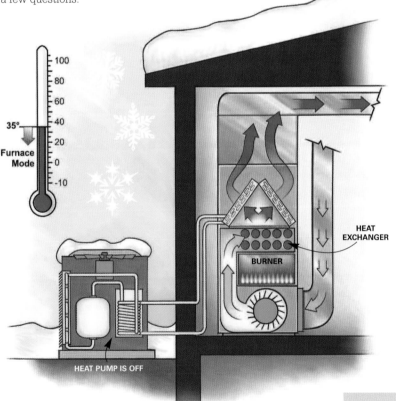

HEAT EXCHANGER

BURNER

HEAT PUMP IS OFF

Figure B: Cold-period operation

During cold periods, the heat pump slumbers while the furnace takes over, supplying the heat by operating like the conventional furnace it is. The burners ignite the fuel (oil, propane or natural gas) and the furnace fan blows air drawn from the cold-air returns and warms it by blowing it over the heat exchanger and on throughout the home.

Check into tax credits

In addition to saving money in the long run, a dual-fuel heat pump might pay you back right away. This upgrade may qualify for an energy-savings tax credit plus rebates. Ask your utility company and HVAC installer about available incentives in your area.

SaveElectricity&Water

EXPERT ENERGY-SAVING TIPS

Clever ideas for using less energy—and saving money!

Over the years, we've shown boatloads of tips for saving energy. We've gone back through our archives to find the best energy-saving tips, and then worked with energy expert Erik Lindberg to add some new ones. These tips are easy to implement, won't cost much (if anything) and will save you money on your heating and cooling bills.

A basic part of an energy audit is the blower door test. The auditor closes all the doors and windows and then places a blower fan in a front or back door. This blower door test measures the "tightness," or air infiltration rate. The pressure and flow gauge (inset photo) shows the difference between the inside and the outside airflow so the auditor can calculate the air leakage rate.

Get an energy audit

An energy audit entails a series of tests, including the blower door pressure test (shown), that tell you the efficiency of your heating and cooling system and the overall efficiency of your home. On the basis of the test results, the auditor will recommend low-cost improvements to save energy and larger upgrades that will pay you back within five to seven years. Audits take two to three hours and cost $250 to $400, but if you set one up through your utility company, you may be eligible for a rebate. For more information, visit thefamilyhandyman/com and search "energy audit."

Best way to find attic leaks

To find out where warm air is escaping into your attic, look in your attic for insulation that has darkened (the result of filtering dirty air from the house). In cold weather, you might even see frosty

areas in the insulation caused by warm, moist air condensing and freezing as it hits the cold attic air. In warmer weather, you'll find water staining in the same areas. For information on sealing the leaks, visit thefamilyhandyman.com.

Stop a draft in 60 seconds

According to Erik Lindberg's energy audits, electrical boxes that hold switches or outlets are major sources of heat loss. Foam gaskets ($3 for a pack of 12 at home centers) won't completely seal the boxes, but they'll help. They're quick to install—just take off the cover plate, stick the gasket over the box, then put the plate back on.

3 Plumbing, Heating & Appliances

IN THIS CHAPTER

EASY WATER SOFTENER FIXES

Is your soft water not so soft anymore? You can often fix the problem yourself. However, if you have an older softener (20 years or so) and none of these fixes work, it may need replacement ($500 and up).

All softeners, whether they have one or two tanks, work the same way. As cold water flows through the resin tank, the mineral content—the hardness—is removed because the minerals stick to thousands of resin beads. When the softener recharges, the flow of fresh water is stopped while salty water from the brine tank is sucked into the resin tank, where it dissolves the accumulated minerals and is flushed down the drain.

Before you tear apart your softener, check the control settings—especially after a long power outage. The timer clock has to show the right time so that the resin tank is cleaned and recharged when no one is using water (usually early morning).

Also make sure the hardness setting is still correct—well water hardness can change over time. Bring a small container of your water to a water softener dealer for a water hardness test, then check the results against your settings.

Note: Set the water supply to "bypass" before working on the softener. And run the hot water after you turn the softener back on to flush out any hard water.

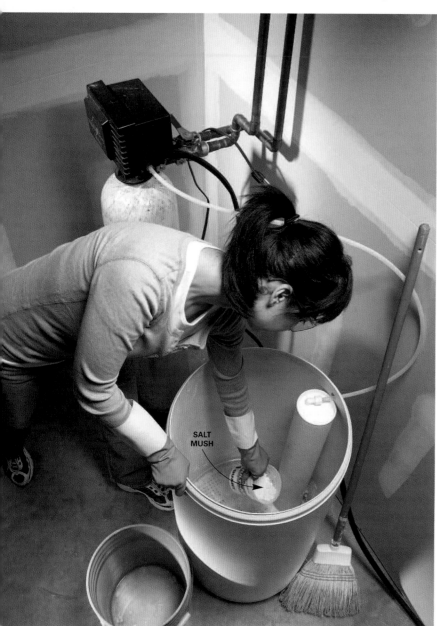

SALT
MUSH

1 Look for salt problems

Check for salt problems in the brine tank. Start by pushing a broom handle down into the salt to break up salt bridges (like a dome), blocking salt from dropping to the bottom of the tank. If too little salt gets dissolved, the resin bed won't get clean and the water won't get softened.

Also, when the salt level is low (or at least once a year), check for a crust of salt mush at the bottom. This thick salt paste doesn't dissolve well, reducing the salinity of the brine solution, and needs to be removed (**photo left**).

Don't use rock salt; it contains dirt and other impurities that can clog the softener.

Scoop out the mush at the bottom of the tank, then pour in hot water to dissolve the rest before regenerating the system.

2 Clean the resin bed

Clean the resin bed twice a year with resin bed cleaner (available at water softener dealers) if you have "clear water iron" (dissolved iron makes a glass of water turn cloudy or rusty after sitting for several minutes). Otherwise the resin bed won't remove the iron (**photo right**).

Pour diluted resin cleaner into the brinewell tube. Lift out the air check valve (or brine valve assembly) and clean it in warm water.

Left: Remove the cap that covers the venturi assembly and filter screen and carefully remove the parts.

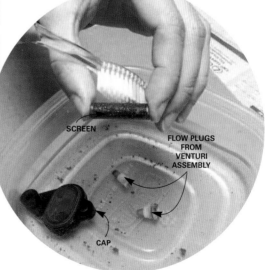

3 Clean the venturi assembly

The salty water flows through these parts from the brine tank to the resin tank. If the screen and nozzle get clogged by sediment, the resin bed won't be cleaned and the water will stay hard (**photos above**).

Gently clean dirt and mineral deposits from the screen and from the venturi assembly parts in a pan of warm water.

HomeCare & Repair

REPLACE A BROKEN ICEMAKER

If your icemaker stops working, there's no need to call the appliance repair service. First, locate the saddle valve that's clamped to the house water supply and turn it off and on a few times to break up any mineral buildup clogging the valve. If that doesn't work, unplug the refrigerator and remove the icemaker (**Photo 1**) to make sure the water inlet at the back of the refrigerator isn't plugged with ice (just heat it with a hair dryer if it is). However, if the water supply isn't blocked and the refrigerator is older, it's time to replace the icemaker. According to appliance repair pros, most icemakers break down long before the refrigerator. The good news is that most replacement kits are in the $100 to $125 range, and installing one is simple.

Locate the model number on the wall of the refrigerator just inside the door, then buy a new ice-maker at an appliance store or online (do a search for "appliance parts").

Unplug the refrigerator and turn the water off, then take the old icemaker out and disconnect the wiring. Plug the new icemaker in (**Photo 2**), hold it in position and screw it to the refrigerator wall.

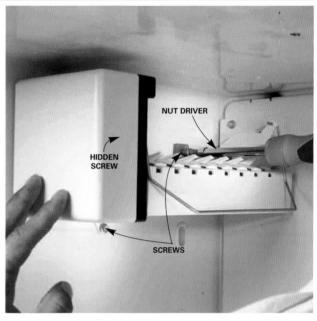

NUT DRIVER

HIDDEN SCREW

SCREWS

1 Use a nut driver or a long screwdriver to remove the screws that hold the icemaker in place.

UPGRADE AN ICEMAKER SUPPLY LINE

Inexpensive plastic water lines and saddle valves sold for icemakers can eventually clog or leak, causing water damage.

You can replace your plastic water line with a copper tee fitting, a high-quality shutoff and a braided steel supply line in a half hour for about $25—and never have to worry about leaks again. Braided steel is a tough, non-kinking alternative to 1/4-in. flexible copper or plastic.

Turn off the house water supply and drain the water from the entire system. Remove the saddle valve and cut out the copper underneath it (**Photo 1**). You may need to cut more, depending on how much play you have in the water line, to make room for a repair coupling and additional copper if needed.

Unscrew the packing nut from the shutoff and remove the handle and core before soldering. Jiggle the water lines to get all the water out, then clean and flux the fittings and solder everything together (**Photo 2**).

Allow the pipe to cool for several minutes, then reattach the shutoff handle. Close the shutoff and turn the house water back on to check for leaks. Attach the braided water line (**Photo 3**), then run the water into a bucket or sink for a few minutes to flush out any corrosion or bits of solder. Finally, fish the water line through the floor or wall to the back of the refrigerator (**Photo 4**).

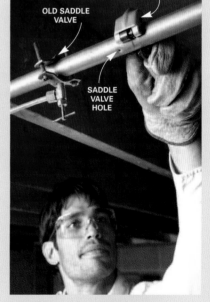

PIPE CUTTER

OLD SADDLE VALVE

SADDLE VALVE HOLE

1 Unscrew the valve and slide it aside. Cut the water line to make room for a new tee fitting.

BRAIDED STAINLESS STEEL SUPPLY LINE

Pull the refrigerator out from the wall, disconnect the water supply from the inlet valve at the bottom of the refrigerator, then replace the old inlet valve (**Photo 3**). Inlet valves should be replaced when the icemaker is replaced, and are usually included with replacement kits. If not, order it separately.

Before you push the refrigerator back, turn the water on and check for leaks.

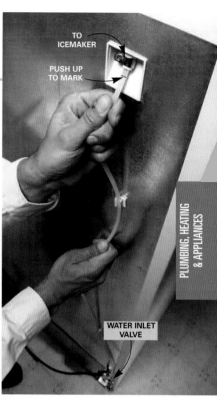

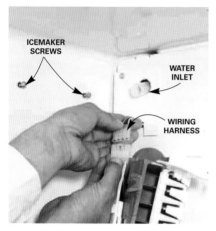

2 Line up the wiring harnesses and plug them together before screwing the icemaker in place.

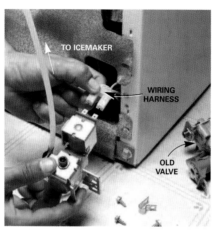

3 Remove the old inlet valve and plug in the new one, then attach it to the frame.

4 Push the water supply from the inlet valve onto the barbed fitting at the top of the refrigerator.

2 Clean, flux and assemble the copper fittings and the shutoff valve, then solder the joints.

3 Hand-tighten the water line to the shutoff, then turn the nut another half-turn with a wrench.

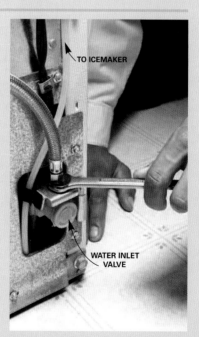

4 Attach the water line to the water inlet valve at the back of the refrigerator.

HomeCare & Repair

PREVENT HOUSE FIRES — CLEAN OUT DRYER LINT

Built-up lint inside dryer cabinets causes more than 15,000 fires every year. Lint escapes through tiny gaps around the edges of the dryer drum and falls into the cabinet, especially when the exhaust vent or vent cap is clogged and airflow is restricted. The lint can get ignited by electric heating elements, gas burners or even a spark from the motor, and the flames then travel through the lint-lined exhaust vent. To make sure this doesn't happen in your house, check the exhaust vent and the inside of the cabinet frequently.

To clean the exhaust duct, shut off the gas and unplug the dryer, then pull the dryer away from the wall and disconnect the duct from the dryer. Use a brush and a vacuum to remove the lint in the duct. If you have a flexible duct (especially the plastic type!), replace it with rigid metal duct.

To clean inside the dryer, unplug it and turn off the gas, then open either the top or the front. The procedure is the same for gas and electric dryers. For dryers with a top lint filter and a solid front panel, remove the lint filter and take out the two screws on the side of the filter opening. Pull the top forward (**Photo 1**). Disconnect the door-switch wires in the front corner, remove the front screws and drop the panel forward (**Photo 2**). The drum will tip as the panel drops, but this won't damage anything. Just hold it up while you clean.

Brush and vacuum under the drum and at the top and back of the dryer. Clean thoroughly around the heating element, but work gently around wires and mechanical parts. Use a long brush to clean the vent, then vacuum it from the top and back (**Photo 3**).

Finally, reassemble the dryer. Put the front into the drum and lift, then drop the front into the catches near the bottom while holding it tight against the sides. Reattach the front screws and wires, then set the top back down.

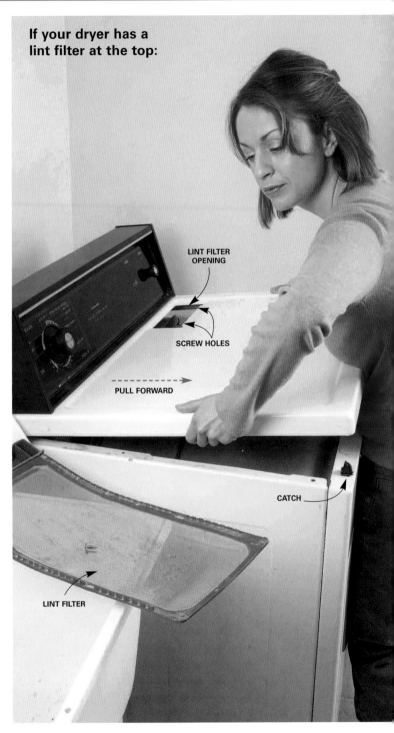

If your dryer has a lint filter at the top:

LINT FILTER OPENING

SCREW HOLES

PULL FORWARD

CATCH

LINT FILTER

1 Remove the screws under the lint filter, then jerk the top forward and lift it up to release it from the catches at the corners.

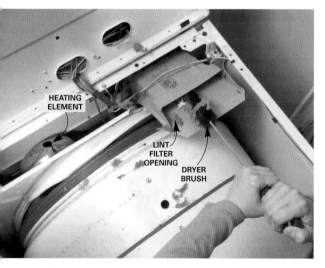

2 Remove the two screws near the top, then tip the front forward and lift it clear of the bottom catches and the drum.

CATCH

CATCH

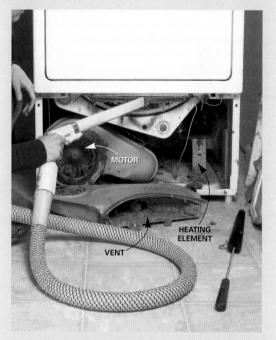

HEATING ELEMENT

LINT FILTER OPENING

DRYER BRUSH

3 Brush out the lint inside the lint filter opening and vacuum all around the drum.

If your dryer has a front access panel:

For dryers with a removable front panel, release the metal catches (or remove screws) and pull the panel off (**Photo 1**). Remove the screws that hold the vent in place, then clean out the lint with a vacuum and brush (**Photo 2**).

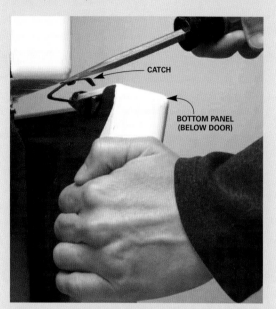

CATCH

BOTTOM PANEL (BELOW DOOR)

1 Slide a screwdriver into the gap at the top of the bottom panel at the two catches to release the panel.

MOTOR

HEATING ELEMENT

VENT

2 Vacuum out the motor, the vent and the inside of the dryer. Clean carefully around wires and small parts to avoid breaking them.

HomeCare&Repair

1 Cut the old caulk with a utility knife and pull out the vent from the outside.

BIRD'S NEST

2 Insert the duct from the dryer into the new vent duct and wrap the joint with metal tape.

METAL TAPE

NEW CAULK

REPLACE A BROKEN DRYER VENT CAP

Dryer vent caps are deliberately lightweight so they'll open easily, but this flimsiness also means they'll break easily. The caps, especially the type with multiple small flaps, also clog easily with lint. (Avoid this type unless you're conscientious about cleaning it.)

To replace an old vent cap, first pull apart the duct at the last joint inside the house. If they don't pull apart easily, look for small screws holding the sections of pipe together. Next, remove the screws or nails used to attach the cap to the siding and cut through the caulk around the edges (**Photo 1**). Pull out the cap, scrape away old caulk and dirt, and then wipe the siding clean so new caulk will stick.

Cut the new vent pipe to the same length as the old one, then slide it through the wall. Screw the cap to the siding and caulk around the edges with paintable caulk.

Finally, join the old duct inside the house to the new vent (**Photo 2**). Vent caps are available for $8 at home centers.

SILENCE A NOISY CHECK VALVE

Waste lines from a sewage ejector or sump pump use a check valve to stop wastewater from flowing back into the basin. When these valves shut, they can make a thud loud enough to be heard throughout the house.

To quiet them, replace the old check valve with a "silent" or "soft close" check valve.

Remove the section of waste line under the check valve, disconnecting it at the union or coupling above the basin—or cutting the pipe.

Drain the water above the check valve, then loosen the clamps and remove it (**Photo 1**). If you don't have a shutoff valve above the check valve, install a "full port" shutoff valve ($10) on the waste line above the check valve. You won't get soaked with dirty water the next time you service the check valve.

Cut the waste pipe to the proper length and attach the silent check valve (**Photo 2**). Reassemble the pipes, open the shutoff valve and turn on the pump.

Silent check valves are available from plumbing suppliers for $35. The type we used is made by A. Y. McDonald (Series 2069). Contact customer service at aymcdonald.com or (800) 292-2737 if you need help finding a local distributor.

1 Push a long screwdriver up into the old check valve to drain the water above the valve.

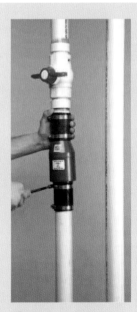

2 Push the pipe fully into the rubber sleeves of the check valve, then tighten the band clamps to seal the joints.

FIX YOUR SEWAGE EJECTION PUMP—SAVE $$

When sewage ejection pumps fail, you can quickly have an ugly mess on the basement floor. Before you panic and call the plumber (minimum charge $250), make sure the "float" switch works. Most sewage ejector pumps and some sump pumps have a floating ball attached to the pump by a separate electrical cord—if you see two cords coming out of the basin, you have a float switch. This switch activates the pump when the water reaches a certain height. The switch is plugged in with a "piggyback" plug, and the pump is plugged into the back of it so it doesn't turn on until the switch does (**Photo 1**).

Unfortunately, these switches may only last half as long as the pump, according to manufacturers. However, universal replacement switches are available at home centers and plumbing suppliers for $20, and replacing the switch is simple.

First check the circuit breaker and GFCI outlet. If they're OK, unplug the pump from the back of the piggyback plug and plug it in directly. If the pump kicks on, the switch is bad. If it doesn't turn on, the pump is bad, but replacing it ($300, including switch) is just as easy as replacing the switch—simply lift out the old pump and put a new one in.

If the pump works, run water for a minute to flush out the dirty water—but don't let the water level go below the pump or you'll burn out the pump. Then remove the basin top. Pull the vent pipe from the top and loosen the coupling or union that joins the waste line together (wrap a towel around the pipe to catch any water).

Lift out the pump and mark the point where the cord that holds the switch is attached to the pump. Attach the new switch at the same point so it will turn on and off at the same water level (**Photo 2**). Also check to be sure there's an air bleed hole near the bottom of the waste pipe (another potential cause of pump failure). If you don't see one, drill a 1/16-in.-diameter hole into the waste pipe about 2 in. from where it enters the pump.

Put the pump back in the basin and reassemble the plumbing. Make sure the float switch moves freely and doesn't get wedged against the sides. Seal around the edge of the basin with silicone caulk if the original gasket or seal is deteriorated.

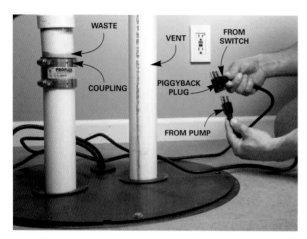

1 Test the switch by bypassing the piggyback plug and plugging the pump in directly to see if it works.

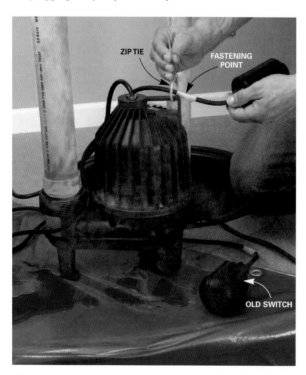

2 Use a plastic zip tie to attach the new switch cord to the pump at the same point the old cord was attached.

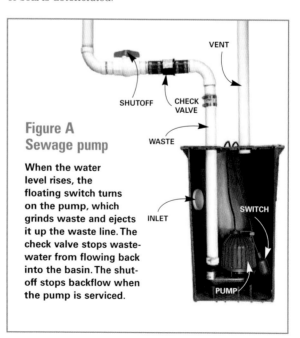

Figure A
Sewage pump

When the water level rises, the floating switch turns on the pump, which grinds waste and ejects it up the waste line. The check valve stops wastewater from flowing back into the basin. The shutoff stops backflow when the pump is serviced.

HOW TO STOP A
RUNNING
TOILET

. . . and get a stronger flush while you're at it

Toilets haven't changed much in the last 80 years. After a flush, water still fills a tank, lifting a float that shuts off the water when it reaches a certain level. A lever still opens a flapper to cause the flush, falling back into place when the water level drops. So it's no surprise (nor any consolation) that we face the same flush problems today that our grandparents did. Sometimes the flush is too wimpy, sometimes the water keeps running, and sometimes the bowl doesn't refill.

Our ace plumber, Les Zell, has a simple four-step strategy to solve 95 percent of these problems. You can complete the first three steps in five minutes. That'll solve most problems. The fourth step is usually easy too, but not always. More on this later. These steps work for most toilets but not for pressure-assist models.

STEP **1**

Check the fill tube

Remove the tank lid and find the fill tube. It's a small flexible tube that runs from the fill valve to the overflow tube. While the tank refills, this tube squirts enough water down the overflow tube to refill the bowl after the completed flush. If this tube falls off or the water stream misses the overflow tube, the bowl won't fill and your next flush will be wimpy (that is, won't develop a strong siphon). Reattach the fill tube and make sure it perches about 1 in. above the rim of the overflow tube. Flush the toilet and watch the water stream to make sure it goes down the overflow tube.

Push the fill tube firmly onto the fill valve. Make sure the fill tube sends water into the overflow tube.

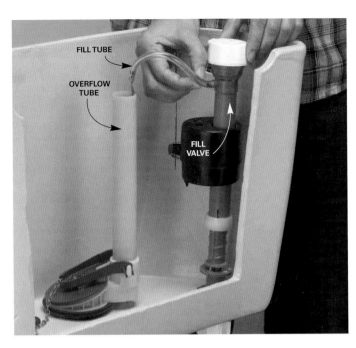

FILL TUBE

OVERFLOW TUBE

FILL VALVE

WATER LEVEL MARK

CLIP

ROD

FLOAT

Adjust the float to set the water level. Pinch the clip and slide the float up or down on the rod. Keep adjusting the float until the water shuts off at the proper level.

STEP **2**

Adjust the fill height

The water level in the tank is controlled by an adjustable float. A float that's set too low produces a weak flush; if it's set too high, water spills into the overflow tube and the fill valve won't shut off. The water will keep running. Look for the fill level mark on the inside back of the tank and mark it on the overflow tube so you can see it more easily. If you can't find it, measure down about 1 in. on the overflow tube and make a mark. Then flush the toilet and see if the water reaches and stops at that mark. If not, adjust the float up or down. If you have an old toilet, you'll have to bend the brass rod that connects to the float ball to make adjustments. But with newer toilets you usually turn a screw or slide a clip along a rod. Flush the toilet after each adjustment.

Also make sure that the water level is at least an inch below the C-L (critical level) marked on the fill valve. You can adjust the height of many valves to raise or lower the C-L.

Occasionally the fill valve simply won't shut off, which means that it's defective. If so, turn the water supply off at the shutoff under the tank. Buy a replacement valve ($6 to $10 at hardware stores and home centers). You don't have to match the old one; many, like the one shown, fit most toilets. It's a 15-minute change-out. For detailed instructions, go to thefamilyhandyman.com and search for "fill valve."

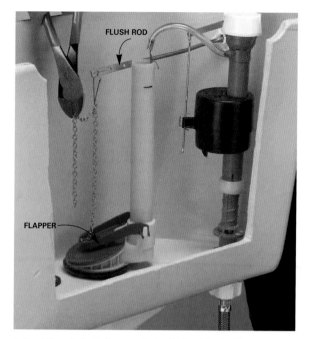

FLUSH ROD

FLAPPER

Adjust the chain to leave a little slack with the flapper closed. Then cut off the excess, leaving about an inch.

STEP 3

Adjust the flush handle/flapper chain

A chain that's too short or tangled won't allow the flapper to close and water will continue to leak into the bowl. This causes the fill valve to cycle on and off to refill the tank. A chain that's too long, or a flush rod that hits the tank lid, won't open the flapper wide enough to stay open for the full flush. You'll find yourself having to hold the lever to complete a good flush.

To avoid these problems, adjust the linkage in the chain to leave only a slight bit of slack when closed. Cut the chain at the rod to leave only about an inch extra to reduce the potential for tangles. Then put the tank lid back on and make sure the flush rod doesn't strike the lid when you press the lever. If it does, bend it down slightly and re-adjust the chain.

Tip

Wear plastic gloves when you remove the flapper. A fine black film often builds up on rubber surfaces and is hard to scrub off your hands.

STEP 4

Replace the flapper

If you've completed the first three steps and your toilet still runs, chances are you have a worn-out flapper. Turn off the water, remove the old flapper and take it to the store to find an exact replacement. (Hardware stores often carry a wide variety.) Most flappers snap over ears on the overflow tube. Others have a ring that slips over the tube.

Now here's the catch. You may not find an exact match. The range of flapper styles has mushroomed over the last 15 years, and you may find 15 to 20 flapper options on the store shelf. Some packages include specific brand and model information (so note yours before you leave home). Others have a "universal" label. If you can't find an exact replacement, try the closest one and pick up a universal type as well. They're cheap ($2 to $3), and the extra one just might save you a second trip to the store! (Avoid the "adjustable" types unless you're replacing an adjustable one.)

Install the new flapper and make sure it opens and closes freely. Then test it. If the water continues to run or runs intermittently, you're not getting a good seal. Try a different flapper.

If you just can't find a flapper that seals, consider replacing the entire overflow tube/flapper (about $10). On most toilets (two-piece), this means removing the tank. It's not difficult and you don't need special tools. It'll take you about an hour, and you'll avoid that $100 plumber service call.

Unsnap the old flapper and take it with you to the store to find an exact replacement. In addition to the closest replacement, pick up a "universal" type.

Handy Hints®

SPARKLING DISHWASHER

Add a cup of vinegar to your empty dishwasher and let it run a full cycle once a month or so. Your kitchen may smell a bit like a pickle jar for a few hours, but hard-water lime buildup will be rinsed away, making your spray arm and other dishwasher parts work flawlessly.

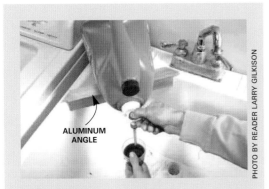

ALUMINUM ANGLE

MINIMIZE LIQUID DETERGENT MESS

Dripless liquid detergent containers always drip just a little. Keep it under control with a special shelf on the corner of the laundry tub. Just cut a 1-1/2-in. aluminum angle long enough to support the front edge of the container, then glue it to the tub with silicone caulk. Rest the container on the ledge and drips will just fall into the laundry tub instead of creating a gooey mess somewhere else.

PHOTO BY READER LARRY GILKISON

VINEGAR

DON'T JUST STAND THERE—SHUT IT OFF!

An overflowing toilet can wreck the floor as well as the ceiling below, so don't let it happen! Next time you see the water in a stopped-up toilet preparing to breach the rim, calmly reach behind the toilet and shut off the valve that feeds the tank. The water will stop instantly, and you'll prevent a big cleanup project.

BETTER DETERGENT DISPENSING

To dispense liquid laundry detergent without lifting it, drill a 1-in. hole through the cabinet bottom directly under the spout. Replace the plastic cap between uses to avoid drips.

GOING ON VACATION?
DON'T COME HOME TO A
DISASTER

*Six easy ways to prevent
catastrophic water damage*

We all think about burglars when we leave town, but when it comes to vacant houses, water does a lot more damage than crooks. This article will show you how to head off the biggest sources of trouble so you can set off on vacation without coming back to any expensive surprises.

Water damage from failed plumbing is responsible for billions of dollars in repair costs each year, and it will cost you plenty if you return home to a flooded kitchen or basement. The main causes of water damage are frozen broken pipes, ruptured washing machine and dishwasher hoses, leaking water heaters, and clogged or leaking icemaker water supply lines.

Regular maintenance can help you prevent water problems in the long term. In the short term, here are six things to do before you head out the door to catch your flight.

1 Shut off the main valve

Shutting off the main valve that controls all the water for your home is the best protection against catastrophic water damage. Everyone in your home should know where the main water shutoff valve is located so they can stop the water in an emergency. And you should turn it off whenever you leave home, even overnight. If you're not sure where it is, look for your water meter; the main shutoff will be located nearby.

Many water meter setups have two valves, one on the street side of the meter and one on the house side. If you live in a colder climate, you'll typically find the main shutoff in the basement near the front of the house. In warmer climates, it will be outside your home attached to an exterior wall or in an underground box with a removable lid.

There are two types of main shutoff valves: the gate valve and the ball valve. The gate valve is common in older homes and has a round handle that must be turned a number of times to open or close the valve. Gate valves are designed to be fully open or fully closed. Water flowing through a partially open gate valve can wear away the metal and cause the valve to fail over time. The ball valve is more common in newer construction and has a lever handle that needs to be turned 90 degrees to turn the water on or off. You can immediately tell if it's open or not: In the closed position, the lever is perpendicular to the pipes; in the open position it's parallel.

If you've never shut off the main water valve before, test it before you leave on vacation. Turn on a faucet somewhere in the house and shut off the main water valve.

Shut off the water supply to your entire home when you leave for overnight or longer.

All water flow should stop. An old gate valve can break, so be gentle when you're handling it. If the valve is stuck, leave it alone. If it leaks or doesn't shut off all the way, have a licensed plumber replace the valve or replace it yourself if you're comfortable with a straightforward plumbing project. You'll need to call your water department (and possibly pay a small fee) to have the water to your house turned off at the curb stop while you make the repair.

If you have a well, shut off the electrical switch for the well when you leave for an extended period so it won't pump any water while you're gone.

Figure A

In warmer climates, the main water shutoff is typically outside, attached to an exterior wall or in an accessible underground box.

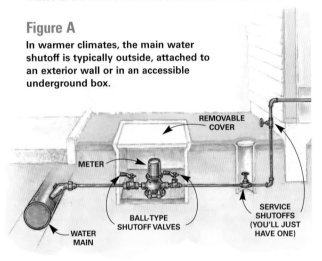

Figure B

In colder climates, the main water shutoff is typically in the basement.

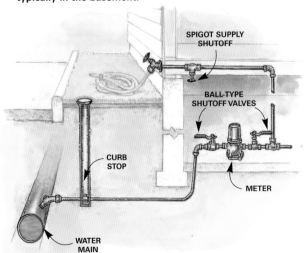

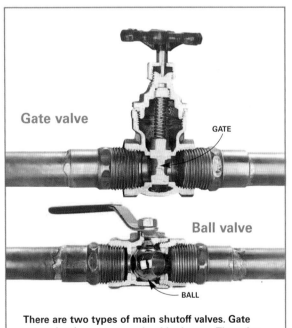

There are two types of main shutoff valves. Gate valves (top) are common in older homes. The valve closes when a wedge-shaped brass gate is lowered into a slot. Ball valves (bottom), which contain a pivoting stainless steel ball with a hole drilled through the center, are less prone to wear.

2 Shut off water supply valves

If you can't shut off the main water supply because you have an automatic sprinkler system or someone watering the plants while you're gone, shut off the valves to the most common sources of water damage such as dishwashers, icemakers and washing machines, in case a hose cracks or lets go. Individual shutoff valves or "stops" are installed on the supply lines leading to most appliances as well as to toilets and faucets. Typical supply stops have a small round or oval handle that you turn clockwise to shut off the flow of water.

The shutoff to your refrigerator's icemaker might be located under the sink or in the basement. If your shutoff valve looks like the one to the right, consider replacing it with a standard shutoff valve (go to thefamilyhandyman.com and search for "plumbing a refrigerator").

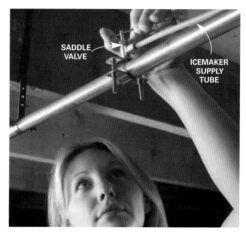

Turn off valves for water-using appliances like dishwashers, washing machines and icemakers.

3 Check your supply lines

Rubber or plastic supply lines that lead from shutoff valves to appliances, faucets and toilets become brittle and can leak or even break as they age. Since you're messing with your shutoff valves anyway, inspect the supply lines too. If you find any leaks, cracks, bulges or signs of corrosion, replace the lines before you leave town. Your best choice is line encased in a braided stainless steel sheath. A pair of washing machine hoses costs less than $20 at home centers. Shorter versions for faucets or a toilet cost about $6 each.

> **Tip**
> Don't wait for a vacation to check your supply lines. With 10 minutes and a flashlight, you can inspect every line in your house.

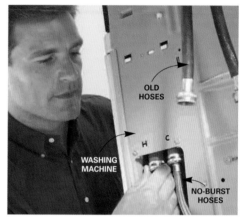

Stainless steel braided (no-burst) hoses last longer than rubber or plastic hoses and are less likely to leak. They also prevent mice from gnawing through the lines.

4 Test your sump pump

Sump pump systems help keep groundwater out of your basement. Before a vacation, test your sump pump by filling the sump pit with water and making sure the pump is actually pumping out the water.

If it doesn't, be sure the sump pump is plugged in (a surprisingly common oversight) and check the breaker as well. Also make sure the outlet pipe isn't frozen or clogged and that it directs water away from your home. Clean the hole in the discharge line and check that the motor is running smoothly. Also consider adding a backup battery to your sump pump so that it functions during power outages, which seem to go hand-in-hand with heavy rainstorms. (To install a backup battery, go to thefamilyhandyman.com and type "sump pump battery backup.")

Test your sump pump: Dump water down the sump pit to raise the water level, and make sure the pump is ejecting the water properly.

5 Check your gutters

A 1,000-sq.-ft. roof will shed about 620 gallons of water during a 1-in. rainfall, or about 103 gallons per downspout if you have six downspouts. That's a lot of water dumped right next to your basement. Although it may seem obvious, clean and properly functioning gutters with downspouts that empty away from the foundation are key to avoiding major and expensive home repairs.

So before you leave for a vacation, take a walk around the house and check your gutters. Check to see if leaves, sticks or other debris are blocking the inlet of the downspout and preventing water from flowing down the spout. Also make sure your downspout extensions are discharging the water far enough from the foundation and that you always reattach them after you mow your lawn.

Downspouts should discharge water at least 10 ft. from the house. If yours don't, consider adding extensions.

6 Shut off the water to exterior faucets

Outdoor faucets are the first plumbing parts to freeze and burst when the temperature drops. So always close the supply shutoff valve inside the house before you head off on vacation (see **Figure B**, p. 109). This is a good idea even if you have a frost-proof faucet, since you'll probably turn down the thermostat when you leave home. After turning off the supply shutoff, open the outside faucets to drain the remaining water out of the pipes. Never leave a hose connected to an outdoor faucet: It traps water in the faucet, which can freeze and crack open the faucet.

Another tip to avoid frozen plumbing is to turn the heat down to 60° F when you leave, but not lower. You want to keep things warm enough inside the house so that water pipes running through exterior walls don't freeze and burst. Leave the doors of bathroom vanities and kitchen sink cabinets open to allow more heat to get to the plumbing, and consider using a temperature sensor.

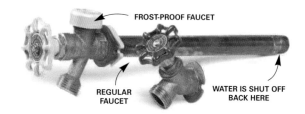

FROST-PROOF FAUCET

REGULAR FAUCET

WATER IS SHUT OFF BACK HERE

Save energy while you're away

- Unplug appliances that consume electricity even when they're not in use such as DVD players, microwaves, coffeemakers and computers (also make sure to disconnect the computer from the Internet). This is both a cost savings and a safety issue. It's not unheard of to have a cat tiptoe across a counter and unwittingly turn on the coffeemaker.
- Turn the water heater down to the "vacation," "low" or "pilot" setting.
- During the winter, set your thermostat to 60° F and have a neighbor check on the house regularly for furnace malfunctions.

- In the summer, set your air conditioner to 85° F so it runs less often but keeps electronics cool and gives the house an occupied appearance. Having no air conditioner humming and no windows open on a sweltering day is a sure signal to a thief that no one is home.
- If you'll be gone for an extended period, clean out the fridge (and freezer) completely, shut it off and leave the door propped open.

Question&Answer

KEEP YOUR WASHING MACHINE FRESH

We bought a front-loading washing machine about six months ago. Lately, I've noticed a moldy smell whenever I open the door to do a load of laundry. Is this normal?

My guess is that, like most people, you leave the washer door closed between loads and only wash a couple of loads per week. This is only a problem because the ultra-tight seal on front loader doors doesn't let the interior dry, and between washings, mold can grow inside the damp confines. And because front loaders use less water than top loaders (which fill up almost to the top), they don't always wash away the mold when you run a load of laundry.

Eliminating the mold is easy. Just run the empty washer through a cycle once a month with mold cleaner tablets designed for front loaders. If you don't want to use the tablets, you can substitute a cup of bleach.

In the future, you can prevent mold by treating the washer monthly and keeping the door open between washings so the interior can dry out.

DIY WASHER PEDESTAL

I'm buying a front-loading washing machine and dryer. The optional pedestals cost $180 apiece. Can I build my own?

Yep, and it's an easy way to save more than $300. The key is to make the pedestal sturdy, especially for front-loading washers, since they have a tendency to move around if they're not on a solid, level surface.

To start, measure the length and width of your washer and dryer. That's your minimum size for the pedestals. You can make them longer and wider if you want the extra space to stand on to reach overhead shelving or to set the laundry baskets on. Or you can make one long pedestal to fit under both the washer and the dryer (see illustration).

Build the pedestal out of 2x10 or 2x12 lumber. Feel free to add an attractive finish. Use shims to level the pedestal before you set the appliance on it.

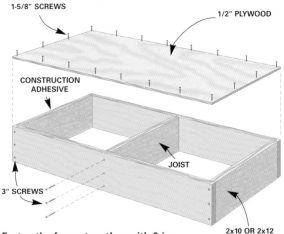

Fasten the frame together with 3-in. screws. Attach a joist in the middle. Apply construction adhesive to eliminate squeaks, then fasten 1/2-in. plywood over the top with 1-5/8-in. screws.

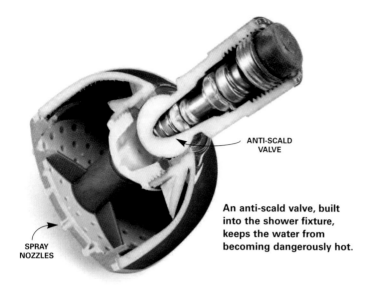

ANTI-SCALD VALVE

SPRAY NOZZLES

An anti-scald valve, built into the shower fixture, keeps the water from becoming dangerously hot.

SIMPLE-TO-INSTALL SCALD PROTECTION

Our water temperature varies greatly even though the water heater is set at 120° F. Sometimes the bath water gets dangerously hot. Can we install anti-scald protection without ripping open the walls?

My parents have the same problem in their 35-year-old house—someone turning on water in the kitchen or flushing a toilet downstairs changes the water temperature for someone taking a shower upstairs. Scalding water is dangerous, especially for young kids who can't turn it off. Approximately 3,800 people are injured and 34 people die each year from excessively hot tap water, according to the Consumer Product Safety Commission.

Anti-scald valves have been required by code for years, but older homes may not have them. And putting them in an existing bathroom means tearing open the walls to access the plumbing pipes.

An easier fix is to replace the showerhead and the tub spout with fixtures that have a built-in scald protection valve. To install, simply unscrew the existing showerhead or tub spout, wrap pipe tape around the exposed threads, caulk around the opening for a tub spout, then attach the new fixture. When the water reaches an unsafe temperature, the fixture automatically cuts the water flow to a trickle. Flow resumes when the water cools. Codes may still require an anti-scald valve (not just an anti-scald fixture). Check with your local building inspector.

Replace showerheads and tub spouts with anti-scald fixtures to avoid dangerously hot water.

Look for the fixtures (starting at $25) in home centers. Two manufacturers are American Valve (americanvalve.com or h2otstop.com) and American Standard (americanstandard-us.com).

SHOWER OUTDOORS WITH PRIVACY

I live near the ocean and have an outside shower. The problem is that the shower is completely open, so I have to wash off, then go into the house to change. Do you know of anything that encloses the shower so I can rinse off and change in privacy?

Outdoor shower enclosures are available in a wide range of prices—from $12 to more than $1,000. The enclosures offer privacy so you can shower in the buff and change outside, without upsetting (or exciting!) the neighbors. They're also good for showering outdoors at lake cabins. To find them you can enter "outdoor shower enclosure" in any Internet search engine.

The enclosures do not include any plumbing—they're simply privacy structures and you're on your own to figure out how to install valves, showerheads and running water.

The lower-price enclosures are portable and often hang from something overhead, like a shower arm. They're lightweight, some less than 4 lbs., and the entrance snaps closed. Higher-priced vinyl enclosures are also available. One company that makes them is Cambridge Molding. Its Lily Pod enclosures are made with an aluminum frame and post system, modular vinyl panels and hidden stainless steel hardware. The door has an aluminum latch and a dead bolt. For buying information, call (866) 440-9357 or visit lilypodinc.com.

NewTools&Gear

AUTOMATIC LEAK BUSTER

A new line of braided stainless steel supply lines from Watts, called FloodSafe Auto-Shutoff Connectors, has a shutoff device built into the inlet that can detect a burst line and shut off the water to prevent water damage. The connectors are great for vacation or second homes, where a busted supply line could leak for days or weeks before someone noticed.

While we don't suggest running out and changing all of your supply lines, if you have old, bulging hoses, replacing them with these new connectors can ward off a giant headache. They're available for faucets, toilets, icemakers, dishwashers and washing machines, starting at $15. Find them at home centers and plumbing supply stores.

Watts, (978) 688-1811. watts.com

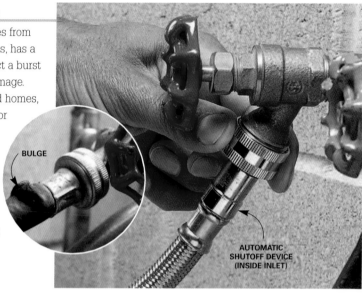

BULGE

AUTOMATIC SHUTOFF DEVICE (INSIDE INLET)

QUICK FIX FOR DIRTY DRYER VENTS

Keep your dryer running efficiently and avoid possible catastrophic lint fires by doing these three things. First, clean the lint screen and filter after each load. Second, periodically clean the inside of the dryer cabinet (see "Prevent House Fires—Clean Out Dryer Lint," p. 100). And third, clean the dryer vent.

The new LintEater ($30) from Gardus has a 4-in.-diameter auger brush attached to flexible rods that extend up to 12 ft. to sweep away lint buildup in the duct. Our appliance expert raves about this thing. He once took enough lint out of a dryer vent to fill a paper grocery bag.

A vacuum adapter (included) attaches to the end of the duct (after it's disconnected from the dryer). Then you connect it to a shop vacuum to suck up loose lint while you feed the brush through the duct from the outside vent opening. If the vent is too long, take it apart and clean it in sections.

Cleaner vents allow the dryer to operate more efficiently and prevent a fire hazard. The LintEater is available at home centers and many online retailers.

Gardus, (888) 985-0208. linteater.com

FLEXIBLE RODS

DRYER ADAPTER

TO VACUUM

VACUUM ADAPTER

LINT BRUSH

AUGER BRUSH

TIME FOR A
NEW WATER
HEATER?

*Replace it yourself and
save hundreds of dollars!*

If your water heater is no longer doing its job, a simple fix may be all it needs. For repair help, go to thefamilyhandyman.com and search for "water heater." On the other hand, a water heater's life expectancy is only about 10 to 14 years, so replacement may be your best move. And if you notice leaks coming from under the tank, replacement is your only move. Rusty puddles mean that the tank is rusting out. Someday—maybe next year, maybe tomorrow—that trickling leak will turn into an instant flood. Don't gamble. Replace that time bomb as soon as you can.

If you have some basic plumbing experience, you can replace a water heater yourself and save $200 to $400 in plumber's fees.

We'll show you how to replace a conventional natural gas water heater. The procedure is the same for a propane heater. If you choose a "power vented" gas model, all the water and gas connections are the same as we show, but the venting steps are different. For more, go to thefamilyhandyman.com and search for "power-vented water heater." Replacing an electric water heater is a little easier. All the water connections are the same and you don't have to deal with gas piping or venting. For details on situations different from the one we show here (such as electric models, plastic water lines or copper gas lines) go to thefamilyhandyman.com and search for "replace water heater."

Time, materials and money

If you have lots of plumbing experience, you might be able to complete this project in half a day. But we recommend you start in the morning so you have plenty of time to get the job done and not leave your family without hot water overnight. You'll need a helper to carry the old unit out and the new one in. Check with your trash hauler or recycling center to find out how to dispose of the old heater.

A new water heater will cost from $250 to $500, depending on the size, efficiency and warranty. The materials you'll need for the installation depend on your situation and local codes.

Even if you've worked with plumbing and gas lines in the past, play it safe and contact your local department of inspections. Get a permit (if required), and go over your installation plans with an inspector.

If your valve doesn't look like this one, see bottom of this page.

1 Shut off the gas by turning the handle a quarter turn. In the "off" position, the handle is perpendicular to the pipe.

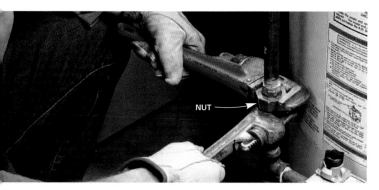

NUT

2 Disconnect the gas at the "union" fitting. Place the larger wrench on the nut and hold the union's collar with another wrench. Start with the wrenches a quarter turn apart.

GATE VALVE

3 Cut the cold water line above the old gate valve to make room for a new ball valve. Cut the hot water line at the same height.

Turn off the gas and water

To get started, turn off the gas at the valve near the water heater (**Photo 1**).

If the "isolation" valve above your water heater is a gate valve (**Photo 3**), we recommend that you replace it with a ball valve (**Photo 4**). Be sure to choose a "full-port valve." Gate valves often leak or won't close tightly. To replace the valve, you'll have to shut off the water at the main valve (usually near the meter). That means your whole house will be without water until you install the new valve. If you already have a ball valve or if you choose to leave the old gate valve in place, you can simply shut it off. That way the rest of the house will have cold water while you work (toilets will still work!).

With the water and gas off, drain the water heater. Attach a garden hose to the drain valve at the bottom of the tank, route it to a floor drain and open the drain valve. To allow air into the hot water lines and speed up the draining process, go to the highest faucet in the house and turn on the hot side only (on single-handle faucets, push the lever all the way to the left).

Disconnect the gas, vent and water lines

Disconnect the gas line at the union (**Photo 2**). Then disassemble the threaded "tee" and "drip leg" and remove the nipple from the water heater gas control valve. Don't throw them away—you'll need them for the new water heater. If your gas line is copper or a flexible supply line, just unscrew the nut.

To disassemble the vent piping, remove the sheet metal screws. Wear gloves; the ends of the metal piping are sharp. You can reuse the vent pipes if they're in good shape. But if you find even slight holes, cracks or corrosion, toss them into the trash. New pipe is inexpensive and leaks can allow deadly carbon monoxide to build up in your home.

Next, cut the copper water lines with a tubing cutter (**Photo 3**). If you have copper corrugated water

Old gas valves can leak

The "grease-pack" valves found in older homes tend to leak as they age. Even if your local code doesn't require replacement, we recommend you install a ball-type gas valve instead ($10). Replacement isn't difficult; you just unscrew the old valve and screw on the new one. But you will have to turn off the main gas valve and later relight pilot lights. If you don't know how to handle these tasks, call in a professional plumber and expect to pay $80 to $150.

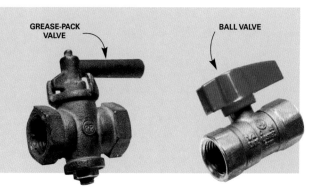

GREASE-PACK VALVE

BALL VALVE

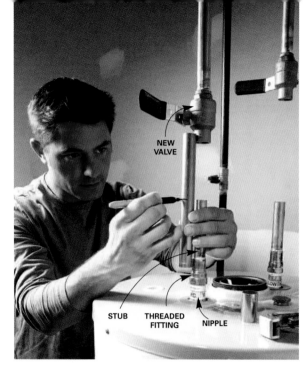

STUB   THREADED   NIPPLE
        FITTING

NEW
VALVE

4 Reconnect the water. Install new valves first so you can turn on the water to the rest of the house. Then install nipples, followed by threaded fittings and "stubs" of pipe. Hold the final section in place to mark the length.

SLIP COUPLER

COLD

5 Make the final connections with "slip" couplers. Be sure the coupler doesn't slide down as you heat it.

lines, simply disconnect the nuts at the water heater. If you have galvanized steel pipes, disconnect unions just as we did with the gas union shown in **Photo 2**. Also unscrew the blow tube from the temperature and pressure (T&P) valve. You may be able to reuse it on the new water heater.

At this point, the old heater should have drained enough so it can be moved off to the side (with a helper). If the heater isn't draining fast enough, sediment may be clogging the valve. Allow it to drain as long as possible and then move the heater outside so you can remove the drain valve from the tank.

Reconnect the water

Set the drain pan into place with the opening facing the floor drain. Get someone to help you lift and set the heater in the pan. If you're replacing the isolation valve, solder on the new ball valve next.

Screw dielectric nipples into the new water heater. These plastic-lined nipples reduce corrosion and increase water heater life. Some water heaters come with dielectric nipples already installed (buy a set if yours doesn't have them). Be sure to coat the threads with pipe thread sealant or wrap with Teflon tape. Next, solder female threaded copper pipe fittings to short lengths of copper tubing and set them aside to cool. Tighten the cooled fittings onto the nipples. Then add short sections of pipe below the valves (**Photo 4**) and make the final connections with "slip" couplers (**Photo 5**). You must use slip couplers—standard "stopped" couplers won't work. For tips on soldering copper pipe, go to thefamilyhandyman.com and search for "solder."

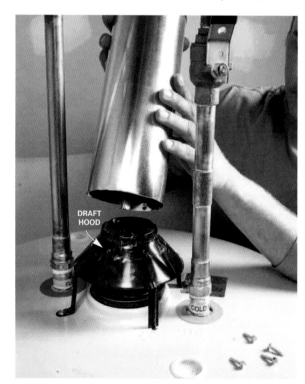

DRAFT
HOOD

COLD

6 Connect the vent pipe to the hood with sheet metal screws. Never use a reducer, even if the hood's opening is smaller than the vent pipe.

Thread a "blow tube" onto the T&P valve. If the old blow tube is too short, you can use 3/4-in. galvanized steel pipe or copper pipe (along with a male threaded fitting). If you use galvanized pipe, cut off the threads on the bottom to prevent someone from capping off the blow tube if the T&P valve leaks.

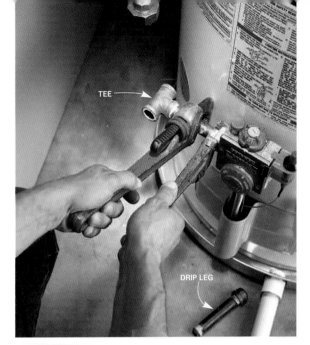

7 Reconnect the gas. Hold back the control valve to avoid damaging it. Then screw the drip leg into the tee.

8 Measure between the union and the tee and add 1 in. to determine the correct nipple length.

Install the new vent

Snap the new draft hood onto the water heater and secure it with sheet metal screws. Check the installation manual for the recommended diameter vent pipe for your new heater. If the recommended vent pipe diameter is larger than the vent hood opening, don't install a reducer. Measure a straight section of new galvanized vent pipe to rise as high as possible before you install the adjustable elbow (the higher the rise, the better the draft). On any horizontal sections of vent, make sure the pipe slopes down toward the water heater 1/4 in. per foot of pipe. Bend out small sections of the pipe and attach it directly to the vent hood with screws (**Photo 6**). Then continue installing new vent pipe sections and connect to the flue. Most plumbing codes require a minimum of three screws for each vent pipe joint. For tips on cutting metal venting, go to thefamilyhandyman.com and search for "sheet metal."

Hook up the gas

Apply gas-rated pipe thread sealant or tape (don't use standard white Teflon tape) to the gas nipple and thread it into the new gas control valve. Tighten the nipple using two pipe wrenches (**Photo 7**). Assemble the tee and drip leg using the same two-wrench technique.

If the old section of pipe below the union no longer fits, you'll need to measure for a new nipple (**Photo 8**). Make sure you assemble and tighten the gas union before you measure the length for the intermediate nipple. Add 3/4 in. to 1 in. to this measurement and buy a new nipple. When the gas connections are complete, turn on the gas and check for leaks (**Photo 9**). You can buy leak detector in a convenient spray bottle ($3) or mix your own solution (one part dish detergent, two parts water).

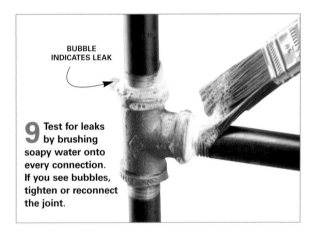

9 Test for leaks by brushing soapy water onto every connection. If you see bubbles, tighten or reconnect the joint.

Open the water valves and an upstairs faucet and fill the tank. Leave the faucet open until water flows out. Then shut it off and check the new water connections for leaks. Open the gas valve and light the pilot light following the manufacturer's instructions. You're in for a pleasant surprise with your new water heater—manufacturers have done away with the old "match-lit" pilot system. Instead of igniting the pilot with a match or lighter, you just push a button.

When the burner fires up, test for "backdrafting," which can allow deadly carbon monoxide into your home. Close all doors and windows and turn on kitchen and bath exhaust fans. When the burner has been running for at least one minute, move an incense stick around the draft hood. The smoke should be drawn up into the vent. If not, the exhaust may be entering your home. Turn off the gas and call in a professional plumber.

Finally, set the thermostat to a safe temperature. (For help, go to thefamilyhandyman.com and search for "water heater temperature.") In about two hours, you'll have enough hot water for a well-deserved long shower.

LOCAL **CODE** REQUIREMENTS

You'll find lots of accessories for your new water heater at the home center. Some are required by local codes; others are just good ideas. Plumbing codes vary, so check with your local inspector.

1. Gas shutoff valve

All codes require a gas valve near the water heater. If you have a "grease-pack" valve, see p. 116.

2. Earthquake straps

These straps prevent a water heater from tipping over and are required in earthquake-prone areas. $12 per pair.

3. Flexible gas line

A flexible gas line can withstand movement and is usually required in earthquake-prone areas. They're easier to connect than steel pipe, but they're not allowed everywhere, so check with your inspector. $15.

4. Drip leg

Any dust or grit in the gas line falls into this short section of pipe before it can reach the water heater's control valve. The required length of the drip leg varies.

5. Isolation valve

All codes require a valve on the cold water line. Though not required by codes, a second valve on the hot line makes future water heater replacement easier. $10 each.

6. Flexible water lines

These flexible lines withstand movement and are required in earthquake zones. But you may want to use them just because they're easy to install. $20 per pair.

7. Overflow pan

Most plumbing codes require a pan and drain pipe in locations where a leak can cause damage. But installing a drain pan is a good idea for any location. $18.

8. Expansion tank

Some codes require an expansion tank to absorb the pressure created when heated water expands. $35.

9. Blow tube

The T&P valve releases pressure, and a "blow tube" directs the scalding hot water toward the floor. The required distance between the blow tube and floor is usually 18 in. or less.

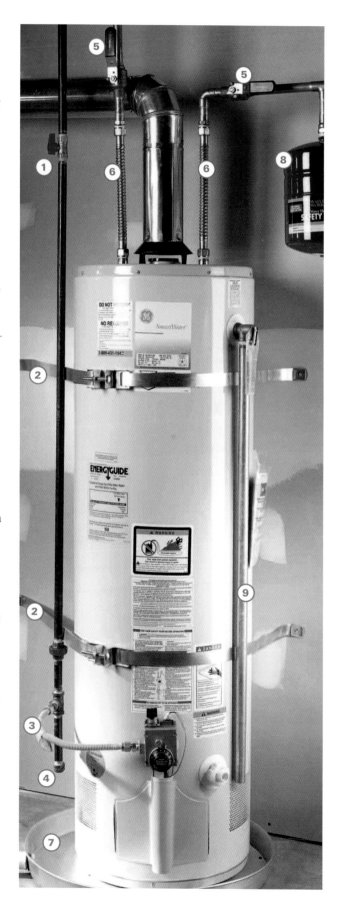

The Family Handyman's Top 10

SPECIAL SECTION

TOP 10 · HOME IMPROVEMENTS

1 Bathroom mini makeover

With a granite-topped vanity from a home center, a new faucet and a mirror, you can upgrade your bathroom for less than $500. The vanity top shown here came complete with an undermounted sink.

2 Halogen track lighting

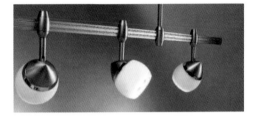

Rail track lighting is practical and decorative. And the price has dropped in recent years. Choose spotlights to highlight pictures and other objects.

3 Add curb appeal

A fresh coat of paint and updated hardware give your front door a quick face-lift. Choose a bold color, but make sure it doesn't look out of place on your home and in your neighborhood.

4 Closet organized

Make the most of your closet space with shelving and accessories. You can outfit an entire closet in one morning.

5 Wallpaper one wall

Wallpaper on one wall adds drama to a dull room with less effort and expense than covering the whole room. It also lets you choose a bold pattern that would be overpowering on all four walls.

6 Laundry center

Equip your laundry room with a spacious clothes-folding table (made from a stock countertop), more storage space and better lighting. Everything you need is readily available at home centers.

Kitchen rollouts

Rollouts turn wasted space deep inside cabinets into accessible storage space. You can even buy rollouts that fit around drainpipes! Be sure to measure the available space carefully so you purchase the right size unit.

8 Backyard oasis

A screened canopy (or gazebo) provides shade from the sun, plus protection from irritating bugs. These backyard retreats are easy to put up, affordable and available at most home centers.

9 Trim and paint

Painted trim requires less skill, time and expense than stained and varnished trim. Be sure to look at the colors you choose in day and night light before you purchase the paint. To create wall stripes, apply easy-release masking tape over a light base color.

10 New bath accessories

Remove the old wall accessories, then repair, clean and repaint the walls. Now you can add mirrors, a towel warmer and shelves for a dramatic upgrade.

TIPS FOR TOUGH CLEANING PROBLEMS

TOP 10

1 Speed-clean chandeliers

CHANDELIER CLEANING SPRAY

For super-simple chandelier cleaning, try a spray-on cleaner that does all the work for you. Buy it for $10 at chandelierparts.com or nancysilver.com.

2 Clean hard floors faster

CLEANING SOLUTION

Cleaning pros love the Swiffer Wet Jet ($20). You can ditch your nasty mop and bucket, and use one of three cleaning solutions and this battery-powered tool instead.

3 Scum-proof your shower doors

Treat cleaned glass shower doors with a water repellent like Aquapel ($8) or Rain-X ($5). These products will keep the glass looking good for six months.

4 Cut grease with a hot sponge

Heat a slightly damp sponge in the microwave for 20 to 30 seconds. Then spray cabinets with an orange-oil cleaner and use the hot sponge to wipe off the cleaner.

5 Blow out the garage

When you need to clean out the garage, open the overhead door, put on a dust mask, earplugs and safety glasses and grab the leaf blower! This method works great in screen porches, too.

6 The right stuff for rust

Tackle rust with a stain remover like Super Iron Out ($10 for a 5-lb. jug). Choose a product that contains diluted hydrochloric acid (aka hydrogen chloride, HCL or muriatic acid). Wear eye protection.

7 Remove bathroom soap scum

SOAP SCUM

PLASTIC PUTTY KNIFE

Wait for the surface of the tile to dry, and then scrape off scum with a 4-in. plastic putty knife. For grout lines, use a Mr. Clean Magic Eraser.

8 Spot-clean food and drink spills

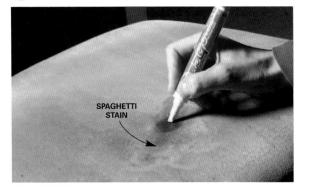

SPAGHETTI STAIN

The best way to prevent permanent stains on upholstery is to treat them immediately. Keep a Tide to Go pen ($3) handy and you'll be ready for anything!

9 Switch to microfiber cloths

MICROFIBER CLOTH

Unlike cotton rags and paper towels, microfiber cloths are made of ultra-fine synthetic fibers that scour effectively without being abrasive.

10 Remove pet hair with duct tape

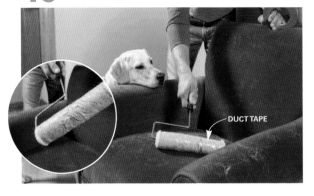

DUCT TAPE

Another use for duct tape! Wrap it sticky-side-out around a paint roller cover and roll it over furniture or carpets to remove annoying pet hair.

TOP 10 TRICKS TO STOP MOLD & MILDEW

1 Check for plumbing leaks

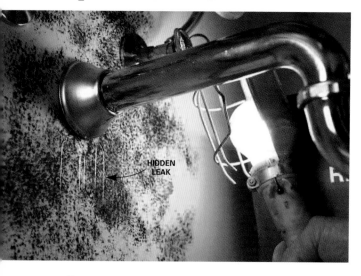

Keep an eye out for mold around water pipes, waste lines, icemaker lines and plumbing fixtures. Drips from this leaky sink drain keep the drywall damp, creating a perfect home for mold.

2 Look for outside leaks

If mold is growing on the inside of an exterior wall, it could be a warning sign of a leak on the outside of your home. Shown here is mold caused by a flashing leak.

3 Inspect the ductwork

Condensation can imitate a leak. Torn insulation allowed condensation to form on this cold-air duct, causing mold on the ceiling just as a roof leak would.

4 Missing insulation feeds mold

Gaps in insulation are a problem as warm indoor air hits the colder surface and then condenses. These conditions feed mold. Lowering indoor humidity can help reduce this problem.

5 Don't let mold make you sick

Breathing mold spores can cause asthmatic reactions, allergic reactions and other health problems. Always wear an N95-rated respirator, rubber gloves and eye protection when removing mold.

7 Win the war against bathtub mold

To prevent mold around tubs and showers (where the moisture source never goes away), spray the wall with an antimicrobial treatment, then seal the grout with two coats of grout sealant to keep water from wicking in.

Seal tile and grout with grout sealant to keep walls from absorbing moisture and feeding mold below the surface.

6 Is it mold or dirt?

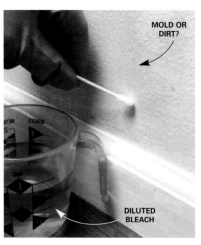

For a quick test, dip a swab in diluted bleach (1 part bleach, 16 parts water) and dab it on the wall. If the spot quickly lightens (or keeps coming back after cleaning), assume it's mold.

Test suspicious-looking spots with a few drops of diluted bleach to see whether it's mold or just dirt.

8 Listen to the air conditioner

If your central air conditioner cycles on and off quickly and you see mold near the diffusers, the unit might be too large for the house, causing the house air to cool before the humidity is removed. The easiest fix is to run a dehumidifier.

9 Stop mold from coming back

Once you have your indoor humidity under control, clean and spray the affected areas with an antimicrobial treatment. In basements or other large areas, you might need to fog the entire room using rental equipment from a home center.

To avoid feeding mold, use paints with mildewcide and materials that mold can't feed on.

MOLD-RESISTANT PRIMER

MOLD-RESISTANT PAINT

10 Don't ignore mold

Mold can be an early warning sign of problems that require expensive repairs, such as wood rot. Avoid the temptation to just wipe away the mold and forget about it—find and stop the water source.

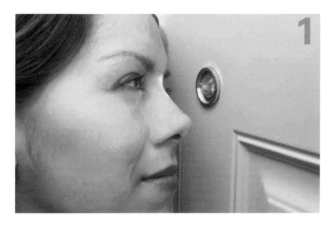

1 Know who's there

Install a wide-angle door viewer so you always know who's at your door. The one shown here from M.A.G. Engineering and Manufacturing (No. 8720, magsecurity.com) costs only $4.20. To install, just drill a hole from each side and screw it in.

WIDE-ANGLE DOOR VIEWER

2 Protect your mail

To help prevent identity theft, use a secure mailbox. Once the mail is dropped in, you need a key to open the box.

3 Pick-proof your deadbolt

To hold a deadbolt firmly in place, install the SIMLock ($10, thesimlock.com). Use this lock with deadbolts that lock in the vertical position.

4 Add inexpensive door and window alarms

CONTACT STRIP

ALARM (INTERMATIC SP440 B)

Wireless alarms for doors and windows are available at home centers ($20 for door alarms; $7 for window). Or check out the products at intermatic.com and doorandwindowalarms.com. These alarms work on any door or window and the batteries last two to three years.

5 Shred papers to protect your identity

It's a good idea to shred all credit card offers, bank statements, bills and other personal papers. Some models will shred credit cards, CDs and multiple sheets of paper as well.

LIGHT

SOLAR PANEL

BATTERY CASE

SENSOR

6 Put motion detector lighting anywhere

Basic motion detector lighting is an inexpensive deterrent. The Heath Zenith model shown here costs $80 (No. SL-7001, heath-zenith.com). The solar panel charges batteries, which power the light.

8 Install a small safe

Purchase and install a small safe that will secure your valuables. Be sure to fasten the safe in the floor or to the wall. The safes shown here are made by Sentry Safe—$100 for the wall model and $120 for the floor model (sentrysafe.com).

7 Reinforce your entry door strike plate

To install a stronger strike plate, use 3-in. screws to penetrate the door frame, wall and studs. This will help keep out a burglar who tries to kick in the door.

10 Beef up your wooden garage entry door

9 Secure patio doors

GROMMETS

Add a secondary lock to your patio door for beefed-up security. Andersen Corp's auxiliary foot lock, shown here, costs $22. Call (800) 426-4261 to find a dealer in your area. Another model that attaches to the top of the door is available for $25 at thedoorguardian.com.

A down-and-dirty way to reinforce a garage entry door is to add plywood and bar the door with 2x4s to stop burglars.

GreatGoofs®

Summer shower

The drain line to my air conditioner was clogged. I called an air conditioner contractor, and he decided to clear it by blasting compressed air down the line from upstairs. My job was to wait outside at the return to see if anything came out.

I stationed myself downstairs but I didn't stand back quite far enough. In an instant, I was showered with putrid water and debris! Shocked, I stood there in disbelief—just long enough for him to send another blast of air, showering me again. Next time, I'll be in charge of the air and someone else can wait outside!

Mucky-faced lie

When I was a youngster, we lived in an apartment complex. One day after work, my father was greeted with the news that the kitchen sink was full of standing water. After studying the situation, my father cleverly reversed the hose on the vacuum so it blew instead of sucked and blasted the clog past the sink trap.

It wasn't long before there was a knock at the door. The next-door neighbor lady was there—covered with soapy water and disgusting goo. She explained that she had been cleaning vegetables in the kitchen sink when there was a sudden, loud—and drenching!—eruption from her kitchen drain. She wanted to know if my father knew what could have caused this disaster. (Apparently the apartment units shared a drain line.) My father looked her right in her mucky face and said he had "no idea" what happened. He enjoyed many years of retelling the story of how his bright idea had led to a bald-faced lie.

F is for flub—and flood

I couldn't get the valves that fed my washing machine to stop leaking, so I replaced the entire faucet assembly. The installation went fine. I reconnected the washer hoses, double-checked for leaks and washed my first load of clothes. Satisfied with my leak-free connections, I went upstairs.

Everything worked perfectly—until I returned to the laundry room and found myself standing in a pool of soapy water. Unfortunately, I'd forgotten to put the drain line back into the laundry tub and an entire washer's worth of dirty water had poured onto my floor. Talk about washed up!

4 Woodworking & Furniture Projects, Tools & Tips

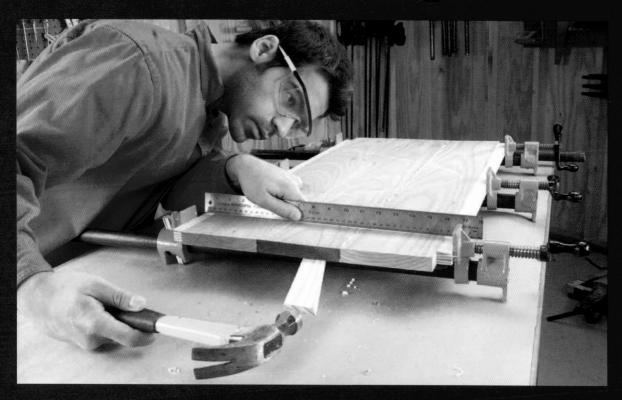

IN THIS CHAPTER

ShopTips™

3" ALUMINUM ANGLE

1x4 FENCE

TWO GREAT DRILL PRESS JIGS

1 Adjustable fence

Add an adjustable fence to your drill press to make it a lot handier for woodworking projects! A fence is especially useful for drilling rows of precisely placed holes. Also, boring holes in a small workpiece is a snap—just clamp the piece to the fence at any angle and drill the hole. You won't struggle with holding small pieces in place while you drill. (That's also dangerous!)

1. Attach a 2-ft. x 1-ft. scrap of plywood or particleboard to the drill press table with countersunk 1/4-in. flat head machine screws, fender washers and nuts. (Run the screws through the slots in the metal table. The fender washers will span the slots.)

2. Create the fence from a 2 ft. x 4-in. x 1-in. board bolted to a 2-ft. piece of 3-in. x 1/8-in. aluminum angle ($10 at a home center for a 4-ft. length). Again, countersink the holes in the board before bolting the board to the angle.

2 Vertical drilling jig

If you've ever tried to drill a perfectly straight and centered deep hole in the end of a board, you know that it's nearly impossible with a handheld drill. But add a drill press and a jig and the job becomes very doable. Make this jig from two 8-in. x 12-in. pieces of 3/4-in. plywood or medium-density fiberboard (MDF). Just screw the pieces together to form a "T" and reinforce the jig with a couple of triangles.

To use the jig, clamp it to the drill press table and the workpiece to the jig. Draw an "X" across the corners to find the exact center of the piece. You'll have to adjust the height of the table and pivot it until you line everything up, but after that, drilling a straight, centered hole is a cinch. This trick will work for rectangular or square boards.

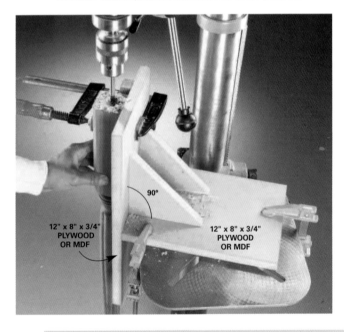

90°

12" x 8" x 3/4" PLYWOOD OR MDF

12" x 8" x 3/4" PLYWOOD OR MDF

FAREWELL, PLANER SNIPE

In a wood shop, a "snipe" is a long, shallow trough that gets carved into boards an inch or two from the trailing end just before a board exits a thickness planer. The smart way to deal with it is to plane boards before cutting them to length, then just cut off any snipes. But sometimes there's not enough length to do that, especially when you buy small, expensive chunks of exotics. Here's what to do then. Trace the last 4 in. of your "beauty board" on a wider scrap board of the same thickness. Saw out the notch, fit the two boards together and plane them as one. Any snipe or gouging will show up on the trailing board, not in your workpiece.

ROSIN PAPER WORKBENCH

Here's instant protection for any kind of messy job. Before you start, just unroll enough rosin paper from this jumbo paper towel holder to protect your workbench. The thick paper absorbs all the glue or finish. When the paper gets too dirty, tear it off and throw it away. A roll of rosin paper is 170 ft. long, so one will last a long time. Here's how to build your paper holder:

Buy a roll of rosin paper ($8) and a length of 1-1/2-in. pipe ($12 for a 4-ft. length) at a home center. Round up some scrap lumber and get ready to do a little bit of head scratching to customize a bracket arrangement that works with your bench design. Our setup should give you the general idea. Bore 1-7/8-in. holes in the scrap wood brackets. Screw keeper strips over the holes to keep the pipe from falling out as you unroll the paper. Use a handsaw to cut the paper roll and a hacksaw to cut the pipe to match the width of your bench. Then load the roll and start dripping stuff all over it.

KEEPER STRIP
BRACKET
ROSIN PAPER
1-7/8"-DIA. HOLE
1-1/2"-DIA. PIPE

"CLAMPING" WITH CLAY

Here's a cushy way to make glue repairs on small or delicate objects without having to hold them together by hand until the glue dries. Flatten out a ball of Play-Doh modeling compound ($2 for a four-pack), then apply glue to the edges of the object you're repairing and press the pieces into the clay. The clay will hold the pieces together while the glue dries, and then you can peel it right off.

MODELING COMPOUND

TOOL TABLE REJUVENATION

Here's a quick, two-step method for cleaning cast iron tables on power tools and protecting them from moisture and corrosion. And as a bonus, your workpieces will slide on the table like silk as you work.

1 Scrub the table by hand with a 3M Scotch-Brite pad or stick the pad on a vibrating sander just like a piece of sandpaper. (A light mist of WD-40 on the table will help loosen even more dirt and rust.) Carefully clean the miter gauge slots as well. Wipe the surface clean with paper towels and mineral spirits.

2 Apply paste wax and buff the surface with a piece of felt stuck on 60-or 80-grit sandpaper on the bottom of a random orbital sander (Felt adheres just like the Scotch-Brite pad to the hooks on the sander.) You could also buff the surface by hand with a cloth.

ShopTips™

ELECTRIC CARVING KNIFE IN THE SHOP

Got some rigid polyurethane foam, Styrofoam or soft upholstery foam you want to cut? Smuggle the electric carving knife out of the kitchen and use that. It works fabulously for any cut you need to make. Just don't get busted at the border by the kitchen cop! But if you do, it's safe to say you didn't wreck the knife.

1-IN. STOP BLOCK FOR MULTIPLE CUTOFFS

To get furniture-grade crosscuts, you have to use a table saw. When you crosscut a whole pile of short pieces to the same length, clamp a specially dedicated block of wood to the table saw fence. This is an old standard trick, but the difference is that this block is laminated for easy sliding, and more important, it's exactly 1 in. thick. Clamp the block on the fence and adjust the table saw fence gauge to the desired length, plus 1 in., and saw the pieces. The 1-in. thickness eliminates any head-scratching and mistakes from using any old scrap block. For safety, position the block so the workpiece loses contact with the block before the cut begins. That all but eliminates any chance of kickback.

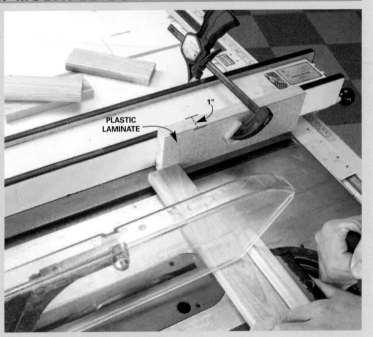

PLASTIC LAMINATE

1"

PERFECT MITER JOINTS EVERY TIME

Here's one way to ensure gap-free miter joints when you're edge-banding plywood. Before you cut the trim board miters, tape 45-degree "fitting" boards to the plywood corners. Now you can cut the trim to fit, shaving off a little wood at a time until you reach perfection. Once you've glued on two opposing sides, fit and trim the other two pieces using the glued-on pieces as guides.

FITTING BOARD

STORAGE POCKETS FOR SKINNY THINGS

Saw off short pieces of 1-1/2-, 2- or 3-in. PVC plumbing pipe with 45-degree angles on one end. Screw them to a board to hold paintbrushes, pencils, stir sticks and just about any other narrow paraphernalia in your shop. Mount them by drilling a 1/4-in. hole in the angled end, and then drive a 1-5/8-in. drywall screw through the hole into the board.

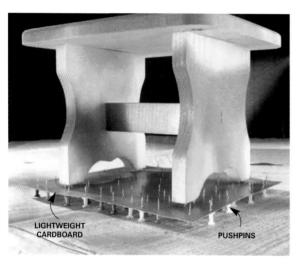

LIGHTWEIGHT CARDBOARD

PUSHPINS

BED-OF-NAILS FINISHING STAND

Paint drips can't collect on the bottom edges of your project if it floats a tad above the worktable while you spray it. To make this magic, push an army of pushpins into a piece of thin cardboard, then set your project on the pins and spray on the finish.

DRILL-DEPTH STOPPER

HOLE DEPTH

Everyone knows the old trick of wrapping tape around drill bits to gauge hole depths while drilling. But after you drill a couple of holes, the leading edge of the tape becomes tattered and less accurate. Here's a simple variation on the theme. Mark the depth on the drill with a bright-colored erasable marker. This tip works great with both twist drill bits and spade bits.

COPY CENTER PROJECT PATTERNS

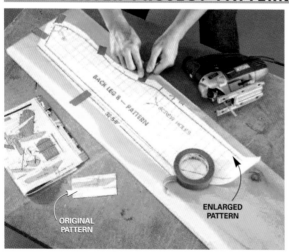

ORIGINAL PATTERN

ENLARGED PATTERN

Enlarging scaled-down woodworking patterns to full scale is a lot of work, and the results are rarely very accurate. But you don't have to go through that exercise anymore. Just about any full-service copy center will do it for you in a couple of minutes for a couple of dollars.

Here's how: Cut the pattern to the actual length of the drawing—our magazine pattern measured 3-13/16 in. Ask to have it enlarged to the size called for in the dimensions. The copy center magician will spin a circular gauge to determine the expansion percentage and punch that info into the copier. In less than a minute, the full-size pattern will roll out. Our 35-3/4-in. Adirondack leg pattern cost less than $2. Stick the pattern directly to the wood with spray adhesive, double-faced tape or masking tape and cut out the part—that's it!

ShopTips™

LEGIBLE SANDING DISCS

Hook-and-loop sanding discs work great on sanding jobs, and you can reuse them several times before they're worn out. But it's almost impossible to read the grit labels on the discs after you've used them once because the markings get scrubbed off by the loops. Here's a solution: Whenever you open a new pack of discs, write the grit label on the back with a permanent marker. Now you'll switch from grit to grit without straining your eyes.

DUST-COLLECTIN', BIT STORIN' ROUTER FENCE

This router fence is a masterpiece of convenience and efficiency. The router is mounted under an extension table attached to the table saw. When routing, slide the table saw fence over and clamp on a 5-in.-wide box with a mouse hole on the side for the bit recess. A drawer for bit storage pulls out of one end, and a shop vacuum hose press-fits in a hole in the other end to spirit away nearly all the chips.

You can glue plastic laminate on the fence so workpieces slide along smoothly, and make the back of the box stick out 3 in. on both ends so it's easy to clamp to the table saw fence.

BIT DRAWER

TABLE SAW FENCE

ROUTER FENCE

SHOP VACUUM HOSE

ROUTER BELOW

BIT STORAGE

2-1/4"

3-1/2" x 3-1/2"

30"   36"

2-1/2"

1" FINGER PULL HOLE

4-1/2"

3-1/2"

DUST BAFFLE

5"   12"

4-1/4"

PLASTIC LAMINATE

1-1/2"

BAND SAW DUST PORT

When band sawing, hook the dust collector hose to a reducer mounted on the saw's lower cover. The saw's factory dust port doesn't always work very well. With a metal-cutting blade in a saber saw, it's super easy to cut out the reducer hole. Just trace a circle, drill a small entry hole for the blade and saw out the circle. Caulk around the reducer on the outside of the cover, hook up the dust collector hose, and now you won't have super-fine band saw dust filling the air.

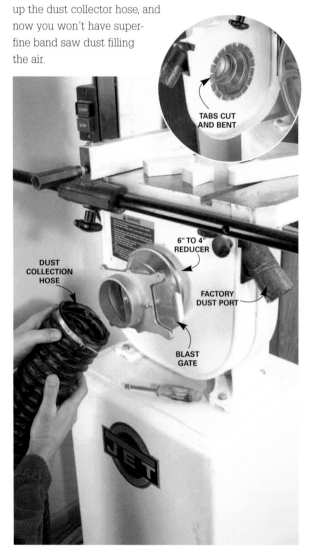

TABS CUT AND BENT

DUST COLLECTION HOSE

6" TO 4" REDUCER

FACTORY DUST PORT

BLAST GATE

DESTINED FOR BURN PILE

SLIDING SHELF

MITER SAW WASTE

Waste-management ingenuity shows up again at the miter saw station. Do you always have a huge pile of cutoff scraps on the table next to your miter saw? Rebuild the miter saw table, and incorporate a drop hole right next to the saw. Directly below the hole place a recycling bin resting on a rollout shelf. When the bin fills up, it's off to the burn pile.

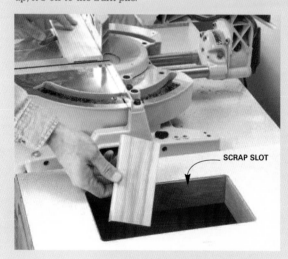

SCRAP SLOT

DO-IT-ALL LAMINATE SAMPLES

Pick up a few free laminate samples on your next trip to the home center and put them to work as glue spreaders, nailing shields, shims, scrapers and spacers. Use them once and you'll discover a dozen other ways they can improve shop life.

GLUE SPREADER

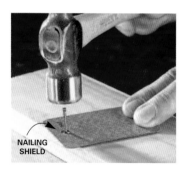

NAILING SHIELD

Paint and finish tips

ZERO-CLEANUP FINISHING

Forget brushes when it comes to varnishing a ton of trim or big, flat areas like tabletops and cabinets. Use a 4-in. disposable roller and a nonstick, lipped baking sheet. Pour some varnish into the tray and use it just like a paint rolling tray. Keep adding varnish as you need it, but try to plan so you end up with an empty tray. When you're through, toss the roller sleeve and let the wet varnish dry in the pan. When it dries, just peel the varnish film right out of the pan.

NONSTICK BAKING SHEET

DRIED VARNISH

DISPOSABLE ROLLER

POLY FINISH WITH NO RUNS, DRIPS OR BUBBLES

If the project you're finishing features spindles, legs, nooks or crannies, switch from a regular to a wipe-on polyurethane. This finish goes on like a hand-rubbed oil finish and won't pool, bubble or drip to leave mini messes to sand off when it's dry. A number of wipe-on poly finishes are available, but we like Rockler's Polyurethane Satin Gel Finish (rockler.com, $10.59 a pint, $19.29 a quart). It wipes on smoothly, dries super-fast and, when applied with a cloth, leaves zero lap marks.

BUG-BEGONE TWEEZERS

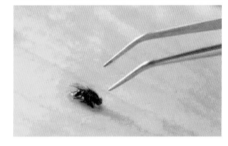

Keep a tweezers handy when you're applying any type of finish. If a mosquito, house-fly, strand of hair, a wood shaving or a speck of sawdust plops onto a wet finish, don't use your fingers or a rag to remove it! That'll always leave a mark. Pluck it out with the tweezers.

TITLE YOUR FINISHING CANS

If you have 10 years' worth of rectangular solvent and finish cans on your shelf, and it's hard to grab the mineral spirits can without first pulling out the acetone, the walnut stain and the denatured alcohol cans, try this great solution. Set all the cans side by side and spray them with white appliance paint. When the paint's dry, write the names with a permanent marker or paint pen on the painted spines like a book title. Now you'll instantly nab the can you need.

APPLIANCE PAINT

MASKING TAPE

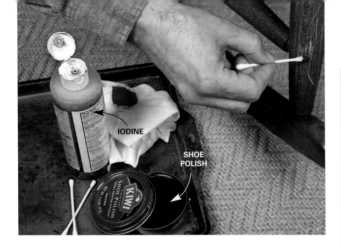

IODINE

SHOE POLISH

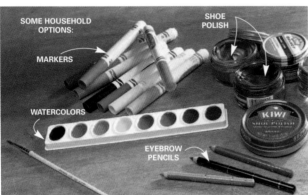

SOME HOUSEHOLD OPTIONS:

MARKERS

WATERCOLORS

SHOE POLISH

EYEBROW PENCILS

FURNITURE DING FIXERS FOR FREE

Fix dings and scratches on wood surfaces without spending a penny. You already have a palette of colors in your closet, desk drawer or makeup kit. Shoe polish, eyebrow pencils, markers, watercolors, fingernail polish and iodine thinned to the right shade with denatured alcohol are just a few of the possibilities. Before applying color to the marred area, try it on the part of the furniture that's the least visible. You can even create a "test" scratch in a hidden spot. When you determine the right color, rub it into the scratch, then wipe off the residue from the adjacent surface.

PENCILS ON THE DOUBLE

Can't find your pencil? Try this! Saw a package of pencils in half with a fine-tooth saw and stick pencil cap erasers on the eraserless halves. You've just doubled your stock of pencils and made them a lot harder to break!

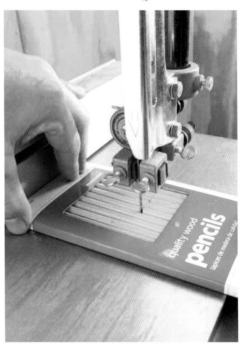

quality wood pencils

FLAWLESS SURFACE PREP

Anxious to put varnish on that freshly sanded project? Well, just hold on for a second! Before applying the finish, rub the project (with the grain!) with No. 0000 steel wool. You'll lift sanding dust from the grain and burnish and shine the surface fibers.

Follow up with a Swiffer Sweeper cloth ($4 a box) to wipe away any specks of dust or steel wool. You've now ensured a pristine surface for perfect results with oil-based (not water-based) finishes.

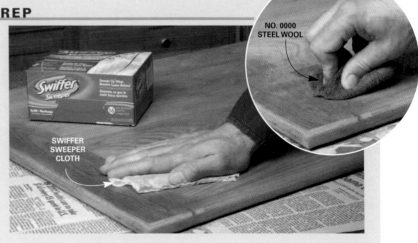

NO. 0000 STEEL WOOL

SWIFFER SWEEPER CLOTH

ShopTips™

Tips from a pro

Custom furniture maker Bruce Kieffer spent two years planning and building his dream shop. Here he shares some of his favorite tips.

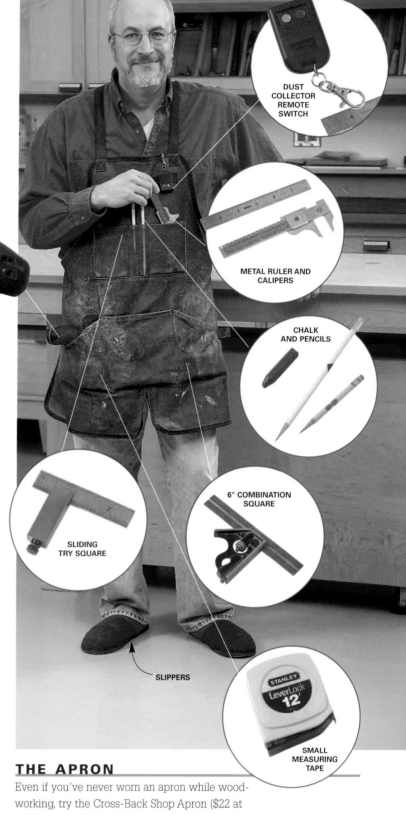

DUST COLLECTOR REMOTE SWITCH

METAL RULER AND CALIPERS

CHALK AND PENCILS

SMALL SCREW GUN

6" COMBINATION SQUARE

SLIDING TRY SQUARE

SLIPPERS

SMALL MEASURING TAPE

AIRTIGHT CAULK TUBE SEAL

Done with the caulking job but the tube's only one-third empty? Dip the nozzle into a can of Plasti Dip rubber coating ($6 at a home center). You'll create an airtight seal that's easy to peel off when the next job calls.

THE APRON

Even if you've never worn an apron while wood-working, try the Cross-Back Shop Apron ($22 at rockler.com). Calipers, tape measure, squares, dust collector remote switch, wood shields for glue clamps—they're right at your fingertips. And a small screw gun is another invaluable. You'll wonder how you ever got along without it.

POLY SQUIRTER

Want to know how to avoid drips and messes when you apply polyurethane varnish to large surfaces or multiple pieces of trim? Use an ordinary squeeze bottle and squirt narrow beads of finish onto the boards, then roll them out. The poly flows neatly onto the wood and rarely drips onto the floor. After practicing a few beads, you can squirt out just the right amount for each board.

FIND-ANYTHING HARDWARE DRAWER

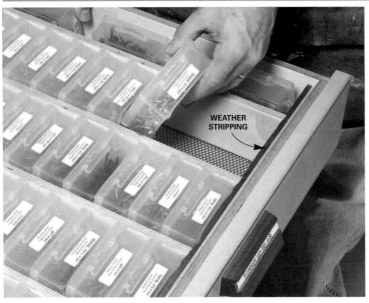

WEATHER STRIPPING

Tired of wondering where to find a 1-in. drywall screw or a 3/8-in. washer? Take a look at this setup.

In the drawer shown, movable partitions are held in place by strips of foam weather stripping at the front and back. The 44-plus boxes rest on edge, labels up, for easy grabbing and stowing. If you want, you can key the labels in on the computer and print them out on sticky labels.

Shop for boxes at craft, tackle, office or dollar stores. But if you want lots of just about any particular size box, check out althor.com. This is for super-organized shop rats, though. The minimum order is $100! But you get tons of high-quality boxes for the money.

STAY-FLAT PLYWOOD SPACERS

Plywood or other sheet stock can warp, especially if it's stored surface to surface. These blocks separate the sheets so air can circulate on both sides. Flat sheets from the lumberyard stay flat this way, no matter how long they're stored. The leather is flexible, so you can use the spacers on any combination of thicknesses of sheet goods.

The blocks are a snap to make from scrap wood and leather. Cut two 1-in.-wide strips of leather (or vinyl or heavy cloth) and space and screw 2-in. x 3/4-in. x 1-in. blocks along the strap. The air space also keeps the sheet stock a lot easier to grab when you need to pull one out. For full sheets, use three sets of spacers, one at each end and one in the middle.

SPACERS

Question&Answer

STABILIZE A WOBBLY BOOKCASE

I recently built a bookcase and I plan to put it in a carpeted room. How do I keep the bookcase level on carpet?

You're right to be concerned. Carpet is held in place by tack strips placed along the perimeter of the room. When you set your bookcase (or any other furniture) over the strips, it won't sit level.

You have a couple of options. The first is to pull the carpet free of the tack strip, cut out a strip of padding where the front corners of the bookcase will sit, and replace the padding with a strip of wood that's the same thickness as the tack strip, usually 1/4 to 3/8 in. (**Option 1**).

A second option is to install adjustable feet (called gliders; $4 at home centers) on the corners of the bookcase (**Option 2**). They're simple to install—just drill a hole and insert the feet. You won't have to mess with the carpet, but the feet may be noticeable, which you might not like.

Resist the temptation to simply remove the tack strip. The carpet can move, even under the weight of the bookcase, eventually resulting in a carpet wrinkle in the room.

Regardless of the option you choose, we recommend securing the bookcase to the wall so it can't tip over. A child climbing or pulling on an unsecured bookcase could knock it over (hundreds of kids are injured each year by falling furniture). Fasten a furniture strap to the wall and the bookcase to keep it from tipping over. The straps cost about $6 at hardware stores. Or, fasten the bookcase to the wall by driving 3-in. screws through the back of the bookcase (at obscure locations) into studs (be sure you hit studs). A total of four screws—two screws into two studs—is plenty.

TACK STRIP

WOOD

PADDING

Option 1:
Pull back the carpet. Measure from the wall the width of the bookcase, cut away the padding, then insert shims for the bookcase corners.

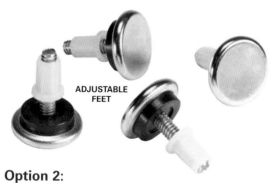

ADJUSTABLE FEET

Option 2:
Drill holes and install adjustable feet on the bookcase corners to level it from front to back and side to side.

RETROFIT AN OLD MITER SAW

I like those laser cutting guides on newer miter saws. Is it possible to retrofit my old saw with a laser?

It's possible, and not terribly expensive. The guide fits alongside the blade, replacing the outer washer. When the saw starts running, the guide shoots a laser beam that shows exactly where the blade will cut.

Quarton makes a product called the Infiniter Laser Cutting Guide, which fits on most miter saws and circular saws. Three small replaceable alkaline batteries provide the power. The centrifugal force of the saw blade automatically starts the laser, so you see the beam as soon as you pull the trigger. Rockler sells the guide for $22 (rockler.com; check the Web site to make sure the guide will work for your saw). It installs in less than five minutes, and the blade will cut exactly on the laser mark.

Replace the outer blade washer with a laser cutting guide for more accurate cuts on your circular or miter saw.

ALKYD VARNISH:
IN SEARCH OF THE FACTS

In a past issue, you mentioned "alkyd" varnish. What is it and where can I find it?

Alkyds are synthetic resins now used in place of natural oils like linseed and sandarac in traditional varnishes. These resins form the varnish film. Alkyd varnishes work well for trim and doors because they're easier to apply and softer, which makes them easier to sand. They're fine where they don't have to withstand abrasion and wear.

You'll find this varnish in any paint store. Look for the words "alkyd varnish" or "oil-based varnish" on the can. Don't confuse them with cans labeled "oil-based polyurethane." Polyurethane usually cures harder than alkyd, which is why it's a popular coating for wood floors and tables.

Note: If you read the fine print on the cans, you may notice that some polyurethanes also contain alkyds. This is one case where reading too deeply into the list of ingredients will sink you into a morass of complicated chemistry. Stick with the basic labels!

New Tools&Gear

Fantastic wood finish

Bruce Wiebe, a long-time "Workshop Tips" editor, once watched a legendary woodworker, Sam Maloof, apply finish to a chair. When the finish was dry, the wood glowed from within, like honey in a jar. Maloof said he'd developed the finish after not liking the plasticky look and feel of lacquer and polyurethane. Rockler now makes and sells the finish as Sam Maloof Poly/Oil Finish and Oil/Wax Finish ($14 a pint, $22 a quart).

TOP: POLY/OIL FINISH
ABOVE: OIL/WAX FINISH

You rub on two applications—oil and polyurethane, and then oil and wax—to create a beautiful finish. Maloof's tip: "When your hand gets hot from friction, you know you're doing it right." The downside is this finish takes five days and a little perspiration, but Bruce says the projects he finished 20 years ago—chairs, dining tables, cabinets—are still glowing today.

Rockler, (800) 279-4441. rockler.com

New Tools & Gear

OLD WORLD CRAFTSMAN, MEET THE COMPUTER

Ever fantasize about being a world-class wood-carver but feel like you don't have the time (or talent) to achieve that lofty goal? Well, now you can spend $1,900 and fake it. Craftsman's CompuCarve produces three-dimensional carvings and scrollwork. Point-and-click computer software creates the designs from a library, or you can draw your own images using CompuCarve's computer interface, which then carves the image. The design software is available for Macs and PCs, then the images are transferred to the CompuCarve via a memory card.

The tool handles workpieces up to 14-1/2 in. wide, 5 in. high and almost any length. Precision sensors measure the board being fed through and detect the position of the cutting or carving bit, then the LCD display walks you through the remaining steps, such as changing the bits. CompuCarve also handles cutting, jointing and routing.

Craftsman, (800) 842-7755. craftsman.com

PYRAMIDS FOR FRESHLY FINISHED DOORS

When you want to finish both sides of doors or shelves without waiting for one side to dry, the Painter's Pyramid is a great solution. Just flip a freshly finished or painted door over and set it on the pyramids so you can finish the other side. The plastic pyramid tips make minimal contact with the wood, so they just barely mar the wet finish. A 10-pack costs $7 on the company's Web site.

K & M of Virginia, (804) 426-4366. painterspyramid.com

INEXPENSIVE (BUT EFFECTIVE) DUST COLLECTION

If you've ever tried using a shop vacuum to improvise a dust collection system, you'll appreciate the Loc-Line Dust Collection system from Lee Valley & Veritas. Rigid plastic pieces inter-lock to create a hose up to 23 in. long that can bend and twist to suit your work area. Attach one end of the hose to a shop vacuum, stick a nozzle on the other end, then place the nozzle

HOSE

NOZZLES

ADAPTER

VACUUM ADAPTER

HOSE ADAPTER

next to any dust-producing power tool to collect dust near the source. Unlike flimsy vacuum hoses, this hose stays where you put it.

Dust collection systems this affordable are hard to find. The hose costs $29.50. Nozzles and hose adapters range from $3.95 to $5.70. Buy the system on the company's Web site.

Lee Valley & Veritas, (800) 267-8735. leevalley.com

HandyHints®

STADIUM-SEATING BOOKSHELF

Cut a hollow PVC fence post ($8 at home centers) to the length of your bookshelf and push it to the back of the shelf. This creates a second tier for paperback storage, doubling the number of books you can put on display.

NYLON

PVC
FENCE POST

NYLONS—FOR THAT POLISHED LOOK

After waxing wood or leather, use a pair of pantyhose for that final buff. It will give your project that extra gleam and make the surface feel smoother.

ALL-NATURAL, ORGANIC WOODWORKING MALLET

Three- to 4-in.-diameter tree branches make great woodworking mallets. Check the brush pile for one with a branch handle, then trim the ends flat with a saw and sand the sharp edges. It doesn't work any better than a store-bought mallet, but it's free—and it's nice to look at too.

ELASTIC-CORD TOOL HOLDER

Use elastic cords to make a portable tool organizer for chisels and other hand tools. Fasten one end of the cord to a 1x8 with an electrical staple, lay the cord straight without stretching it, then staple the other end. Add staples every 3 in. to create holders, leaving the staples just loose enough so the cord can still move. Then fasten the 1x8 to the wall.

ELASTIC
CORD

Do's & Don'ts

EDGE-GLUING BOARDS

Here's how to get great results with minimum hassle!

Gluing boards together to make wider panels is a handy woodworking skill that's easy to learn. Woodworkers with well-equipped shops often buy rough lumber and then rip, plane and joint the lumber to get straight edges for tight-fitting joints. But you can get the same results by carefully choosing boards from a home center or lumberyard. Look for boards with similar color and grain patterns. Then sight down the edge of each board to be sure it's straight. Finally, make sure the boards are flat and not twisted.

Do arrange boards for the best appearance. For projects like tabletops where one side of the glued-up boards will be more visible, choose the best-looking side of each board to face up. If the boards vary in shade, arrange them so differences blend as well as possible. Don't put a dark board between two light ones, for example. Finally, flip the boards end for end and shuffle them until the grain patterns look natural and pleasing. When you're happy with the results, draw a "V" (**photo right**) across the boards with chalk or pencil. If you're assembling several panels, also number them. When it's time to glue the boards together, simply align the marks to make sure the boards are properly arranged.

CHALK MARK

Do apply an even bead of glue. Use white or yellow woodworking glue for interior projects. For projects exposed to moisture, use water-resistant glue. Spread a 1/8- to 3/16-in.-diameter bead of glue along the edge of one board. For an even bead that's perfectly centered on the edge, hold the glue bottle with one hand and the spout with the other hand. Move the glue bottle along the board quickly, letting your index finger ride along the board as a gauge to keep the bead of glue centered. Use a spring clamp to hold the board upright while you apply the glue. You only need to apply glue to one of the two boards being joined.

Don't apply too much glue. Using too much glue won't adversely affect the strength of the joint, but it will make a mess that will require extra time to clean up. The goal is to apply just enough glue so that when the boards are clamped there will be an even, 1/16-in.-wide bead of squeezed-out glue along the length of the joint. Also try to avoid getting glue on the face of the boards, where it will cause trouble with finishing later.

Do slide glued edges together. Press the two boards together and slide them back and forth against each other. This is the best way to spread the glue evenly on the edges of both boards.

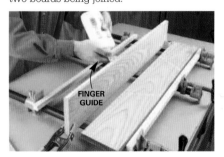

FINGER GUIDE

Tip

Cover the top of the clamps with masking tape to avoid staining the boards and to make cleanup easier.

Do inspect the glue joint before clamping. Separate the boards and inspect the edges. The goal is to have a thin, even layer of glue on each edge. If there are areas where the glue is thin or missing, apply a little more glue to these sections before clamping the boards together.

ADD GLUE HERE

NO SQUEEZE-OUT

Don't skimp on clamps. A good glue joint should have an even bead of squeezed-out glue along its entire length. Add clamps to areas where there is no squeezed-out glue.

Do align the top surfaces carefully. You'll save yourself tons of sanding by making sure the top surfaces are as close to perfectly flush as you can get them. There are a couple of tricks to make this easier. First, glue and clamp only one joint at a time. It takes a little longer, because you'll have to wait for the glue to set up before removing the clamps and adding the next board. But it's much easier to get good results if you focus on one joint at a time. Second, start clamping at one end and work your way along the boards, making sure the top surfaces are flush as you tighten the clamps. Feel the surface with your finger and adjust the boards up or down until the tops are flush with each other. Then apply enough clamping pressure to close any gaps and squeeze out about a 1/16- to 1/8-in. glue bead.

FEEL THE JOINT

Do scrape glue while it's soft. At room temperature and average humidity, the squeezed-out glue will be ready to scrape in about 20 minutes. Wait until the glue changes from liquid to a jelly-like consistency. Then scrape it off with a chisel or putty knife. If the clamps are in the way, you can safely remove them after about 20 minutes in normal conditions. Handle the glued-up panels carefully, though, since the glue won't reach maximum strength for several more hours.

Don't walk away from bowed glue-ups. Glue-ups with bows are impossible to flatten after the glue sets. Hold a straightedge across the glued-up boards to make sure they're flat. Flatten them by driving shims between the boards and the clamps. If the assembly is bowed up, add another clamp on top of the boards.

EDGE PROTECTOR
GAP
SHIM

Tip Place strips of wood between the clamps and the boards to protect the edges of the boards.

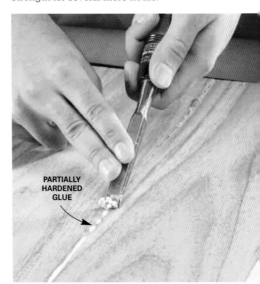
PARTIALLY HARDENED GLUE

Do's&Don'ts

SPRAY FINISH ON WOOD

ORGANIC
VAPOR
RESPIRATOR

Flawless results with aerosol cans

Brushing on liquid finishes is one way to apply clear coats. But don't discount spray finishes, especially for smaller projects.

Off-the-shelf aerosol cans of shellac, lacquer and polyurethane allow you to quickly apply a finish that's free of brush marks. Spraying is also an efficient way to finish complex shapes. Here are a few simple but important tips and techniques that all but guarantee the best results.

Do get set up for spraying. Spraying is fast and gives a smooth finish, but it also creates a fine mist of solvent and finish that drifts and settles on everything in sight and is dangerous to breathe. To avoid problems, work outdoors if possible. If you spray indoors, cover everything with plastic sheeting or drop cloths and wear a respirator fitted with organic vapor filters, especially if you're spraying lacquer. Also put an exhaust fan in the window. Read the label on the spray can for additional safety precautions.

Do start the spray off the edge. It's hard to get even coverage if you start or stop spraying on the surface you're coating. The spatters that happen when you first push the button can blemish your work, and spray builds up in one spot if you don't move fast enough. An easy and foolproof way to avoid these problems is to start spraying before you reach the edge of the project, move across the project at an even pace, and stop spraying after you've gone past the far edge. This technique guarantees an even, spatter-free coat of finish across the entire surface.

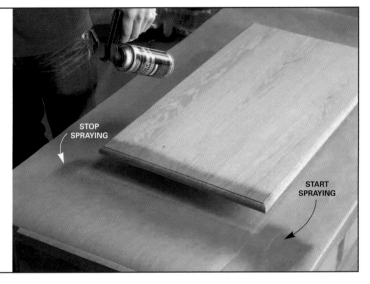

STOP
SPRAYING

START
SPRAYING

Don't swing the can in an arc.

It's natural to swing the spray can in an arc, but this results in uneven coverage. The finish will build up in the center and be light on the edges.

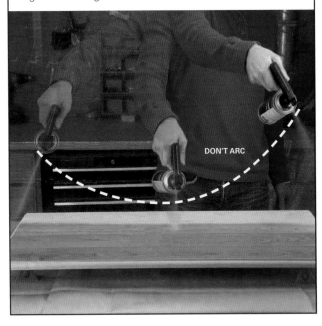

DON'T ARC

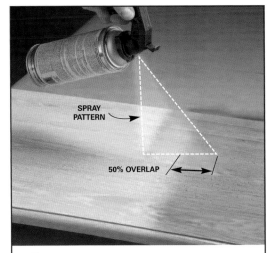

SPRAY PATTERN

50% OVERLAP

Do overlap the spray.

To get even coverage, overlap the spray about halfway onto the previously sprayed section. If you just overlap the edges, you'll get a narrow band of thicker finish where the two strips meet. Overlapping at least 50 percent solves this problem—you'll apply about the same amount of finish everywhere.

Do keep the spray tip parallel to the surface.

Focus on keeping the spray tip an equal distance from the surface as you move it along. At the same time, keep the can moving at a steady pace to get an even coat. The goal is to apply just enough finish to wet the surface without creating runs. Prevent runs by applying several thin coats rather than one or two thick coats. The finish may look blotchy after the first coat, but additional coats will produce a uniform finish.

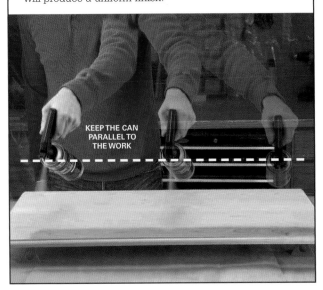

KEEP THE CAN PARALLEL TO THE WORK

Don't dent your finger.

If you've ever used spray cans to finish a large project, you know how sore your fingertip can get from pressing down on the spray tip. A spray-can trigger handle saves your finger and gives you better control of the spray. You'll find spray-can trigger handles at home centers and hardware stores for $4.

SORE FINGER

TRIGGER HANDLE

Do's&Don'ts

Do seal dark stains and exotic wood with a mist coat. Spraying a heavy coat of finish over a dark stain or over some oily exotic woods can ruin your project's appearance. The solvent in the finish can dissolve the stain or the color in the wood and cause it to bleed or get muddy looking. To avoid this, prime these types of projects with several thin mist coats before applying a thicker coat of finish. Apply a mist coat by raising the can higher than normal and moving the can faster than usual. This will reduce the amount of spray hitting the surface. Mist coats dry quicker than a full coat, so you can typically apply several mist coats with less-than-normal waiting time. Wait for the previous coat to dry to the touch before recoating.

MIST COAT

BLEEDING

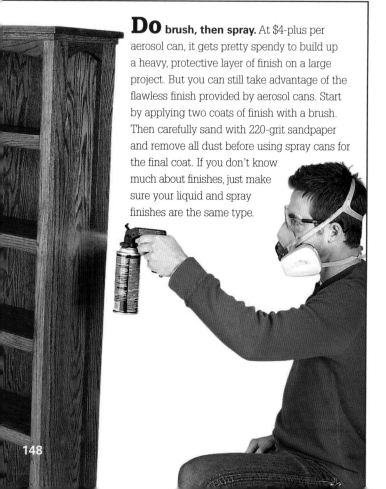

Do brush, then spray. At $4-plus per aerosol can, it gets pretty spendy to build up a heavy, protective layer of finish on a large project. But you can still take advantage of the flawless finish provided by aerosol cans. Start by applying two coats of finish with a brush. Then carefully sand with 220-grit sandpaper and remove all dust before using spray cans for the final coat. If you don't know much about finishes, just make sure your liquid and spray finishes are the same type.

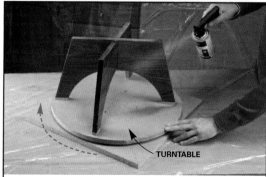

TURNTABLE

Do spin your project.
When you have a small project with many sides to spray, placing it on a turntable will speed up your job and make it easier to get good results. Instead of trying to move around the project as you spray, just give the turntable a little spin. You can build a turntable like this by mounting lazy Susan hardware to a scrap of particleboard or plywood, and then mounting a plywood or particleboard disc to the hardware. Lazy Susan hardware is available for about $4 at hardware stores and home centers. Check the instructions before leaving the store so you can pick up any screws you'll need.

MUD-BUSTING
BOOT SCRAPER

Ordinary doormats simply can't handle serious muck, but you can clean out packed dirt from even the deepest boot treads with this boot scraper made from 2x4s.

1. Screw the base pieces (A and B) together upside down so that the screw heads are hidden.
2. Fasten the uprights (C) to the sides (D), then screw the side brushes on with 2-in. screws.
3. Screw the bottom brushes to the base with 2-in. screws.
4. Space the side pieces so that the bristles are roughly 4-1/2 in. apart.
5. Add a piece of aluminum angle to the front edge so you can scrape boots before brushing them.

Use stiff-bristle brushes—either "bilevel" brushes or deck scrub brushes. You may need to cut off part of the handle so the brush will lie flat.

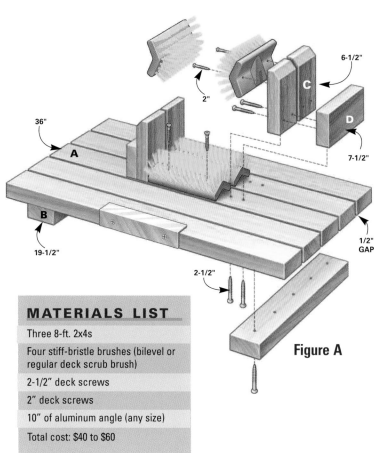

Figure A

MATERIALS LIST

Three 8-ft. 2x4s
Four stiff-bristle brushes (bilevel or regular deck scrub brush)
2-1/2" deck screws
2" deck screws
10" of aluminum angle (any size)
Total cost: $40 to $60

TWO ESSENTIAL
SAW GUIDES

For straight and square cuts every time

With these two saw guides, you can use your circular saw to make cuts that rival a table saw's for speed and accuracy. Building the guides is a quick and easy project. You can complete both in two or three hours. And if you use medium-density fiberboard (MDF) like we did, the total cost will be less than $15.

We'll show you how to build the guides and make sure they produce accurate cuts. You can get all the parts for both from a 4 x 8-ft. sheet of 1/2-in. MDF. We chose MDF because it's inexpensive, stable and readily available at most home centers and lumberyards. Cutting MDF creates a nasty dust storm, though, so wear a mask and put a fan in the window if you're cutting inside. Since you'll use the factory edges as guides, inspect the sheet to make sure the edges aren't dinged up or dented. Then handle it carefully while you're getting it home to avoid damaging the edges. If you can't haul a full sheet, ask to have the sheet ripped into two 2 x 8-ft. pieces that are easier to handle. You'll also need wood glue, three No. 8 x 7/8-in. round head screws and one 1/4-in. washer.

Square-cut guide
Build this handy circular saw accessory in an hour and use it the next time you need a perfectly square cut on a shelf or other wide board. (See p.152.)

Straightedge guide
Cut big sheets down to size quickly with this straightedge guide. Line the guide up with your marks, clamp it down, and run your saw along it to make a cabinet-quality cut.

STRAIGHT-AS-AN-ARROW CUTS

Make wavy cuts a thing of the past with this easy-to-build guide

This straightedge guide allows you to make perfectly straight cuts up to 8 ft. long with your circular saw. It's great for ripping shelves or cabinet parts from a 4 x 8-ft. sheet of plywood. Even if you own a table saw, it's often easier to use a guide and a circular saw than to wrestle a big sheet of plywood through your table saw. You'll customize the guide to your saw, allowing you to simply align the edge of the guide with your cutting marks and clamp it down. You don't have to measure back from the cutting line as you would if you were using a regular straightedge.

Constructing the guide is straightforward. **Photos 1 and 2** show how. The key is to make sure the fence is perfectly straight. Start by drawing a line 6 in. in from the edge of the MDF sheet. Saw along the line with your circular saw. Then flip the 6-in. strip (fence) over onto the remaining MDF and align the two saw cut edges. Clamp the fence in this position while you draw a fine line along the factory edge. You'll use this line to make sure the fence stays perfectly straight as you glue and clamp it.

Flip the fence over again, back to its original position, and spread wood glue on the surface that will face down. Finally, align the factory edge of the fence with the line. Let the fence hang over the end of the guide by 2 in. (**Figure A**). Make sure it's the end where you'll start the circular saw cuts. This will help the saw get a straight start when you're using the guide. Clamp the fence and let the glue set for 20 minutes. Then run your circular saw along the fence to separate the straight-edge guide from the rest of the sheet (**Photo 2**).

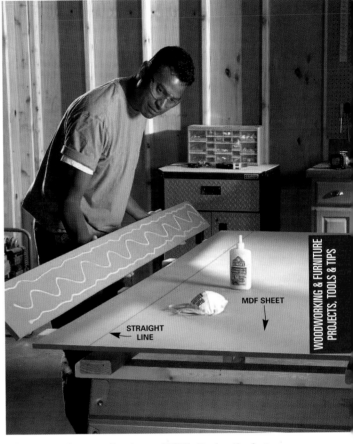

1 Glue the fence to the sheet of MDF, aligning the factory edge with the straight line. As you clamp the fence, make sure you don't push it off the line.

2 Run the saw along the fence to separate the base from the remainder of the MDF sheet. Now you have a guide that will give you perfectly straight cuts up to 8 ft. long.

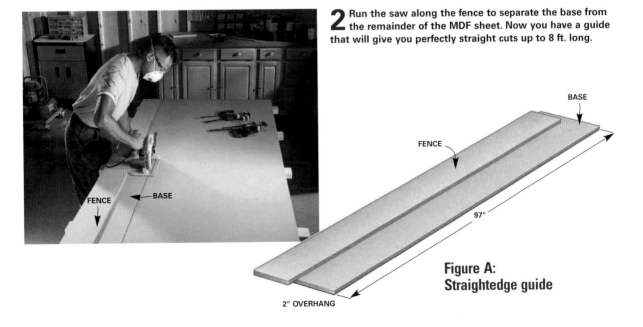

Figure A: Straightedge guide

RIGHT-ON
RIGHT ANGLES

Make precision right-angle cuts quickly with this crosscut guide

This guide allows you to make perfectly square crosscuts on pieces up to 18 in. wide. Like the straightedge guide, the crosscut guide is customized to your saw so you can simply line up the edge of the guide with your cutting mark and clamp it. Then run your saw along the fence to make the cut.

Start by cutting a 22-in. square from the corner of the MDF sheet. Then cut a 3-in.-wide strip from the remaining factory edge of the sheet. Cut the strip into two 22-in.-long pieces. In one 3-in. x 22-in. piece, drill a 1/8-in. hole at one end and a 3/8-in. hole at the other. This will be the adjustable stop that you'll screw to the bottom of the base. **Photos 1 and 2** show how to build the guide. Start by aligning the edge of the stop with a factory edge of the base and attaching it with the "swivel" screw and the "adjustment" screw (**Figure B**). The critical step is making sure the stop is at an exact 90-degree angle to the fence.

Build the guide and make a test cut (**Photo 2**). Then check the cut with a framing square. If the cut isn't square, loosen the adjustment screw and nudge the stop a bit. Then retighten the screw and make another test cut. Make a reference mark next to the stop before you adjust it so you can gauge the distance. Repeat this process until the guide delivers perfectly square cuts. Then drive another screw through the stop into the base, next to the adjustment screw, to lock the stop into place.

1 Screw the fence to the base. Align a framing square with the bottom edge of the base and clamp it. Then align the fence with the square before attaching it with screws.

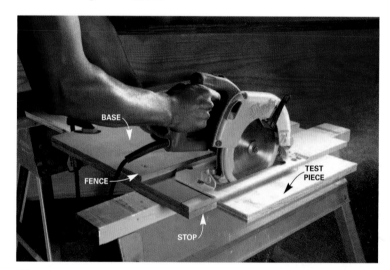

2 Cut through the excess base material and a test piece with your circular saw. Check the end of the test piece with a framing square and adjust the stop to correct the cut if necessary.

Figure B: Crosscut guide

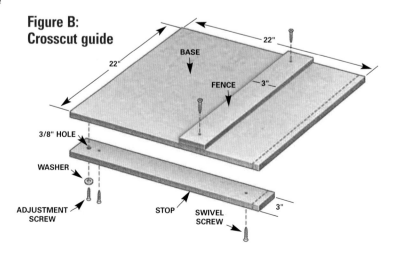

5 Exterior Maintenance & Repairs

IN THIS CHAPTER

Question&Answer

BLACKENED, STREAKY ROOF

What are these black streaks on my roof? The shingles are less than 10 years old, and there are no trees anywhere near the roof.

READER MYSTERY PHOTO

You have hardy algae called Gloeocapsa magma. As the blue-green algae accumulate, they develop a dark, hardened outer coating, which results in the black stains you see. The algae feed on the limestone in your shingles.

The algae will worsen and become more noticeable each year, trapping moisture and causing premature shingle aging and granule loss. If you don't like the streaks, reshingle with algae-resistant shingles. If the streaks don't bother you or you're not ready to invest in a new roof, install zinc or copper strips (available at roofing centers) along the top course of shingles. When rain hits the strips, it produces a solution that runs down the roof and keeps algae, moss and fungus from growing. However, the strips won't eliminate the existing algae.

FINISHED FOUNDATIONS WITHOUT TERMITE WORRIES

You have recommended rigid foam insulation panels to cut heat loss and dress up foundation walls. I was told not to use them in the South because they're not termite resistant. What gives?

The panels we showed from Styro Industries (888-702-9920; styro.net) are not termite resistant and could provide a bridge for termites to access the house. A termite specialist told us that installing the panels also makes it difficult to inspect along the bottom of the siding for termites. However, Dow Chemical (dow.com/Styrofoam) now offers a termite-resistant insulation panel, called Styrofoam Blueguard, that you can install on the foundation's exterior, then trowel a finish over the surface. The 4 x 8-ft. panels are available in 1-, 1-1/2- and 2-in. thicknesses. But they're new and not yet widely available (call 866-583-2583 to find a distributor in your area).

Wear gloves and a long-sleeve shirt when handling the insulation. Adhere the insulation to the foundation with foam-compatible adhesive, butting the joints tightly together. To cut the panels to size, score them with a utility knife and then snap them. Some building codes require a 2- to 6-in. gap between the panels and the siding for termite inspection.

Once the panels are installed, apply a stucco-like finish. We show a premixed acrylic finish by Styro Industries (styro.net) called TUFF II Pre-Mixed Coating ($68 for a 5-gallon bucket that covers 80 sq. ft.). Etch the insulation with a wire brush just enough to take the sheen off the surface (this allows for better adhesion of the finish). Apply Sticky Mesh HD tape (also made by Styro; $40 for a 9-1/2-in. x 150-ft. roll) over the insulation, overlapping seams by 2 in., then apply two coats of the coating with a trowel or putty knife. Paint the coating using an exterior acrylic paint, if desired.

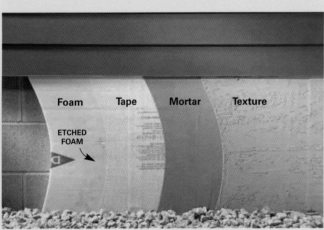

Foam | Tape | Mortar | Texture

ETCHED FOAM

DISTINCTIVE GARAGE DOORS

Your "Great Garage Contest Winner" had an overhead garage door that looked like French doors. Where can I get a garage door like that?

That garage door struck a chord—like you, a lot of other readers wanted to know where they could get it. The door that got all the attention is one of three French door styles made by FrenchPorte (866-545-4561; french-porte.com). The translucent frosted panes are made from polycarbonate sheet, not glass. Prices start at $2,100 for an 8-ft. 2-in. x 7-ft. door.

If you're interested in other ideas for the garage, including door styles, openers and accessories, visit garagewownow.com. The site has a lot of helpful design tips for garages and features manufacturers that have interesting door designs. You'll be surprised at how much an updated garage door can improve your home's curb appeal—and add value.

BETTER TRACTION ON CONCRETE

I'm worried about my elderly mother slipping on our front steps or sidewalk. I plan to paint the concrete. Is there anything I can do to make the surface slip resistant?

Paint stores sell additives that you mix with a gallon of any type of paint or solid-color stain to give you better traction on concrete surfaces. The additive won't change the color of the paint or stain, but it provides texture to improve traction. Don't expect a completely slip-resistant surface.

Stir the additive into the paint (one package per gallon), then apply the paint with a paintbrush or roller. If you're applying more than one coat, put the additive in the final coat. The additive costs about $4.

Mix the nonskid floor additive with the paint. Then apply the paint to give the surface a rough texture to help prevent slips.

CHOOSING 4x4s

I heard that 8-ft. pressure-treated 4x4s contain the pith. Longer 4x4s are less likely to, and are therefore more decay resistant. Is this just old carpenter's talk?

Chalk one up for the crotchety old guys. Pressure-treated 8-ft. 4x4s are typically made from "peeler cores," which are the byproduct of plywood production. When a log is turned on a lathe to produce plywood veneer, the center that remains, called the peeler core, is used as a post. These cores often contain the pith, or center of the log, which doesn't accept pressure treatment as well. Peeler-core posts are more likely to warp and twist than posts cut farther away from a tree's center.

When shopping for 4x4 posts, look at the ends. If growth rings start near the center of the post and expand outward, it's almost certainly made from a peeler core (**see photos**). If the rings are off center, it's not the log's center. Buy 10-ft. posts instead of peeler-core 8-footers and trim them to fit.

Centered growth rings indicate the post is made from peeler core and won't accept pressure treatment well (right), while off-center rings mean the post is not the log's center (left).

TIPS FOR TROUBLE-FREE CONCRETE

Avoid hassles now and cracks later

KICKER

OVERBUILD YOUR FORMS

Every builder has a horror story about forms that bulged or even collapsed under the force of wet concrete. To avoid a horror story of your own, build strong forms. Use 1-1/2-in.-thick boards (2x4s, 2x6s, and so on) except on curves. If you're using 2x4s or 2x6s, place stakes no more than 3 ft. apart. If the forms extend belowground, pack soil against them. If they extend more than 6 in. aboveground, reduce the spacing between stakes and brace each one with a second stake and a diagonal "kicker."

HARDBOARD

FORM CURVES WITH HARDBOARD

Hardboard siding is intended for exterior walls, but it's also great stuff for forming curves because it's flexible and cheap. A 12-in. x 16-ft. plank costs about $10 at lumberyards and you can cut it to any width you need. Because it's so flexible, hardboard needs extra reinforcement to prevent bulging against the force of the concrete. If the forms are belowground, place stakes no more than 3 ft. apart and pack soil against them. For aboveground forms, space stakes 16 in. apart. To form consistent, parallel sides for a curved sidewalk, build one side first. Then use a "gauge board"—a 1x4 with blocks screwed to it—to position the other side. In wet weather, hardboard can swell and your perfect curves might become wavy. So if rain is forecast, be prepared to cover your hardboard forms.

KEEP STAKES OUT OF THE WAY

Stakes that project above forms create a hurdle for your screed board—and screeding concrete is hard enough without obstacles. So before you pour, take five minutes to cut off any protruding stakes. If the tops of your forms are near ground level, make sure your screed board won't drag against the ground; you may have to skim off a little dirt to clear a path for the board.

STAKE

PUT DOWN A SOLID BASE

A firm, well-drained base is the key to crack-free concrete. The best plan for a solid base usually includes compacted soil followed by several inches of a base material such as gravel. But the best base depends on climate and soil conditions. So talk to a local building inspector who's familiar with conditions in your neighborhood. Packing the soil with a rented plate compactor ($40 per half day) is always a good idea, but you may be able to skip the gravel altogether if you have sandy soil.

PLUNGE OUT THE BUBBLES

When you pour concrete, air pockets get trapped against forms, leaving voids in vertical surfaces. That usually doesn't matter on sidewalks or driveways. But aboveground, on stairs, curbs or walls, the results can look like Swiss cheese. To prevent that, just grab a 2x4 and "plunge" all along the forms. Then go all along the forms with a hammer, tapping the sides.

Recipe for a lasting driveway

Too many builders—pros and DIYers alike—treat a driveway just like a patio or sidewalk. But because they support vehicles, driveways deserve some extra effort and expense. Whether you're hiring a contractor or doing it yourself, here are three suggestions for a stronger slab:

THICKNESS: Most driveways are 4 in. thick, but consider a 5-in. slab. That extra inch of concrete increases the strength of the slab by about 50 percent but increases the cost of a typical driveway by only $200 to $300.

REINFORCEMENT: There are two ways to reinforce a concrete driveway: with rods of rebar or with wire mesh. The purpose of reinforcement is to reduce cracking and to hold the slab together if it does crack. Rebar does both jobs better and costs only a few bucks more for a typical driveway.

BASE: What goes under your driveway is just as important as the driveway itself. The best base varies according to climate and soil conditions. It may be a 16-in. layer of special base material or 6 in. of compacted gravel. To get advice, talk to a building inspector who's familiar with soil conditions in your area. If you're hiring a contractor to do the job, be sure the bids describe the base in detail. And don't choose a low bid that skimps on the base work.

BULL FLOAT

Avoid too much water

When you have concrete delivered, the first words out of the driver's mouth may be "Should I add some water?" Unless the concrete is too dry to flow down the chute, your answer should be "No, thanks." The right amount of water is carefully measured at the plant. Extra water weakens the mix. More water makes it easier to work with right away, but will lead to a weaker slab.

If you're mixing your own concrete, do this test: Plow a groove in a mound of concrete with a shovel or hoe. The groove should be fairly smooth and hold its shape. If it's rough and chunky, add a smidgen of water. If it caves in, add more dry concrete.

DON'T DELAY FLOATING

After screeding concrete, the next step is to "float" it. Floating forces the stones in the mix down and pulls the cement "cream" to the surface so you can trowel or broom the surface later without snagging chunks of gravel. If you wait too long and the concrete begins to stiffen, drawing the cream up is difficult or impossible. So the time to float is right after screeding. On a long sidewalk or driveway, it's best to have a helper who can start floating even before all the screeding is done. There is one reason to delay floating, though: If puddles of water form on the surface after screeding, wait for them to disappear before floating.

On small projects, you can use a hand float made from wood ($6) or magnesium ($20). The "mag" float glides easier for less arm strain. But for bigger projects like driveways or patios, don't mess around with a hand float. Instead, rent a bull float (shown above; $20 per day). The long handle extends your reach and makes the job easier, while the broad head covers the surface quickly and flattens out any bulges or depressions. To make the surface as flat as possible, float it in both directions.

"MAG" FLOAT

Top 10 concrete mistakes

1. ORDERING JUST ENOUGH. If you're ordering concrete, it's much better to pay $60 for an extra half yard of concrete than to come up short. You don't have to use it all. The driver will haul away the leftovers.

2. IGNORING THE FORECAST. A little rain can destroy a freshly poured slab. Beware of hot, dry weather too. The concrete may set faster than you can finish it, especially if you're a beginner.

3. WORKING SOLO. Line up more help than you think you'll need. Extra help not only lightens the workload but avoids situations where the concrete hardens faster than you can work.

4. NOT BEING READY. A big concrete pour is a rush job. Don't add stress by waiting until the last minute to finish forms or gather tools. Have everything done and all your tools handy long before the truck pulls up.

5. USING WIMPY WHEELBARROWS. A heavy load of concrete can crush a garden wheelbarrow. Use heavy-duty models only, even if you have to rent them ($15 per day).

6. RELYING ON FIBER. The tiny fibers added to some concrete mixes may reduce surface cracking, but fiber is no substitute for metal rebar or wire mesh.

7. FINISHING WITH EXTRA WATER. It's tempting to sprinkle a little water on the surface while you're troweling to help you get a smooth finish. But it weakens the surface and will lead to flaking later.

8. GETTING BURNED. Some people can tolerate hours of skin contact with concrete. Others end up in the emergency room with severe burns. Don't risk it: Wear gloves and long pants, and wash concrete off skin immediately.

9. TEARING OFF FORMS TOO SOON. It's easy to break off concrete edges while removing forms. So let the concrete harden for at least two days first.

10. FORGETTING YOUR AUTOGRAPH. Be sure to scratch your initials (and the date) in the concrete before it hardens.

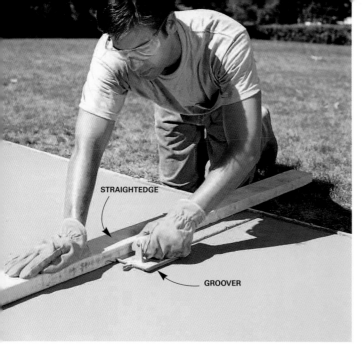

STRAIGHTEDGE

GROOVER

CONCRETE BROOM

CUT DEEP CONTROL JOINTS

The grooves in concrete are called "control joints" because they control cracking. Concrete shrinks as it dries, so cracks have to happen somewhere. Control joints create straight breaks rather than an ugly spiderweb pattern. They also limit cracks that form later. On a sidewalk, space joints 5 ft. apart or less; on a slab or driveway, no more than 10 ft. apart.

There are two ways to make control joints: Plow them in the wet concrete right after floating or cut them the following day with a saw. You can buy a diamond blade for your circular saw for $35. Creating joints with a "groover" in wet concrete is less work and less mess. Joints should be at least one-fourth the depth of the concrete. A groover that cuts 1-in.-deep grooves costs about $25. If you have an inexpensive version ($7) that doesn't cut deep enough, use it to create the initial joint, then deepen the cut with a stiff putty knife.

GROOVER

FINISH WITH A BROOM

A smooth, steel trowel finish is too slippery for outdoor concrete. Instead, drag a broom over the concrete. You'll get a nonslip texture and hide imperfections left by floating or troweling. You can use a plain old push broom, but a concrete broom ($10) cuts finer lines. The sooner you start, the rougher the finish. Make your first pass about 15 minutes after floating. If the texture is too rough, smooth it over with a mag float and try again in 15 minutes. Drag the broom over the concrete in parallel, slightly overlapping strokes. You may have to rinse off the broom occasionally to avoid a too-rough finish.

WEIGHTS

PLASTIC SHEETING

SLOW THE CURING

Water is essential for the chemical process that makes concrete harden—the longer concrete stays damp, the harder and stronger it gets. One way to slow down drying is to cover concrete with 4-mil plastic sheeting. When concrete is hard enough so you can't make an impression with your finger, gently spread the plastic. Stretch it out to eliminate wrinkles and weigh down the edges to seal in moisture. When you see signs of drying, lift the plastic and gently sprinkle on more water. Keep a sidewalk or patio damp for three days. Seven days is best for a driveway. Plastic can cause mottled coloring on concrete, but the splotches disappear in a month or two.

Pros often skip the plastic and spray on a waxy liquid "curing compound" to slow down evaporation. Although not as effective as plastic, curing compounds are easy to apply with a garden sprayer. Curing compounds are available at home centers (a $20 jug covers 200 sq. ft.).

This&That

MIXING-BUCKET HOLDER

To hold a 5-gallon bucket for mixing up a batch of mortar or drywall compound, create a "bucket vise" from a milk crate and wood. Screw the crate onto a piece of plywood. Secure the bucket in the crate by wedging in a 2x4 scrap. With your feet firmly straddling the crate, you're ready for high-speed mixing!

WOOD WEDGE

BUCKET

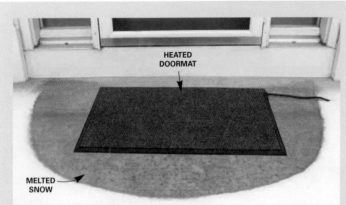

HEATED DOORMAT

MELTED SNOW

HEATED MATS FOR SLIP-FREE ENTRANCES

Nothing sets the heart racing like walking out the front door, stepping on an ice patch and crash landing onto the concrete. Heat Trak's Heated Entrance Door Mat won't let that happen. Set it outside your door, plug it in (the cord is 6 ft. long) and you'll always have a slip-free entrance, no matter what the weather. The mat doesn't have a timer or a switch, so either leave it plugged in or plug it in when the snow starts falling. The company says it'll melt 2 in. of snow per hour.

The mat is ideal for entryways where water drips off the roof and freezes. It also provides a clean area to wipe or stomp the snow off your boots before going inside. Only use it outside (it smells like a new car tire). At $130, it's expensive as doormats go, but it can prevent accidents—and maybe even a lawsuit! Find retailers on the company's Web site.

Heat Trak, (866) 766-9628. heattrak.com

SNAKE OUT SPOUTS

Your plumber's snake is a great tool for pulling clumps of wet leaves out of clogged downspouts.

A ROUND OF PROTECTION

To prevent your ladder from marring your home's exterior, slip golf club covers on the ends of the ladder. It may also motivate you to get your household chores done and get you out on the links.

GreatGoofs®

PORCH BELLY FLOP

I'm an emergency medical technician with our local Volunteer Rescue Squad. I've always prided myself on being able to get up and out the door within two minutes of the pager going off—even after a tough day of major renovation on my house.

At 2:30 one morning, the pager went off and I was out of bed, rescue shirt on, boots pulled up and flying out the door—literally. I was in midair when I remembered that my dad and I had ripped most of the old porch off my house just hours before. I did a heck of a belly flop in the gravel driveway. As I pulled into the Rescue Station and hobbled into the ambulance, my partner asked, "How's the new deck going?" and "Do you need an ambulance?"

"K" HIDES THE SPOT

When I was replacing my garage door, I installed the door's four panels from bottom to top in the same order as they came out of the box. When the second section was in place, I drilled the holes for the lock and handle. This worked great because I could easily reach both sides of the door panel.

But when I had all four sections in place, something wasn't quite right, so I broke down and read the directions. I discovered that the "second" door section out of the carton goes on the top!

Needless to say, the large "K" centered in the top section isn't just for vanity—it covers the holes I drilled in the wrong place!

LOOK OUT BELOW!

A few years ago, my wife and I bought a 100-year-old house. This house needed every fix-up project you could imagine, but we thought we'd better tackle the leaky roof first. The house had one layer of shabby-looking shingles. To save time and money, we decided to skip the tear-off and just add a second layer of shingles. After carrying the first bundle up the ladder, I slammed it down onto the roof. I couldn't believe my eyes. It broke right through the roof and fell onto the floor below. That's how I found out that some of the wood beneath the old shingles was rotting. A whole new roof was the only project we did that year!

WRENCH TOTE

Here's a gripping, portable organizer for all those wrenches and sockets. To make your own, cut a 5-in. handle slot in a piece of 14-in. x 11-1/2-in. x 3/4-in. plywood and screw it to the middle of a piece of 14-in. x 8-in. x 3/4-in. plywood. Band the bottom with strips of 1-1/4-in. x 1/2-in. plywood to reinforce the tote and keep the sockets and accessories onboard. For wrench storage, fasten 13-in.-long magnetic tool bars ($13 each at leevalley.com; No. 99K45.01) halfway up on both sides of the handle board. Tack or glue divider strips to the floor as needed for better socket sectoring. That's it—load and tote!

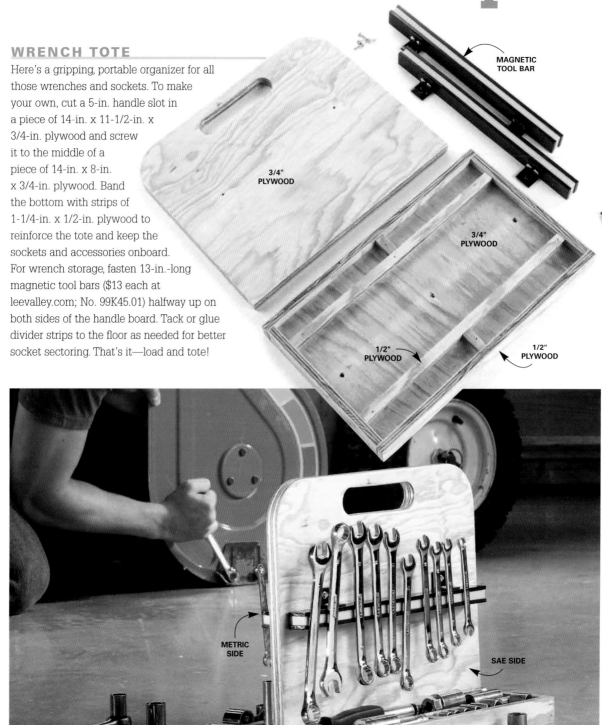

MAGNETIC TOOL BAR

3/4" PLYWOOD

3/4" PLYWOOD

1/2" PLYWOOD

1/2" PLYWOOD

METRIC SIDE

SAE SIDE

Question&Answer

DOUBLE THE LIFE OF YOUR PAINTBRUSHES

I just spent a lot of money on synthetic paintbrushes to paint my house. What's the best way to preserve them so I won't have to buy new ones next time I paint?

To ensure you get a lifetime of use out of your paintbrushes, clean each one immediately after using it, before the paint has a chance to dry. Start by wiping the brush on newspaper to remove excess paint. Then stick the brush into a bucket of warm water (**Photo 1**). Move the brush around to remove as much paint as possible. Next, hold the brush under running water. Run a wire brush (or a kitchen fork) down the bristles to remove dried paint, especially near the handle (**Photo 2**). When the water running off the bristles turns clear, the brush is clean.

Let each paintbrush air dry, then wrap it with the cardboard cover it came in or heavy paper (like grocery bag paper). To keep the bristles straight, hang the brushes from a nail or hook, or store them flat.

1 Move the paintbrush around in a bucket of water to wash out the paint, then run it under water.

2 Use a wire brush to remove the paint from the bristles.

CHECKING A LEVEL'S ACCURACY

How can I tell if my level is still giving me accurate readings? It's been dropped more than once.

The best method is to place the level on a relatively level surface. Shim up the low end until you get a level reading. Make sure to stand perpendicular to the vial when looking at it. Once you get a level reading, turn the level around 180 degrees. If the vial still shows level, you're getting accurate readings.

Check the vial that gives you a plumb reading by placing the level against a door frame. Tape paper shims to the jamb until it's plumb, then flip the level upside down and check for plumb again.

Some levels have vials that can be adjusted. But our advice is to buy a new level if yours is out of whack.

Put sheets of paper under the level until you get a level reading, then switch ends to see if you get the same reading.

OUR **FAVORITE TOOLS**

Once you know about 'em, you're gonna want 'em!

Here at *The Family Handyman*, we're passionate about our tools. We spent a seemingly endless amount of time discussing (and arguing about!) which tools would make the cut for this article. Then we consulted our favorite pros and pared our list down to tools that we use regularly, but ones that you might not be familiar with yet. Let us know what you think!

Cut dust, save time

"The best addition to my woodworking shop over the past 10 years was a basic, low-cost dust collection system," said Gary Wentz, senior editor. "My goal was cleaner air, but I soon found that a dust collector has an even greater benefit: It's a time-saving tool. It drastically cuts cleanup time—I don't have to sweep off every surface and tool. I used to do the dustiest work, like sanding or cutting MDF, outdoors. Now I do these jobs in the shop—no need to drag tools and cords outside."

A dust collector is basically a big vacuum, but it sucks in a lot more air (and dust!) than the most powerful shop vacuums.

"Complete with hoses and fittings, my small-scale dust collection system cost less than $300," Wentz said.

Some home centers carry dust collectors, but the best place to browse is online. Just search for "dust collector."

Gary Wentz

Fast screw guns

"What I like about the automatic-feed screw guns is their speed. You don't have to handle individual screws—the screws come in strips that you feed into the gun," said Jon Jensen, set builder for *The Family Handyman* and former contractor. "They're wonderful tools for drywalling, fastening decking—any job where you need to drive a lot of screws. You can adjust the depth for sinking screws and for different types of screws. That's what makes it really versatile."

The DuraSpin 14.4-volt model by Senco ($150; senco.com) and the Autofeed Screwdriver by Makita ($110; makita.com) are two automatic-feed screw guns. And the cordless option is another big benefit.

"You just keep the tool running, and it drives each screw to the exact same depth each time," Jensen said. "You can really get a lot of work done fast."

TWO-HOLE DRILL GUIDE

FACE CLAMP

Fast and easy joinery

Jeff Gorton

"A Kreg Jig will let you make a joint in about two minutes. I first saw the jig during a product demonstration at a tool show years ago," said Jeff Gorton, associate editor. "I was impressed enough that I went out and bought one. It's become one of my favorite tools because it lets me build furniture, cabinets and bookcases without having to cut fancy (and time-consuming) joinery."

A Kreg Jig lets you drill pocket holes, then screw the pieces together with special screws. You'll leave visible holes, which you can hide inside the project or fill with pocket-hole plugs.

Kreg sells several different pocket screw kits. At a minimum you'll need a two-hole drill guide similar to the one shown above, a step drill with a stop collar, a long driver bit for the pocket-hole screws, and a face clamp. These will cost you about $75. To see the full range of Kreg products or to find a dealer, go to kregtools.com.

Easy-to-handle air hoses

Travis Larson

"I've gone through many, many air hoses over the years—rubber, plastic, synthetic, you name it," said Travis Larson, senior editor. "They all get hard and inflexible in cold weather, they're hard to coil, black ones leave marks all over walls when you're trimming, and they're very heavy. The four or five survivors are all hanging neatly in my shop, unused for the three years since I converted to polyurethane lines."

Polyurethane is soft, so it's more flexible than rubber. The air hoses are lightweight, flexible and easy to coil up at the end of the day, even in low temps. They don't leave scuff marks, so you can use them inside without marking up the walls. And the hoses are tough enough to withstand use and abuse on job sites.

"I love the way the hose's slippery surface glides over everything. You don't have to constantly pull on them to drag them, and they don't get hung up like the old-fashioned hoses did," Larson said. "They're well worth the premium price tag."

A 50-ft. polyurethane hose costs $30, versus about $10 for a traditional hose. Polyurethane hoses are available at some home centers or online.

Dual-use wire stripper

Ken Collier

"I used to use two tools for wiring projects—a goofy little stamped metal tool to strip off sheathing and a pair of wire strippers to strip insulation off individual wires," said Ken Collier, editor in chief.

"Those days are gone. My new wire strippers do both tasks admirably.

"I've rewired my cabin, my workshop and most of my 100-plus-year-old house. Wire strippers that strip the sheathing and the insulation make wiring faster, easier and more pleasant."

These strippers start at $15 at home centers.

Home Improvement Tools & Techniques

Lights that last (almost) forever

"LED (light-emitting diode) flashlights and work lights are fabulous because the bulbs seem to last forever and so do the batteries—making cordless trouble lights feasible (finally!)," said Elisa Bernick, associate editor. "LEDs are great on a variety of levels. Unlike traditional flashlights or work lights, LEDs have unbreakable bulbs that last 50,000 hours or more. They cast a clear white light that's easier on the eyes than the yellow-white light of standard bulbs."

Elisa Bernick

LEDs consume only one-tenth the battery power of regular flashlights and work lights. Sure, LED flashlights and work lights cost a bit more on the front end, but you won't have to replace the batteries or bulbs for years. They're worth checking out!

Eric Smith

Smooth rollers, smooth finishes

"Before a painter friend turned me on to foam rollers, I had a hard time getting a smooth finish on doors and woodwork," said Eric Smith, associate editor.

"These mini rollers, only 4 or 6 in. long, are made of dense foam that spreads the paint or varnish smoothly for a uniform, mark-free finish (unlike nap rollers, which leave tiny bumps). I was amazed the first time I used one.

"But the rollers aren't perfect. They spread the finish thin, so you usually need two coats. And the rollers are a pain to clean, but since most cost less than $5 at home centers and paint stores, you could toss them when you're done."

Three tools in one

The Japanese cat's paw has three intended uses: It pulls nails, works as a pry bar (the thin blade will get under just about anything) and acts like a small hammer to whack things. Once you own one, you'll find other uses for it too.

"It has a permanent place in my tool belt," said Ken Collier, editor in chief. "I use it for prying open cans, as a rough-and-ready scraper, and for pulling small nails that would slide out of the hammer claw. It's an always-with-me tool."

Japanese cat's paws and other small cat's bars start at $10 at home centers.

Ken Collier

Air compressor that fits on your belt

Brett Martin

"When Kobalt hit the market with its portable compressed CO2 regulator kit last year, my first thought was, 'What took so long?' It's a great idea that seems long overdue," said Brett Martin, associate editor. "The cylinder powers pneumatic nail guns and staplers with up to 120 psi, so you don't have to drag around a bulky (and loud!) air compressor and hoses for small jobs.

"The cylinder fits on your tool belt and has a 10-ft. hose. I hooked mine up to a nail gun and installed the baseboards in my kitchen. The 20-oz. cylinder gives you up to 675 shots with a nail gun. It's great for projects in finished rooms when you don't want to run air hoses and worry about them scuffing the floor or walls. New cylinders cost $6 for 9 ozs. and $9 for 20 ozs. when you trade in your old tank."

Mighty midget batteries

"I've tossed a dozen perfectly good cordless drills because the batteries died and new ones cost as much as a new drill. That's one reason I love new lithium-ion batteries: They have a longer life span—twice as long, according to some manufacturers," said Gary Wentz, senior editor.

Gary Wentz

"But the best thing about lithium-ion batteries is that they're about half the size and weight of other batteries. That means power-guzzling tools like saws can pack more punch and run longer without being too heavy. And the screwdrivers are small enough to drop in your tool pouch, but powerful enough for just about any job."

For more, visit thefamilyhandyman.com and search "lithium-ion battery."

WASHING WINDOWS

Try washing windows with a squeegee and you'll never go back to a spray bottle and paper towels. Squeegees get your glass clear and streak free in a fraction of the time it takes with paper towels.

The same high-quality window washing tools the pros use are readily available at home centers and full-service hardware stores. The whole setup costs less than $30 and will last many years. You'll need a 10- or 12-in. squeegee ($6 to $12), a scrubber ($4 to $8), a bucket (a 5-gallon plastic bucket will work), hand dishwashing liquid (we recommend Dawn) and a few lint-free rags or small towels.

Yes, you can use a squeegee inside the house, too

The pros do it all the time, even in houses with stained and varnished woodwork. The key is to squeeze most of the soapy water out of the scrubber to eliminate excessive dripping and running. Then rest the scrubber on the edge of the bucket rather than dropping it in the water after each window. Depending on how dirty your windows are, you may be able to wash five or ten windows before

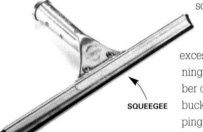

SQUEEGEE

rinsing the scrubber. Keep a rag in your pocket to wipe the squeegee and quickly clean up soapy water that runs onto the woodwork. Use a separate clean rag to wipe the perimeter of the glass. Microfiber rags (top left **photo, p. 169**) work great for window cleaning. They're available at discount stores, home centers and hardware stores.

SCRUBBER

Get your window sparkling clean in less than 30 seconds—

WIPE PERIMETER

MICROFIBER RAG

Use a microfiber rag to wipe up excess water along the bottom edge of the window. Then poke your finger into a dry spot on a separate lint-free rag and run it around the perimeter of the window to remove any remaining suds. Wipe off any streaks using a clean area of the lint-free rag. Change rags when you can't find any fresh, clean areas.

NARROW SQUEEGEE

DIVIDED-LITE WINDOW

Wash divided-lite windows with a sponge and a small squeegee. If you can't find a small enough squeegee, you can cut off a larger one to fit your glass size. Scrub the glass with a wrung-out sponge. Then use the tip of the squeegee to clear a narrow strip at the top. Pull the squeegee down and wipe the perimeter.

CLEAN STRIP

TOUCHING GLASS

Tips for hard-to-clean windows

Dried paint, sticky labels, tree pitch and bug crud may not yield to plain soap and water. Here are a few tips for removing this tough grime.

- Scrape wetted glass with a new, sharp razor blade to remove dried paint.
- Remove tree pitch or bug droppings with a fine (white) nylon scrub pad. Wet the glass first and rub in an inconspicuous area to make sure you're not scratching the glass.
- Add 1/2 cup of ammonia per gallon of water to help remove greasy dirt.
- Loosen sticky residue left from labels or tape by soaking it with a specialty product like Goof Off. You'll find Goof Off in the paint department at hardware stores and home centers. Then scrape off the residue with a razor blade.

just scrub, squeegee and wipe!

Do's&Don'ts
DRIVING SCREWS

With the right techniques, screws will go in easier, and you'll stop stripping out screw heads

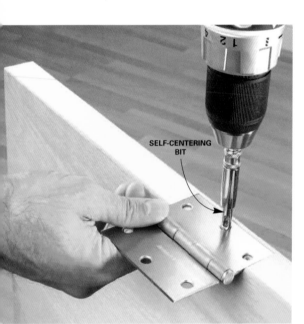

SELF-CENTERING BIT

Do use a self-centering bit when mounting hardware. Even with a steady hand and a sharp eye, it's tough to drill a perfectly centered pilot hole for hardware installation. And if the hole is off-center, the screw won't seat properly. But there's an easy solution. Self-centering bits ($8 to $20) drill a centered pilot hole, resulting in perfectly centered screws. There are several sizes of self-centering bits available. Choose one to match the size of screw you're using.

SELF-CENTERING BIT

Do use the clutch. At times, drills can provide too much power, causing screw heads to snap off or strip, especially with small brass or aluminum screws. Most newer cordless drills are equipped with a clutch, which can eliminate this problem. Set the clutch by twisting the ring near the chuck to the smallest number. Try driving a screw. If the clutch releases (you'll hear a ratcheting noise) before the screw is fully driven, move the setting to a higher number. Choose a setting that drives the screw fully before the clutch releases.

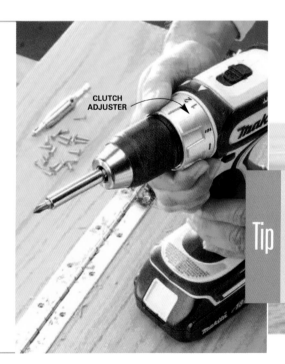

CLUTCH ADJUSTER

Tip

Using square or star-drive screws and bits reduces the tendency for the bit to slip off the screw head.

170

Do line it up and push hard. Driving screws with a drill can be tricky until you master the technique. The most common mistake beginners make is applying too little pressure. Coupled with bad alignment, this spells trouble. If the bit is skipping out of the screw head and you already know that the bit isn't worn, then improving your technique will help. First, be sure the driver bit is aligned with the screw shank. If the bit's sitting crooked in the screw, it won't engage firmly and will slip. Then, with the bit firmly seated, start the drill slowly (assuming you have a variable-speed drill) while pushing hard against the screw. Apply extra pressure with a hand on the back of the drill body. The combination of correct alignment, pressure and slow speed will ensure that the screw goes in without bit slippage, which can damage the screw head and driver bit.

Do drill clearance holes. Have you ever screwed two boards together but not been able to pull the two pieces tight together? This happens when the screw threads engage in both pieces of wood while there's still a gap between them. One solution is to clamp or nail the boards together before making the permanent screw connection. If you don't want to mess with clamps or nailing, you can drill a clearance hole through the first board to solve the problem. Choose a clearance hole bit that's large enough to allow the screw to spin freely. Even cupped or twisted boards are easily drawn tight with this method.

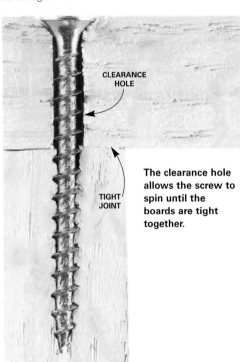

CLEARANCE HOLE

TIGHT JOINT

The clearance hole allows the screw to spin until the boards are tight together.

BIT AND SCREW ALIGNED

Don't mount the bit directly in the chuck. Magnetic bit holders are so handy that it's surprising they're not included as a standard accessory with every cordless drill. Bit holders are readily available wherever cordless drills are sold ($3 to $8). Some have a sliding sleeve that keeps your fingers safer by allowing you to drive long screws without holding the screw shank. Here are a few other advantages of using a bit holder:

- Driver bits are easier to install and remove.
- The extra length allows better visibility and makes it easier to keep the bit aligned with the screw.
- Long bit holders allow easy access to hard-to-reach areas.
- You can stack two bit holders for an extra-long reach.

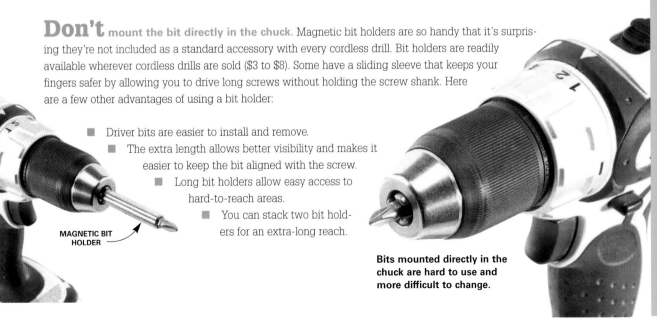

MAGNETIC BIT HOLDER

Bits mounted directly in the chuck are hard to use and more difficult to change.

Do's & Don'ts

Do drill pilot holes for toe screws. Driving screws at an angle (toe-screwing) is a common technique for making right-angle connections. But if you simply angle the screw in the desired direction, it will usually just slip down the board. The key to successfully driving screws at an angle is to use this two-step process to create an angled pilot hole. Choose a drill bit with a diameter equal to the screw shank, not including the threads. First, estimate the entry point based on the length of the screw. Then start the bit at a right angle to the wood at this point (below left). As soon as the drill bit engages the wood, tilt the bit to the desired angle and finish drilling the pilot hole (below). Now drive the screw into the angled pilot hole to complete the job.

STRAIGHT STARTER HOLE

1 Start the bit at a right angle to the piece you're fastening.

ANGLED PILOT HOLE

2 Tip it to the correct angle and drill the hole.

Do use a countersinking drill bit. Countersinking bugle head screws so they are flush or slightly recessed leaves a neat appearance. You can drill a pilot hole and a countersink in one step with a combination countersink and drill bit. For straight-shank screws, the less expensive ($3 to $5) straight-bit design works fine. For tapered-shank wood screws, use a countersink fitted with a tapered-shank bit ($10 to $15).

STRAIGHT-SHANK COUNTERSINK BIT

TAPERED-SHANK COUNTERSINK BIT

Countersink bits are available with or without stop collars. An adjustable stop collar lets you set the maximum depth of the countersink for more consistent results. Also, you can hide the screw by drilling a deep countersink, called a counterbore, and gluing a plug into the hole. Countersink drill bits are available in sizes to match screw sizes. If you're an avid woodworker, it's worth buying a full set. Otherwise, a No. 7 or No. 8 will cover the most common screw size.

Don't use a worn bit. Using worn driver bits is a common mistake. If you're using the right technique and the bit is still skipping in the screw head, it's time to replace the bit. The trick is to have spare bits on hand so you can replace them at the first sign of wear. The next time you're at the home center, buy a 10-pack of No. 2 Phillips bits for about $8 and you'll always have spares. Don't forget to get a few of the other sizes and shapes too.

WORN-OUT PHILLIPS BIT

Tip Match the driver bit size to the size of the recess in the screw head. The three common sizes of Phillips bits, smallest to largest, are No. 1, No. 2 and No. 3. Can't tell by looking? Pick the bit with the tightest fit.

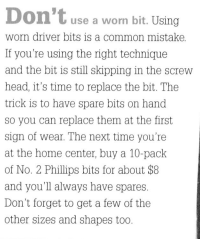

The worn bit on the right should have been replaced with a new one before it became this bad.

CIRCULAR SAW
TIPS AND TECHNIQUES

Brush up on the basics with this collection of circular saw do's and don'ts

Cutting safely with a circular saw is one of the most valuable skills a DIYer can learn. Most homeowners have a saw lying around the garage but may not use it often enough to learn safe cutting skills. It's the lack of familiarity and experience that can lead to poor-quality cuts or worse, bad accidents. In this article, we've assembled a few tips for using your saw safely and improving your cutting skills to help you out on your next carpentry project.

DEPTH
LEVER

1/4" TO 1/2"
BELOW BOARD

Do set the blade depth before cutting. Determine the blade depth by unplugging the saw and holding it alongside your board with the blade guard retracted. Then loosen the depth-adjusting lever or knob and pivot the saw's base until the blade extends about 1/4 to 1/2 in. below the board. Tighten the lever or knob and you're ready to saw.

Don't set the blade too deep. Setting the blade too deep causes a few problems. First, it's more dangerous than a correctly set blade because more blade is exposed while cutting. In addition, the saw is more likely to bind and kick back if the blade is too deep. Safety issues aside, blades cut more efficiently when properly set.

TOO MUCH BLADE
EXPOSED

Do's&Don'ts

Do support plywood for cutting. Crosscutting plywood without supporting it across its entire length can cause the saw to bind or the plywood veneer to tear or splinter as the cutoff piece drops. If you're using sawhorses, simply span them with a pair of 2x4s. This will provide the support needed.

Do allow the cutoff to fall away freely. Always make sure the end of the board you're cutting is free to fall or move away. For rough cuts in framing lumber, let the cut end fall. Be aware, though, that the falling piece can take a sliver of wood with it as the cut nears completion. To avoid this splintering when you're cutting boards for nicer projects, support the board continuously. But don't clamp, hold or otherwise restrict the cutoff piece.

Don't cut wood that's supported on both ends. It's sort of like cutting off the tree limb you're standing on—a guaranteed disaster. The reason is that as the cut nears completion, the board bows downward, which pinches the blade in the cut and causes the saw and/or board to buck. This is dangerous and usually makes a mess of the board, too.

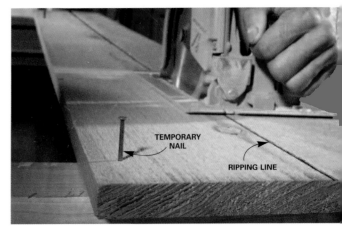

Do secure the board for rip cuts. In most cases, a table saw is a better choice for ripping lumber than a circular saw. But if you don't have a table saw handy, and the rip cut doesn't have to be precise, then a circular saw works fine. The trick is to hold the board in place while you rip it. Unless the board you're ripping is very wide, clamps will get in the way. So a good alternative to clamping is to tack the board down to your sawhorses. We let the nails protrude here because they don't interfere with the saw bed. But you can drive the nails (or screws) flush and still easily pull the board off when you're done. To reduce damage to better-quality boards, use finish nails, and pull them through the back side when you're done.

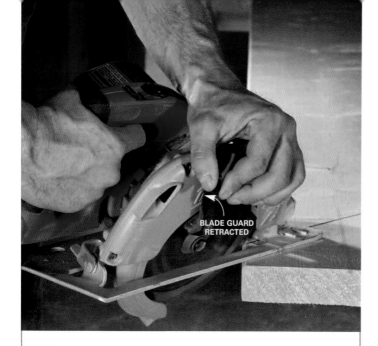

BLADE GUARD
RETRACTED

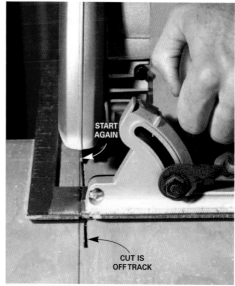

START
AGAIN

CUT IS
OFF TRACK

Do hold the blade guard up to start angled cuts.
Some newer saws have blade guards that are designed to
retract even when you're sawing at an angle. But even with
these newer designs, it's easier to get an angled cut started if
you first retract the blade guard. Once you're a few inches into
the cut, slowly release the blade guard so it rests on the board.
If you try to start an angled cut without retracting the blade
guard, the guard can catch on the wood and cause the saw
blade to bind or the cut to wander off course.

Do cut heavy boards without sawhorses.
When you're cutting joists or other heavy pieces of lumber,
it's often easier to cut them where they lie rather than
hoist them onto sawhorses. An easy way to do this is to
simply rest the board on your toe and lean it against your
shin. Then align the saw with your mark and let gravity
help pull the saw through the cut. Do be careful to keep
the saw cut at least 12 in. from your toe.

12" OR MORE

Do start over if the saw wanders from
the line. Cutting along a straight line is a skill
that takes practice. Once the saw blade is
aligned and cutting along the line, it doesn't
take much effort to keep the blade on track.
But if you get off to a crooked start, it's difficult
to guide the saw back to the line. Don't try to
steer the blade back onto the line. Instead, stop
and let the blade stop spinning. Then withdraw
the saw from the cut, sight along the line and
start again. With practice, you'll be cutting
straight every time.

Do guide rip cuts with your finger.
Making long narrow rip cuts with a circular saw is
easy if you use your index finger as a guide. Align
the blade with the line. Then pinch the saw base
between your thumb and index finger and let your
finger ride along the edge of the board to guide the
cut. This technique is safe as long as you grip the
saw before turning it on and don't release it until
the blade stops.

New Tools&Gear

See-behind-the-walls tool

When this remote camera gizmo arrived at our office, everyone wanted to play with it. No one quite knew exactly what they'd do with the Ridgid SeeSnake micro ($200), but everyone wanted one. It's a little cordless TV fed by a camera on the end of a 3-ft.-long flexible probe. It has its own headlight so you can see in dark areas. Use it to see just about anywhere your melon won't fit into, under or behind. Check inside walls for wires before cutting them open and electrocuting yourself (first drill a 1-in. hole for the probe). Send it into dark confines (engine, furnace, ductwork, and so on) to see what you need to see. Included are attachments that fit around the camera head to let you retrieve small items. Find retailers online.

Ridgid, (800) 474-3443. ridgid.com

Double-action rotary sander

Craftsman's 5-in. Vibrafree random orbit sander (model No. 25927) has noticeably less vibration (the company says 68 percent less) than other sanders. The sander has two discs that work independently of each other, a system that balances the tool as it operates. It also reduces vibration, making it easier on your arm.

If you've done lots of sanding, you know that the outer edge of the disc wears faster than the middle. Since the hook-and-loop discs are replaced separately, you can replace the outer one by itself and get more mileage from the inner disc.

The tool's dust collection system does a better than average job of collecting dust. According to Craftsman, the sander removes 40 percent more dust than other sanders.

Craftsman, craftsman.com

The two sanding discs move in opposite directions to reduce vibration, making the tool more comfortable to use.

SUPER SLIM AND LIGHT BATTERY

CHARGER

CHARGER GAUGE

BELT CLIP

Rugged but light-as-a-feather drill

We've been playing in our shop with Milwaukee's new 18-volt Compact Drill/Driver and it's turned into everybody's favorite drill. The tiny lithium-ion battery charges in only 30 minutes and has a built-in fuel gauge that lets you know how much run time the battery has left. Even more impressive, this powerful drill weighs just 4 lbs., so it won't wear you down. The drill is perfectly balanced and fits your hand like a glove, making it very comfortable to use.

The $200 price tag may scare off casual hole drillers, but if you're a serious DIYer, it's worth the ransom. Consider this: If you take care of the tool, it may very well be the last drill you'll ever buy (although you'll probably need to buy new batteries eventually). The drill comes with two batteries and a charger. A belt clip on the handle keeps the drill at your side—no more stretching for it during one of those need-three-hands moments. Find this treasure at home centers.

Milwaukee, (800) 729-3878. milwaukeetool.com

Portable power and more

Husky's Portable AC/DC Power System ($90) gives you two voltages, 12 (DC) and 120 (AC), for running anything from a camcorder to small power tools. It has a built-in inflator for tires or sports equipment, and jumper cables to jump-start vehicles with dead batteries.

The rechargeable unit will provide power for hand tools that use less than about 6 amps. We used it to run a drill and a sander, but it didn't have enough power for a circular saw. It's compact and lightweight enough to take camping or use for roadside emergencies.

Husky, (800) 916-7004

New Tools&Gear

Portable, cordless wet/dry vac

Lugging around a gigantic wet/dry vacuum for spills and then dealing with extension cords can be more trouble than it's worth. Ridgid's 3-gallon MaxSelect Wet/Dry Vac makes household chores, like cleaning up small spills, a lot easier. It's lightweight, portable and cordless.

The $70 vacuum is an especially good deal if you already have a 24-volt lithium-ion or an 18-volt NiCad Ridgid battery (it'll run on either one) from another cordless power tool. (The vacuum doesn't come with its own battery.) No battery? A home center will hook you up with a battery and charger.

Ridgid, (800) 474-3443. ridgid.com

Versatile vise that fits (almost) anywhere

Dremel developed its Multi-Vise (No. 2500-01) for people who need a versatile vise that's easy to set up and take down. This less-than-$40 gem is a must-have for any hobbyist. It clamps onto any surface (like a kitchen table) up to 2-1/2 in. thick. Because the jaws are cushioned, you can tighten delicate items without marring their surface.

The clamp rotates 360 degrees and tilts 50 degrees, so you're sure to find a comfortable working angle. The vise is available online at dremelstore.us, as well as at home centers and hardware stores.

Dremel, (800) 437-3635. dremel.com

Magnet-backed work light

American Fluorescent's Multi-1 Worklight ($44) is perfect for a garage or workshop. The 18-watt fluorescent bulb throws out enough light to illuminate your work area. Plus, it's easy to move and magnetically clings to any steel surface (or can be screwed to walls for permanent mounting).

The gooseneck arm is flexible and the lamp rotates 350 degrees to cast the light anywhere you need it. A 120-volt outlet in the base lets you plug in power tools without running an extension cord to your work area. The light is available at completegarage.com (No. AF-MLT118ECT).

American Fluorescent, (847) 249-5970. americanfluorescent.com

OUTLET

STEEL PIPE

Recip saw blades for tough jobs

Reciprocating saw blades were dramatically improved when "bimetal" versions became available a while back. They were much more resistant to bending and breakage, but more important, they were so much tougher than their steel predecessors that you could cut through nail-embedded wood. They made recip saws the go-to tool for demolition work. Now, even bimetal blades have been one-upped by Milwaukee's Ice Edge blades. The addition of cobalt and a cryogenic heat treatment improves the blade's hardness and wear resistance, while deeper grooves (gullets) between the teeth keep the blade cooler during cutting, so they last longer. Buy the metal and general-purpose blades from distributors listed online for $22 for a five-pack.

**Milwaukee, (800) 729-3878.
milwaukeetool.com**

Single-squeeze caulk gun

Have a ton of caulking to do? Don't strain your arm squeezing a caulk gun handle for hours. Instead, get a battery-powered caulk gun. Professional ones have been around for years, but they cost big bucks. Now there's an affordable homeowner version.

With Black & Decker's new Powered Caulk Gun, which runs on four "AA" batteries, all you have to do is squeeze the trigger once for a smooth, uniform, continuous bead of caulk. No more gaps or pileups between trigger pulls. Two speeds lets you control the flow rate. Best of all, when you release the trigger, the plunger backs off slightly so the caulk doesn't keep squirting out of the tube and make a mess. The barrel unscrews for loading and changing caulk cartridges.

It's not worth spending the $33 for the tool if you only have one or two windows to caulk, but if you're going to tackle the whole house, the Powered Caulk Gun will make your job a lot easier.

**Black & Decker, (800) 544-6986.
blackanddecker.com**

New Tools&Gear

High-tech earmuffs

Sure, you can buy $20 safety earmuffs at a home center and they'll reduce some noise, but if you spend a lot of time with power tools or lawn equipment, it's worth upgrading to more serious hearing protection. The NoiseBuster Active Noise Reduction Safety Earmuff from Pro Tech Communications is designed to eliminate noise from a wide range of frequencies. It uses a microphone inside the ear cup to monitor incoming noises, then uses electronics to send an "antinoise wave" that's directly opposite to the one coming in to negate the sound.

We put the earmuff to the test while running a planer. The earmuff blocked most noises before we even turned it on. Turned on, the earmuff eliminated most of the planer noise—noticeably better than earplugs or the other earmuffs we tried. A single "AA" battery powers the NoiseBuster earmuff for 65

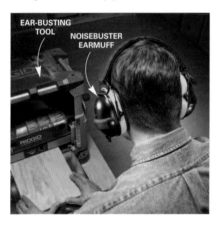

EAR-BUSTING TOOL
NOISEBUSTER EARMUFF

hours. It also has an audio plug-in so you can listen to tunes while you work. Buy them on the company's Web site for $150.

Pro Tech Communications, (877) 226-1944. noisebuster.net

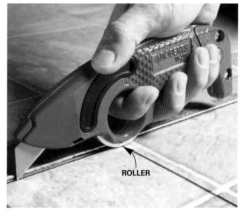

ROLLER

Rolling knife for heavy-duty cutting

The Roberts Roll-O Knife uses standard utility knife blades, but this is not your standard utility knife. First, it's about twice the size of a utility knife. Second, it has an aluminum roller that glides along the surface as you cut, letting you cut straighter and bear down harder without risking scraped knuckles on slips. Third, the knife opens with the push of a button to change blades.

Now for what we didn't like: You can't retract the blade (although you can remove it), and it's a little tricky to use with a straight-edge because of the roller. Still, this heavy-duty knife works great for slicing through hard-to-cut materials like flooring and architectural shingles. Buy it at tools4flooring.com for $15.50 (No. 10-208).

Roberts, (800) 423-6545. robertsconsolidated.com

Quick-to-adjust wrench

Cooper Hand Tools' new Crescent brand RapidSlide adjustable wrench is a lot more user friendly than a traditional adjustable wrench. Instead of the knurled turning adjuster, it has a slide adjuster. You simply slide the lever along the handle to move the jaws, letting you quickly change the jaw opening width. No more fine-tuning those stubborn knob adjusters. Once the jaws are set, they hold in place; you don't need to keep pressure on the slide while turning fasteners. The wrench is available at home centers for $14.

Cooper, (919) 362-1670. cooperhandtools.com

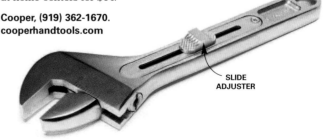

SLIDE ADJUSTER

6 Outdoor Structures & Landscaping

IN THIS CHAPTER

OUR EXPERTS' BEST
LAWN AND GARDEN TIPS

The best way to learn how to get a healthy,
beautiful lawn and garden is to listen to an expert

George Dege

George Dege (aka "Mr. Lawn")
is the owner of Dege Garden
Center, a family-run firm begun
in 1906 (although he's only been
running it for 42 years). During
growing season, he hosts a
weekly call-in radio show
devoted to lawn care. He has
also educated thousands of
homeowners over the years
through seminars and personal
consultations.

Jeff Timm

The owner of a successful
landscaping business, Jeff
Timm designs and constructs
patios and paths, retaining
walls, stonework and other
large landscaping projects for
residential and commercial
clients. He has a degree in
landscape architecture from
the University of Minnesota
and is a contributing editor to
The Family Handyman.

Melinda Myers

Nationally known garden expert
Melinda Myers has written 20
books and numerous articles on
gardening, and is a contributor to
Birds and Blooms and *Backyard
Living* magazines, two of our sis-
ter publications. She hosts "Great
Lakes Gardener" on PBS and
"Melinda's Garden Moments" on
network stations throughout the
country. She has a master's
degree in horticulture and is a
certified arborist.

Best Internet lawn and garden information

All states have agricultural extension services that provide a wealth of free information and services
for homeowners and gardeners. Look for "extension service" for your state on the Internet to get
answers about soils, plants, trees and growing conditions in your region.

Feed shady areas less

"People tend to overapply fertilizer to shady areas because the grass is struggling. But that just kills it faster!

"Many people really have two lawns—a lawn that gets full sun for most of the day, and a shaded lawn that may get only two to four hours of direct sun—and their water and fertilizer needs are different. The grass in shady areas needs less water because less evaporates, and it needs less fertilizer because with less sun it doesn't grow as much. When you go into shade, shift the controls on the spreader so you're spreading about half the amount."

— *George Dege*

Plant trees as if they were full grown

"Before you buy a tree, look at the shade pattern it'll have when it's grown. You're going to start with this cute little tree, and it's going to look good when you plant it near the house, but once it grows up, it's going to be a problem with the roof and gutters."

— *Jeff Timm*

For healthy grass, adjust your soil pH

"Soil pH (acidity level) is very important, and just because your dirt looks rich and black doesn't mean it's the right pH for grass. Take samples around the yard and get them tested. If the pH is too low (acidic) or too high (alkaline), the grass isn't happy to be there. But you can fix the problem by adding lime to raise the pH or iron to lower it. Most grasses prefer a pH of 6.0 to 7.2." — *George Dege*

Note: Lawn and garden centers sell do-it-yourself pH testers; more accurate tests can be performed by extension services.

Mulch plants more—fertilize less

"Overfertilizing with chemical fertilizers can cause excess leaf and stem growth and even burn your plants. Never apply more than the recommended amount.

"Instead of just relying on fertilizers to make your plants look good, concentrate on proper soil preparation to give your plants a healthy growing foundation. Work in several inches of compost in the top 8 to 12 inches of soil. This amazing material improves drainage in clay soils and increases water-holding capacity in sandy soils."

— *Melinda Myers*

Save $$ on mulch

"If you're mulching a big area, use a cheaper hardwood mulch for most of it, then top-dress it with cedar or cypress. You can also top-dress old, ratty-looking mulch—just sprinkle on a fresh 1-inch layer and it'll look brand new. That way you're not paying for something you don't see."

— *Jeff Timm*

Healthy grass is the best weed preventer

"Lawns that are nutrient-stressed are a breeding ground for weeds, so the best defense is a healthy lawn.

"Test the soil to see what type and quantity of fertilizer are needed to help your lawn. Proper fertilization improves lawn health, so grass can compete better and crowd out weeds—without a lot of weed killer."

— *Melinda Myers*

Stop raking and turn leaves into mulch

"As long as at least a quarter of the grass is still showing through the leaves, you can mulch the leaves with your mower. But if the lawn is 80 to 90 percent covered, you'd better rake some of it up. That much mulch creates too much residue, it won't degrade well, and in spring it'll be a matted mess that kills the grass." — *George Dege*

Solve landscape problems with ground covers

"Ground covers are an easy way to soften rock features and patios or control erosion on slopes. If the soil's good, kill the existing vegetation and leave it in place on the slope to stabilize the bank and serve as mulch. Then plant through the layer of dead material.

"Add another layer of shredded bark or other mulch after planting to conserve moisture and reduce weed problems while your ground cover becomes established."

— *Melinda Myers*

The best lawn advice is locally grown

"One-size-fits-all doesn't work for fertilizer, weed killer and grass seed, even though that's what the chain stores sell. Lawn products that work great in Georgia clay may not be good for Kansas or Oregon. The best way to find out about growing conditions in your area and what to put on your lawn, and when, is to talk to a local garden center or your agricultural extension service."

— *George Dege*

Plants don't like rocks

"Rock mulch will reflect heat back into shrubs and heat up shallow roots, so it's not as good for the health of the plant. Shredded mulch holds moisture better and stays cooler."

— *Jeff Timm*

Protect trees with mulch

"Protect exposed tree roots at the surface of the yard. Wounds from lawn mowers create an entryway for insects and disease to move in. However, you shouldn't just bury exposed roots in soil.

"I suggest mulching around the root area instead. A 2- to 4-inch layer of wood chips or shredded bark protects the roots and creates a good growing environment." — *Melinda Myers*

Know how much you water

"To see how much water your sprinkler is putting on the lawn, set out a few cake pans and measure the water they collect in an hour. Put 1 to 2 inches of water on the grass every week—depending on temperature and soil conditions—preferably in the earlier part of the day so the grass dries out before dark."

— *George Dege*

The best garden edging depends on your yard

"Plastic edging will go up and down hills as long as you spike it in well, but over time, straight lines will get a little wavy. Steel edging, on the other hand, will hold a good, straight edge, but it won't roll up hills well. Brick edging looks good, but grass will creep into the cracks, so you've got a little more maintenance.

— *Jeff Timm*

PLASTIC | BRICK | STEEL

LONG LIVE YOUR
LAWN TRACTOR!

Professional tips that prevent expensive repairs

Following the maintenance advice in your tractor's manual is the best way to keep it humming along smoothly. But owner's manuals usually only tell you basically what to do and when to do it—they seldom include the tips and real-world wisdom gained through experience. So we asked veteran mechanics which steps are the most important and how to make maintenance faster and easier. Here's what we learned.

Remove the belt guards and blow off the debris that wrecks belts and pulleys. Scrape away any debris buildup under the pulleys with a screwdriver.

Save $150 in one morning

Dealers typically charge more than $200 for routine maintenance that includes an oil change and new spark plugs and filters. But you can do all these things—and more—in just a few hours. A maintenance kit from your dealer (less than $75) might cost a few bucks more than buying parts separately but ensures that you get all the right stuff.

Blow the mower deck clean

You might think that the belt guards on top of a mower deck protect the belts and pulleys from grass clippings, dirt and other debris. But just the opposite is true. The spinning belts and pulleys suck in debris and the guards trap it inside. Then it swirls around, grinding away at the pulley surfaces and tearing up your belts. Once a pulley wears, it will quickly chew up every new belt you put on. Avoiding expensive belt and pulley replacements is easy; just blow the deck off with an air compressor or leaf blower after every third or fourth mowing.

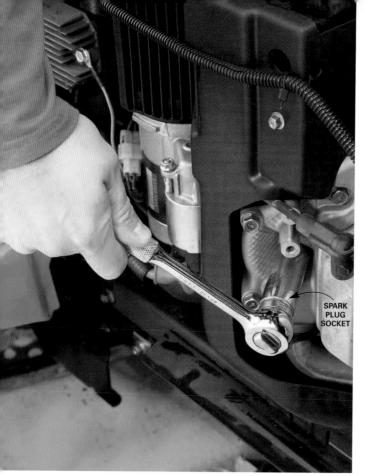

Spark plug pointers

Worn spark plugs cause a variety of problems, from hard starting and poor fuel economy to misfires and even engine damage. So replace them at the manufacturer's recommended intervals. Changing plugs is a simple matter of unscrewing the old ones and screwing in new ones. But there are a few things to keep in mind:

- Prevent debris from falling into the cylinder by brushing or blowing around the plug before you remove it. After removing the plug, wipe out the spark plug seat with a clean rag.
- If an old plug won't turn, don't resort to a bigger wrench. Brute force can cause major engine damage. Instead, use a spray that instantly cools the plug, causing the metal to contract and loosen. The spray is available at most auto parts stores ($6) or online (search for "CRC Freeze-Off").
- Don't forget to set the gap of the new plugs before installing them. Check the manual for gap specifications and use a gap gauge (less than $2 at any auto parts store).
- Use just the right amount of force to tighten the plugs. If you don't have a torque wrench, follow this general rule: First, finger-tighten the plug. If the plug has a gasket, tighten it an additional half turn using a plug wrench. If the plug has a tapered seat, tighten it an additional one-sixteenth turn.

SPARK PLUG SOCKET

Spark plugs are the most important but least expensive components in the engine. Change them regularly for easy starting and fuel economy.

Other models

We show a John Deere tractor in this story, but the maintenance is similar for other brands. Just be sure to follow the procedures, service intervals, and lubricant and torque specifications shown in your owner's manual.

Zero-turn mowers

"ZTR" mowers like this one have a hydraulic steering system, requiring you to change the hydraulic fluid and filter occasionally (typically every 300 hours). It's a quick, simple job, a lot like changing the motor oil.

Get parts (and more) online

- You can find parts online for just about any tractor ever made. Just go to any search engine and type in the brand followed by "parts."
- Lost the owner's manual? Search for the manufacturer and "manual." If you're lucky, you'll find an online version. If not, you'll have to order one—and likely pay $30 or more.
- Mytractorforum.com lets tractor owners share questions and advice on everything from selecting a new tractor to servicing an older model. Just scroll down to "lawn and garden tractors" and select a category.

Service schedules

Every manufacturer recommends different "service intervals" for things like oil, filter and spark plug changes. These intervals can vary a lot. Many manufacturers recommend greasing moving parts every 50 hours, but some call for it every 25 hours. So don't follow general guidelines—follow your manual.

Replace the fuel filter

An old fuel filter can cause hard starting, poor fuel economy, maybe even an expensive carburetor rebuild. Check your owner's manual to find out how often to replace the filter.

Replacing the fuel filter is easy. But there's a trick to doing it without getting drenched in gasoline. First, pinch the fuel line leading from the tank with a clamp. Then move the spring clamps away from the filter with pliers. Slip on a pair of nitrile gloves, tilt the inlet side of the filter up and remove the inlet hose. Drain the small amount of fuel from the fuel line into a drain pan. Then, plug the filter inlet with your thumb, tilt the entire filter down, and pull it out of the outlet hose. This technique keeps most of the fuel inside the filter, reducing spillage. Place the old fuel filter in the drain pan and install the new filter. Pay attention to the fuel flow direction arrows—the arrow must point toward the engine. Move the fuel line clamps back into place and remove the "pinch-off" clamp from the fuel line.

Tip Get a smaller gas can. Old gas (stored for more than 30 days) is the most common cause of starting problems.

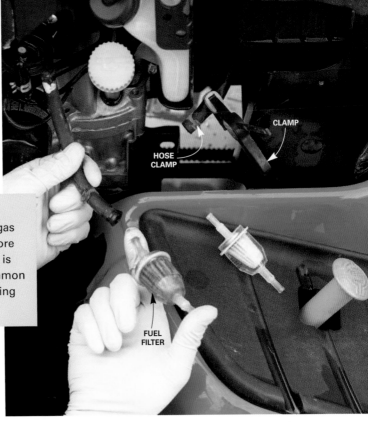

Replace the fuel filter without making a mess. Pinch off the fuel line with a clamp to stop any gas flow. As you remove the old filter, plug the openings with your fingers.

Choose the right oil

Just like your car, your tractor needs regular oil changes. If your owner's manual suggests a brand of oil, you can ignore that advice. But do pay attention to the recommended viscosity (such as 10W-30). If you use your tractor for snow removal, check the manual for a "winter weight" oil recommendation. Never, ever change the oil without also changing the oil filter. To prevent a buildup of gunk on the engine, wipe up any spilled oil. Bottle the old oil and take it to your nearest oil recycling center for disposal.

Screw on the new oil filter until the rubber gasket touches the seat. Then give the filter another half turn. Spread a light coat of oil on the gasket so it doesn't bind against the seat. Check the "donut" on the back of the container and be sure to buy oil with an "SM" rating.

Blade-changing tips

Dull blades make the engine and belts work harder. They're bad for your grass, too. Instead of slicing off the grass cleanly, they leave a torn edge that takes longer to heal.

- To change blades safely, remove the mower deck instead of working from underneath the tractor.
- If the deck has wheels, it tends to roll away as you try to flip it over. Lock one wheel with a clamp as shown to the left. Lay the deck on a couple of 2x4s to prevent damage to the pulleys.
- Lock the blades in place with a clamp and blocks as shown. Don't simply wedge a block between the blade and deck; the blade can break free and cut you.
- If you're an Olympic weightlifter, you can loosen the blade bolts with an ordinary wrench or ratchet. If not, use a 25-in. breaker bar and six-point socket ($25 for both at home centers and hardware stores).
- Blade changes are less hassle if you keep a spare set handy. You can sharpen the dull ones in your spare time or take them in for professional sharpening. For sharpening tips, go to thefamilyhandyman.com and search for "mower blade."
- Grass buildup on the underside of the deck reduces cutting efficiency. Scrape off big chunks with a flat pry bar and clean up the rest with a putty knife.
- To avoid overtightening blade bolts, check the specs in the owner's manual and use a torque wrench ($50 at home centers and hardware stores). Truth is, many tractor owners get by without a torque wrench. But if you ever break a bolt, remember that we warned you.

1 Loosen stubborn blade bolts with a long breaker bar. Hold back the blade with wood blocks and a C-clamp. A clamp on the rear wheel stops the deck from rolling as you flip it over.

2 Position the new blades in a "U" pattern for better balance and less vibration. Tighten blade bolts with a torque wrench to avoid breaking them.

Tip Cutting tall grass is very hard on belts. If you've let the grass go too long between cuttings, mow in half swaths to reduce the load and extend belt life.

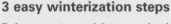

3 easy winterization steps

Before your tractor hibernates for the winter, take a few minutes to prevent springtime troubles.

- Moisture inside an unused engine leads to corrosion. "Fogging" the engine—spraying an oily mist into each cylinder—prevents this. All you have to do is remove the spark plugs and blast in some aerosol fogging spray ($6 at auto parts stores). Then reinstall the spark plugs.
- Storing a battery that isn't fully charged can lead to permanent damage, especially in cold weather. Connect the battery to a battery charger and charge it until you get a reading of 12.7 volts.
- Stored gas will slowly gum up the whole fuel system, and the repairs can be expensive. So add a fuel stabilizer such as STA-BIL or Seafoam ($4 at auto parts stores) to the gas tank before winter. (Adding stabilizer to your gas can year-round is also a good idea.) But remember that stabilizers aren't effective in gas that contains ethanol. If you don't know whether the gas contains ethanol, run the engine until the tank is empty.

Cover the air intake and exhaust openings with plastic wrap or aluminum foil to keep critters from homesteading in your engine over winter.

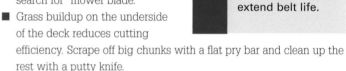

Clean the air filter between changes

You already know that it's important to change the air filter as often as the owner's manual recommends. But it's also a good idea to clean the filter between changes. If your tractor has a foam prefilter, wash it with soap and water; never use a solvent or other cleaner. Blow out the pleated paper filter with a light blast from an air compressor. Keep in mind that this is not a substitute for regular filter changes. Even if the filter looks clean, replace it with a new one at recommended intervals.

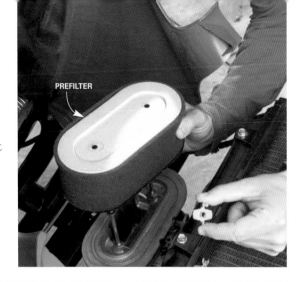

PREFILTER

Wash the foam prefilter and blow off the filter at least once a month during the dusty mowing season.

Grease guidance

It isn't exactly rocket science, but many tractor owners goof up greasing. The biggest mistake is using the wrong grease. The brand doesn't matter, but use the type recommended by the manufacturer, whether it's plain lithium, lithium with molybdenum disulfide, or poly urea. Grease every fitting every time you change the oil. Check your owner's manual to locate them all. There may be grease fittings on your mower deck and other attachments, too. A flexible hose makes reaching the fittings a lot easier. Pick up a grease gun and hose at any home center or auto parts store (about $25 for both).

Pump grease into the fitting until all the dark old grease is purged and fresh new grease oozes out.

Keep your engine clean and cool

A buildup of grass clippings and dirt restricts airflow and prevents the engine from cooling properly. And an engine that runs too hot is headed for major repairs. Even worse, that debris can catch fire.

To clean the engine, vacuum out the engine compartment and the engine itself, including the air cleaner assembly. (Don't be surprised if you find a mouse nest!) If you can't get all the debris with the vacuum, you may have to remove the engine covers and pull it out by hand. Next, spray the engine with an environmentally friendly household cleaner such as Simple Green. Apply the spray cleaner when the engine is cool and let it soak for a few minutes. Then gently hose it off. Don't use a pressure washer—high pressure may damage plastic components. If your engine is coated with oil, don't even think about cleaning it in your driveway or garage. The oil can stain concrete, kill plants and even land you in a heap of trouble with your local EPA. Instead, take the tractor to a shop to have the oil leak repaired and the engine professionally cleaned.

Clean the engine at least once a year to keep it running cool. Just spritz the engine with a household cleaner, then rinse it with a gentle stream of water.

Question&Answer

TROUBLE-FREE TREE PRUNING

What's the best way to cut off a tree branch without damaging the tree?

Prune midsize branches without damaging the tree by cutting them in three stages. Make the first cut (1) on the underside about 8 in. from the trunk, cutting a third of the way up. Make the next cut (2) at the top of the branch 3 in. past the first cut.

Finally, cut the remaining stump off at the trunk (3), just past the slightly raised area, called the branch bark ridge, making the cut perpendicular to the branch to minimize the exposed surface.

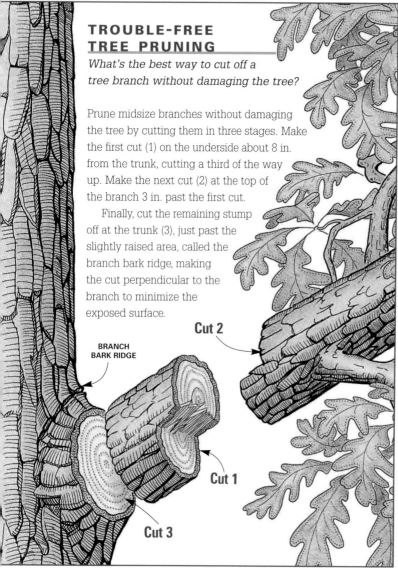

BRANCH BARK RIDGE

Cut 2

Cut 1

Cut 3

THE BEST WAY TO COVER PLANTS

You advise people to cover their house and plants with plastic tarps when power washing their deck. If I do that in the summer, won't it cook the plants alive?

If it receives direct sunlight, clear plastic can create a greenhouse effect on plants on a hot day. However, if you thoroughly wet your plants before covering them and only cover them for a couple of hours, you should be fine.

But you're right—you could cook the plants if you covered them with plastic for a day or more. If you need to cover your foliage for a project, do it on a cloudy day so the sun won't heat up the area under the plastic. If that's not possible, use a light fabric drop cloth instead of plastic.

If you're using a chemical that could harm your plants, such as a deck cleaner, cover them first with plastic, which blocks chemicals, then place a drop cloth over the top to block the sun. Always wet the plants first, and leave an opening along the bottom for air to circulate.

READER MYSTERY PHOTO

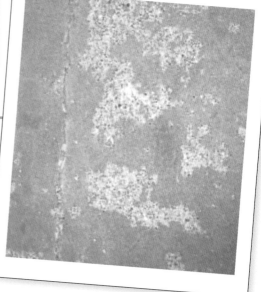

CONCRETE-ATTACKING DEICERS

I used a product on my driveway to thaw the ice. Then the surface started deteriorating. What happened?

You probably used a deicer containing ammonium nitrate or ammonium sulfate—these deicers are made with ingredients typically found in plant fertilizers. But they chemically attack concrete and cause the surface scaling that you experienced. In the future, stick with deicers that contain sodium chloride (rock salt) or calcium chloride. Just be sure to keep them off your yard and away from metal (they can harm vegetation and corrode metal).

SHED-BUILDING TIPS

Easier building, longer-lasting materials and practical features

A yard shed should be easy to build, a pleasure to look at and a practical storage or work space. We've been designing sheds with these goals in mind for more than 50 years. And with each new design, we add a few fresh ideas to our "shed tips" list. The next three pages feature some of the best selections from that long list.

Fast and lasting roof

Metal roofing costs about twice as much as asphalt shingles. But that's not as bad as it sounds. On a midsize shed, you'll only spend an extra $100 to $200. And that's a bargain when you consider the benefits. A metal roof typically lasts 30 to 50 years, so chances are you'll never have to replace it. Metal roofing saves labor, too. Instead of covering the whole roof with plywood, you just nail a few 2x4 "purlins" across the rafters. Screwing the big metal panels to the purlins is much faster than nailing on hundreds of shingles. It's all very simple—if the roof is simple.

If your roof has features like hips, valleys or a dormer, the job gets more complicated. So be sure to check out the manufacturer's instructions before you choose a metal roof. Home centers sell metal roofing, though usually by special order only. You can often order panels precut at the factory, so you don't have to cut them to length. To find manufacturers, installation guides and online suppliers, search online for "metal roof."

Big doors the easy way

A pair of swinging doors can give your shed a wide entrance for your lawn tractor or boat, but a sliding door is a lot less trouble. Sliding doors are easier to build because they don't have to be as stiff and sturdy. And since you don't have to fuss with hinges, installation is much simpler. Years down the road, sliding doors won't sag and stick the way swinging doors do. But sliding doors have two drawbacks. First, they don't fit as tight; critters or snow can sneak in around them. Second, you need a long wall for a wide door—the door's width can only be about half the length of the wall. The sliding closet door hardware available at most home centers costs less than $30, but check its weight capacity. To find heavier-duty hardware, search online for "barn door hardware."

SLIDING DOOR TRACK

RAFTER TAIL

BRACKET

Dress it up with details

A few decorative details make all the difference between a show-off shed and a backyard eyesore. A dormer or front porch can dress up a shed, but smaller details can do the trick, too. Features like exposed rafter tails, simple decorative brackets, corner boards, a cupola or a gable window are great ways to add charm without adding a lot of work.

PAVER FLOOR

WOOD FOUNDATION

Simplified floor and foundation

A concrete slab makes a great foundation and floor for a shed. But you can have a stable foundation and sturdy floor without the cost and hard labor of a slab. Pressure-treated lumber laid on a bed of gravel gives you a fast, easy foundation that will last for decades. To add a floor fast, you can lay joists on the wood foundation and cover them with plywood, just like the floors in most homes are built. To see an example of this approach, go to thefamilyhandyman.com and search for "compact shed." For a floor that's more durable than plywood, fill the wood foundation with gravel and lay cement pavers, just like for a paver patio. A paver floor allows water to drain through, so it's perfect for a gardening shed; spilled water drains away and you rinse the floor clean with a hose.

Don't paint wood

If you want your shed to have a rustic, natural look, you can't beat stained wood. But if you plan to paint your shed, wood just doesn't make sense anymore. The following widely available materials stand up better to time and the elements:

PVC TRIM

- Fiber cement usually costs less than wood, holds paint much longer and never rots. You can buy it in 4 x 8-ft. sheets or planks for lap siding. There are versions for trim boards and soffits too. It's available at home centers and lumberyards. For more info, go to jameshardie.com or certainteed.com.
- Composite trim (made from wood fiber and plastic resins) can be cut, nailed or shaped with a router just like wood. But it holds paint better and costs less than wood. For more information, search online for "primetrim" or "miratec."
- PVC plastic trim is a more expensive alternative, costing about the same as perfect, knot-free wood. But it will last virtually forever, even under the worst conditions, and holds paint better than wood. And if you want white trim, you'll never have to paint it at all. To find manufacturers and dealers, search online for "plastic trim." For tips on installation, go to thefamilyhandyman.com and search for "pvc trim."

Easy tool access

A shallow tool locker on the side or back of a shed offers quick, easy access to lawn and garden gear. To build this tool locker, we constructed an interior wall 12 in. from the back of the shed, covered the studs with pegboard and installed a pair of steel prehung doors ($110 each) inside out so they swing outward. Homemade or sliding doors would work well, too.

A better way to trim

Most builders nail on exterior trim with a heavy-gauge finish nailer or a big framing nailer. But you don't need to buy an expensive nailer for exterior trim. An inexpensive little 18-gauge brad nailer can do the job almost as fast. Since those skinny brads don't have enough holding power to keep large trim in place permanently, you need to first lay on a couple of generous beads of construction adhesive. Then tack the trim into place, using just enough brads to hold it while the adhesive hardens. Unlike thicker nails, brads rarely split the trim and you'll have only a few tiny holes to fill.

Quick, inexpensive skylights

Skylights are the best way to brighten a shed. They let in a flood of overhead light and—unlike windows—leave wall space free for hanging storage and shelving. Skylights made for houses are pricey, but there's an inexpensive alternative. Plastic dome skylights start at about $45 and are easy to install. Just cut a hole in the roof sheathing, nail the skylight into place and shingle around it. Plastic skylights aren't exactly attractive, but you can place them on the side of the roof that's least visible. You can special-order them at most home centers or lumberyards, or buy online (search for "plastic skylight").

Frame the roof flat on the ground

If you frame your roof the traditional way, one rafter at a time, you'll spend half the day crawling up and down ladders. With prebuilt roof trusses, you'll cut out most of the ladder work, saving time and sparing your knees. Manufactured roof trusses in standard sizes are surprisingly cheap—often just a few bucks more than the lumber alone would cost. Contact any home center or lumberyard for prices and options. If you need a custom size or a steep roof pitch, however, manufactured trusses cost more, making building your own trusses worthwhile. It's easy, too. Assembling the first one takes some careful layout. But you can churn out the others fast, using the first one as a pattern.

Cheap windows with charm

"Barn sash" windows are the simplest windows you can get—basic wood frames, single-pane glass and dividers for classic charm. That simplicity makes them inexpensive ($45 for a 22 x 42-in. version) and versatile. You can install them upright or sideways, screw them in place permanently, or hinge them on the side or top. The only difficult thing about barn sashes is finding them. Some home centers carry them, but most don't. Call local lumberyards first. If that fails, ask a manufacturer to recommend a local dealer. To find manufacturers, search online for "barn sash."

PATH & WALL TIPS

Pro tricks for easier, faster, better building

There's no way around it: Building paths and walls with heavy materials like brick and stone is hard work. But whether it's digging, hauling or cutting, there are ways you can work smarter. Several of the following tips help you save time and effort while you're building your wall or path. And after all that hard work, you want your project to last, so we've also included some tips to make sure your paths and walls look as good in 20 years as they do the day you finish.

Get rid of soil, dirt cheap

Path projects seem to breed dirt. And hauling it away can be costly. Rented roll-off trash containers (Dumpster is one brand) are great because you can roll the wheelbarrow right into the container and dump it. But you'll pay about $300 per container load. Here are other ways to get rid of dirt.

- Ask around the neighborhood. Someone may have a low spot to fill or need soil to build up around a leaking foundation.
- Check the Internet. In large cities, there are often companies that match people looking for dirt with people looking to get rid of it. Go to dirtfill.com to see if this service is available in your area.
- Form a berm or build a raised planter bed.
- Put up a sign that says "Free Dirt."

Skip the mortar

Mortar is traditionally used to secure the top courses of stone on a wall. But polyurethane adhesive does the same thing without the hard work and mess of mixing mortar or the skill needed to trowel it on. Also, polyurethane stays flexible, so it doesn't crack and fall out like mortar does. Combine stone chips with the adhesive to shim stones to keep them steady until the adhesive cures. Polyurethane adhesive is available at home centers and is at least as strong as dedicated landscape adhesives. If the materials are dry, use caulk tubes of polyurethane adhesive. For damp materials, you can use liquid polyurethane glue.

POLYURETHANE ADHESIVE

STONE CHIP SHIM

Gorilla Glue is one brand. The materials must fit tightly together for a liquid glue like this to work.

Build in drainage for long-lasting walls

Water-soaked soil is the worst enemy of retaining walls because it exerts enormous pressure behind the wall. Adding good drainage behind block or stone walls is crucial for long-lasting, bulge-free walls. Start by laying perforated plastic drainage tubing along the base of the wall slightly above ground level so it can drain to daylight. Slope the tubing about 1/4 in. per foot. Then add outlets at about 16-ft. intervals (**photo above**). Cover the tubing with crushed stone. Then continue filling behind the wall with crushed stone as you build it.

DRAINAGE TUBING

OUTLET

Snap lines on the sand

You can stretch a string between stakes to create a layout line for setting bricks, but simply snapping a chalk line in the sand is quicker, plus you don't have a string in the way. With layout lines snapped on the sand, laying bricks is faster and easier. The chalk won't stick to dry sand, so you may have to mist the sand with water before snapping lines. Then snap layout lines directly on the sand using a standard carpenter's chalk line reel.

CHALK LINE

Rental tools to save time and toil

- Digging out for your path is easier if you get rid of the sod first, and a rented sod cutter makes short work of this job. Rent a kick-type sod cutter ($14 per day) for small paths or a gas-powered sod cutter ($50 per day) for big jobs.
- Carrying bricks a few at a time is time consuming and hard on your hands. Take a tip from the pros and rent a brick tongs ($5 per day).
- Cutting brick is quick and nearly dust-free with an electric paver saw ($64 per day). Save all the cuts for last to reduce the amount of time you'll rent the saw.

Keep sand in the cracks

POLYMERIC SAND

Sweeping dry sand over paver-brick or stone patios and walks is the traditional way to fill the joints. The problem is, the sand tends to get washed away or swept out of the joints, and can be a nuisance when it gets tracked into your house. One solution is to use special polymeric sand that binds together when wetted. You can buy the polymeric additive and mix it with dry sand yourself, or you can buy premixed bags of sand. Premixed sand is the most convenient solution. A bag ($24) covers about 120 sq. ft. on paver bricks. Check with local landscape suppliers or call Pave Tech at (800) 728-3832 for help finding a local dealer of SandLock additive. Make sure there is no sand on the surface of the path or patio before you wet it.

Another option is to apply a stabilizing sealant after you finish the walk or patio. The sealant soaks into the sand and glues the grains together. Sealing a patio helps prevent staining from spilled red wine or greasy meat. So if you plan to apply a sealer anyway, you can save time by stabilizing the sand joints while you're at it. One brand is TechniSeal Stabilizing Sealant for Pavers and Sand Joints ($47 per gallon). Call TechniSeal at (800) 465-7325 for help finding a local dealer. Follow the recommended coverage instructions carefully.

LIQUID STABILIZING SEALANT

POLYMERIC SAND   **SAND ADDITIVE**

Keep the dust down

Spray water on the diamond blade when you're cutting concrete, bricks or blocks. The small, controllable stream from a garden sprayer works best. The water also cools the blade and speeds the cutting process. Make sure the saw is double insulated or has a grounded plug and is plugged into a working GFCI outlet or GFCI-protected cord.

GFCI PROTECTION

GARDEN SPRAYER

DIAMOND BLADE

PVC PIPE

HEAVY-DUTY DOLLY

Save your back

Heavy-duty two-wheel dollies ($40 and up) work great for moving flat stones and piles of brick. Special dollies called ball carts have a curved back to fit the root ball of a tree. These are available at some rental centers (about $24 per day) and are perfect for moving boulders. Move really heavy stones by rolling them over lengths of PVC pipe. A lot like the ancient Egyptians did.

1-1/2"
ATHLETIC TAPE

Save your fingertips

Handling brick or stone all day can scrape the skin off your fingertips, even to the point of bleeding. Gloves are OK, but they limit dexterity and wear out quickly. Here's a tip from our favorite landscape consultant. When you're laying bricks, pick up a roll of 1-1/2-in.-wide athletic tape at the drugstore and put a few wraps of it around each of your fingers. You can still get a good grip on the bricks and your fingers won't be raw at the end of the day.

ATHLETIC TAPE

Cover your grass

Bricks and stone really tear up grass. If you're not careful, you'll have to lay new sod. Plywood keeps shards and soil from mingling with grass and makes it easy to clean up with a shovel. You can also prevent wheelbarrow ruts by covering the route with strips of plywood.

Pack the gravel in layers

Depending on the type of soil, most paths, patios and walls require an 8- to 12-in.-deep compacted base of gravel. But if you just dump 8 in. of gravel into a trench and run a plate compactor over it, only the top few inches will be fully compacted. The uncompacted gravel will settle later, creating waves in the wall or path. For a fully compacted base that won't settle, add the gravel in 2- or 3-in.-deep layers, and run the plate compactor over each layer before adding the next one.

PLATE COMPACTOR

Get deliveries right

- Don't have bricks or stone delivered until you've completed the digging, installed the gravel or other base material, and hauled away excess dirt; otherwise they're likely to be in the way. You'll have to work around piles of stone as you move tons of soil and gravel.

- Ask about truck-mounted forklifts. Most landscape suppliers offer truck-mounted forklifts that can drop materials right next to your worksite. This service can cost $50 or more, but that's a bargain compared with hauling two tons of brick to your backyard in a wheelbarrow.

- Make sure the material gets placed where you want it. If you won't be home when the material is delivered, post a sign that says "put bricks here" to eliminate any chance for misunderstandings.

Handy Hints ®

DRIVE-BY WEEDING

Attach a bottle of herbicide to your lawn tractor with a hook-and-loop strip (like Velcro) in a spot where you can easily grab it. When you're mowing your lawn, pause the tractor and spray weeds right when you see them for weed control on the fly.

HOOK-AND-LOOP STRIP

HOOK-AND-LOOP STRIP

ENGINE MARK-UP

Use a permanent marker to write the exact oil blend needed for your two-cycle engines on any clean surface. It'll save you from running to the file cabinet to find your manual or grabbing the wrong mix.

EASY-READ RAIN GAUGE

Drip food coloring into the bottom of your rain gauge the next time you empty it out. When it showers, the coloring will reconstitute and tint the water to make the gauge easier to read.

EASY WATERING

Stop dragging your garden hose all over the yard by attaching it to your fence with conduit straps (available in the electrical section of home centers). Then just hook up the hose at the spigot end, whatever sprinkler you want at the other end, and open the valve. It will make watering "the back 40" an easy task.

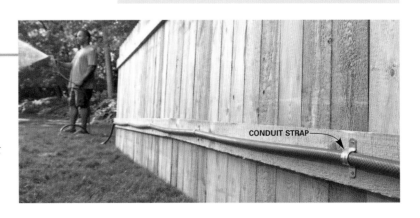

CONDUIT STRAP

OUTDOOR STRUCTURES & LANDSCAPING

HandyHints®

SHIELD FOR FERTILIZER SPREADER

When you're using a broadcast spreader for weed-and-feed fertilizer or even a sand-and-salt mixture for an icy sidewalk, protect your flowers, bushes and grass with this simple clamp-on shield. Hang it on the side of your spreader with a couple of spring clamps.

SPACE-SAVING HOSE STORAGE

If you have a small yard, don't waste any precious real estate on a bulky hose reel. Pound a 4-ft. length of galvanized steel pipe ($7 at home centers) into the ground, coil up to 50 ft. of hose around it and top the end with a nozzle that hooks into the pipe's end. This hose holder's narrow profile is both space saving and attractive.

STEEL PIPE

NewTools&Gear

Feed the birds, not squirrels

A lot of bird feeders are designed to be squirrel-proof. The problem is that most of them don't work. Or they look so hideous that you wouldn't want them in your yard anyway. The Squirrel Stopper from Liberty Products solves both problems—it looks nice and it keeps squirrels from getting fat off your birdseed. A "floating" baffle, connected by three stainless steel springs, moves up and down and side to side so squirrels and other four-legged critters can't climb up.

You can assemble the feeder post in less than 10 minutes without any tools. It holds up to eight bird feeders or plants from S-hooks.

Liberty Products, (616) 450-3890. Squirrelstopper.net

S-HOOKS

BAFFLE

FLAT SURFACE FOR JACK

NO-SWEAT FENCE POST PULLING

To remove a stubborn 4x4 fence post, fasten a 2x4 vertically to the post with five or six screws. Set a car jack on a board or block underneath the 2x4 and jack the post right out of the hole.

PORTABLE POTTING

Cut a piece of plywood roughly to the shape of your wheelbarrow's back end and screw a few wood cleats along the sides to keep it from slipping off while you wheel. Now you'll have both soil and a potting surface right at hand when you take the wheelbarrow to the garden.

STAY-PUT CLEAT

GO WITH THE FLOW

Got an old garden hose with a couple of leaks? Repair it if it's a high-quality hose. But if it's a hopeless case, make it into a soaker hose. Cut lots of 1- to 3-in. slits with a utility knife. The water seeps through the holes fairly evenly, and it's a great way to water gardens.

POSTHOLE HELPER

When digging a hole in very hard soil, dig down a few inches and fill the hole with water. Allow the water to seep down and soften the soil. It'll take a while and you may have to repeat the process, but your back will thank you.

CARDBOARD TUBE

GARBAGE BAG HOLDER-UPPER

Tired of the garbage bag slipping down into the trash can? Cut out the middle of the lid with a utility knife and just snap the outer rim over the bag to keep it in place. This works great for recycling, not so great for stinky stuff!

WEEDY TIP

When you sow seeds, it can be hard to tell little weeds from the young sprouts. Cut cardboard tubes from toilet paper into one-third sections to encircle the seed and keep you from plucking out your young plants.

OUTDOOR STRUCTURES & LANDSCAPING

IS YOUR DECK
DANGEROUS?

7 minutes, 7-point inspection and 7 easy repairs!

A well-built deck will last for decades. But a deck that's rotting or missing fasteners, or that moves when you walk on it, may be dangerous. Decks built by inexperienced do-it-yourselfers, not inspected when they were built, or more than 15 years old (building codes were different back then!) are susceptible to serious problems. Every year, people are severely injured, even killed, when decks like these fall down. This has usually happened during parties when the deck was filled with guests.

Now for the good news. Most of the fixes are quick, inexpensive and easy. Home centers and lumberyards carry the tools and materials you'll need. Or visit strongtie.com to find local stores that stock anchors, post bases and connectors.

In this article, we'll show you the warning signs of a dangerous deck—and how to fix the problems. If you're still not sure whether your deck is safe, have it inspected by your local building inspector.

The checklist:
1. Lag screws in ledger?
2. Missing nails in joist hangers?
3. Rotted posts?
4. Weak post connections?
5. Deck wobbles?
6. Missing ledger flashing?
7. Loose railings?

NEW LAG SCREWS (WITH WASHER)

LEDGER

EXISTING LAG SCREW (WITHOUT WASHER)

SOCKET

Fasten the ledger to the house with lag screws. Drive them fast with a corded drill and socket. Every lag screw must have a washer.

1 No lags in the ledger

The ledger board holds up the end of the deck that's against the house. If the ledger isn't well fastened, the deck can simply fall off the house. A building inspector we talked with said the most common problem with DIY decks is ledger boards not properly fastened to the house. For a strong connection, a ledger needs 1/2-in. x 3-in. lag screws (or lag bolts if you have access from the inside to fasten the washers and nuts) driven every 16 in. This ledger board was fastened mostly with nails instead of lag screws (and no washers).

Starting at one end of the ledger board, drill two 1/4-in. pilot holes. Offset the holes so the top isn't aligned with the bottom hole. Then drive the lag screws (with washers) using a drill and an impact socket (you'll need a socket adapter that fits in your drill). Don't countersink the screws—that only weakens the ledger board.

---

2 Missing nails in joist hangers

Granted, there are a lot of nail holes in a joist hanger—but they all need to be filled. Otherwise, the hangers can pull loose from the ledger board or rim joist. Deck builders sometimes drive a couple of nails into the hangers to hold them in place, then forget to add the rest later. This deck had only a single nail in some joist hangers. In other areas, it had the wrong nails. Joist hanger nails are the only nails acceptable. These short, fat, galvanized nails are specially designed to hold the hangers in place under heavy loads and resist corrosion from treated lumber.

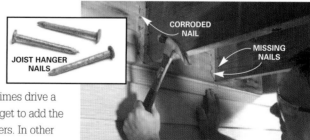

CORRODED NAIL

MISSING NAILS

JOIST HANGER NAILS

Fill every nail hole in joist hangers, using joist hanger nails only. If you find other types of nails, replace them with joist hanger nails.

3 Rotted posts

Deck posts that rest directly on footings soak up water and then they rot, especially posts that aren't pressure treated (like this one, which is cedar). As the post rots, it loses its strength and can't support the deck's weight. Newer decks keep the concrete footings a few inches above ground and use a special base bracket to keep the posts dry. Replacing a rotted post is the best solution. Before removing the post, be sure you have everything you need for the replacement, including a wedge anchor.

Clear grass or stone away from the bottom of the deck post. Prod along the bottom of the post with a screwdriver or an awl. If the wood is spongy or pieces easily peel away, you'll need to replace the post. Start by nailing 2x4s or 2x6s together to use as temporary braces. Place scrap wood on the ground for a pad within 3 ft. of the post being replaced, then set a hydraulic jack over it. Cut the brace to size, set one end on the jack and place the other end under the rim joist. Slowly jack up the brace until it's wedged tight. Be careful not to overdo it. You're just bracing the deck, not raising it. If you hear the joist boards creak, then stop. Then place a second brace on the other side of the post (Photo 1). (If you don't have jacks, you can rent them for $10 each.) Or you can set your temporary braces directly on the pads and drive shims between the posts and the rim joist.

Mark the post location on the footing, then remove the post by cutting through the fasteners that tie it to the rim joist. Use a metal blade in a reciprocating saw (or knock out the post with a hammer). If there's already a bolt sticking out of the footing, use it to install a new post base. If not, you'll need to add a 3/8- by 4-in. wedge anchor. Do this by placing the post base at the marks where the old post sat, and then mark the center. Remove the post base and drill the center mark with a 3/8-in. masonry bit. Drill down 3 in., then blow the dust out of the hole.

Tap the anchor into the hole with a hammer (Photo 2). Install the post base over the anchor. As you tighten the nut on the anchor, the clip expands and wedges tight against the hole walls to hold itself in place.

Cut a treated post to fit between the post base and the top of the rim joist. Set the post into place and tack it to the post base with 8d or 10d galvanized nails (Photo 3). Place a level alongside the post. When it's plumb (straight), tack it in place to the rim joist. Then install a connector and drive carriage bolts through the rim joist (see the next repair).

1 Prop up the deck with temporary braces so you can remove the rotted post. Stop jacking when you hear the deck begin to creak.

2 Tap a wedge anchor into a predrilled hole in the footing, then tighten the post base over it.

3 Set the new post into place and nail it to the base. Plumb the post and fasten it to the rim joist or beam.

OUTDOOR STRUCTURES & LANDSCAPING

4 Wimpy post connections

Ideally, posts should sit directly under the beam or rim joist to support the deck. If the posts are fastened to the side of the beam or rim joist, like the one shown here, the weight is put on the fasteners that connect the post to the deck. This deck had only three nails in the post—a recipe for collapse. Nails alone aren't strong enough for this job, no matter how many you use. For a strong connection, you need 1/2-in.-diameter galvanized carriage bolts.

Add two of these bolts by drilling 1/2-in. holes through the rim joist and post. An 8-in.-long 1/2-in. drill bit costs $10. The length of the bolts depends on the size of your post and the thickness of the rim joist (add them and buy bolts at least 1 in. longer than your measurement). We used 8-in. bolts, which went through two 1-1/2-in. rim joists and a 3-1/2-in. post. Tap the bolts through with a hammer, then add a washer and nut on the other side.

Strengthen post connections with carriage bolts. Drill holes, knock the bolts through, then tighten a washer and nut on the other side.

Stiffen a wobbly deck with a diagonal brace run from corner to corner. Drive two nails per joist.

5 Wobbly deck syndrome

If your deck gets a case of the shakes when you walk across it, there's probably no reason for concern. Still, in some cases, the deck movement puts extra stress on the fasteners and connectors. Over time, the joists can pull away from the rim joist or ledger board and twist out of their vertical position, which weakens them. Fastening angle bracing under the deck will stiffen it and take out the sway. The braces are mostly hidden from view and let you walk on your deck without feeling like it's going to fall down at any moment.

Run a treated 2x4 diagonally from corner to corner, under the deck. Drive two 16d galvanized nails through the brace into each joist. If a single board won't span the distance, use two, overlapping the braces by at least two joists. Cut the bracing flush with the outside edge of the deck.

6 Missing ledger flashing

The area around the ledger board should be watertight. Even small leaks can lead to mold inside the walls of the house and, even worse, the house rim joist (which supports the ledger) will rot and the ledger will fall off. Stand or crawl under the deck and look at the ledger board. If you don't see a metal or plastic lip over the top of the ledger board, add the flashing. Flashing was completely missing from this deck.

To add flashing, first remove the deck board that runs alongside the house. If the boards run diagonally, snap a chalk line 5-1/2 in. from the house, then set the blade in a circular saw to the depth of the decking boards and cut off the board ends. (Replace the cutouts at the end of the job with a 5-1/2-in.-wide board installed parallel to the house.)

For vinyl, wood or other lap siding, work a flat bar under the siding and gently pull out the nails (**Photo 1**). Insert the flashing behind the siding (**Photo 2**). If you have a brick or stucco house, you probably won't see any flashing because the ledgers are often installed directly over brick or stucco.

We used vinyl flashing, but you can also use galvanized metal or aluminum flashing. At each joist location, make a small cut in the flashing lip with a utility knife so it'll lie flat over the joists. The rest of the lip should fit over the top edge of the ledger board.

You should have flashing under the bottom edge of the ledger, too. But since there's no way to add it without removing the ledger board, run a bead of acrylic caulk along the bottom of the ledger board to seal out water (**Photo 3**).

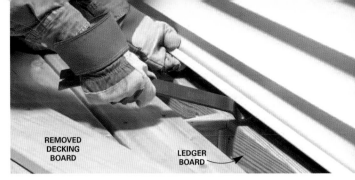

REMOVED DECKING BOARD   **LEDGER BOARD**

1 Pry the siding away from the house and remove the deck board that's over the ledger to clear the way for new flashing.

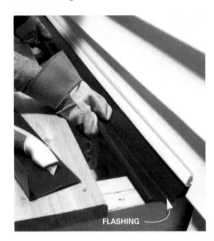

2 Slide the flashing behind the siding so the lip covers the top of the ledger. Reattach the siding.

FLASHING

3 Seal out water along the bottom edge of the ledger, if the bottom flashing is missing, by running a bead of caulk.

LEDGER BOARD

---

7 Rickety railing posts

1/2" BIT

Loose railings won't lead to your deck falling down, but you could tumble off your deck. Railing posts attached only with nails are bound to come loose, and no matter how many new nails you drive into them, you won't solve the problem. Instead, add carriage bolts.

Measure the thickness of the post and rim joist, then buy 1/2-in.-diameter galvanized carriage bolts that length plus 1 in. Also get a nut and washer for each. Drill two 1/2-in. holes through the post and rim joist. Offset the holes, keeping one about 1-1/2 in. from the top of the joist and the other the same distance from the bottom (make sure to avoid drilling where a joist abuts the rim joist). Tap the carriage bolts through the holes, then tighten the nuts until the bolt heads are set flush with the post.

OFFSET HOLES

1/2" CARRIAGE BOLT

Strengthen a loose railing post with carriage bolts. Drill a pair of holes through the post and framing. Angle the hole to avoid joist hangers.

KILL ANY WEED

With the right herbicide at the right time, you can wipe out your weeds in one hour!

When *Family Handyman* Associate Editor Brett Martin bought his house, the lawn was filled with weeds. Dandelions and ground ivy mostly, with a few generous patches of clover and thistles. He poured some weed killer into a dial-up sprayer, hooked the sprayer up to the outdoor spigot, doused the entire lawn, and an hour later he was done. Within a couple of days, the weeds were wilting, and they didn't grow back after he mowed them. Not bad for an hour's worth of weed treatment!

In this story, we'll show you how to kill your weeds in an hour or less. Although there are hundreds of kinds of weeds, they all fall into one of three categories—broadleaf, annual grassy weeds or perennial grassy weeds—and specific types of herbicides target each weed group.

Whether you want to eliminate weeds before they start growing again (early in the year is the best time to attack weeds) or kill weeds that are already overtaking your lawn, we'll show you how. Most of the weed treatments you need are available at home centers, and the others at garden centers (see the Buyer's Guide, p. 207).

KILL **BROADLEAF** WEEDS

A broadleaf weed is any undesirable lawn plant that isn't a grass. The plants have actual leaves on stems, and contrary to the name, many have narrow rather than "broad" leaves. Dandelions, plantain, ground ivy (creeping charlie) and ragweed are a few of the most common broadleaf weeds.

Early

Before broadleaf weeds start growing in the spring, apply a product called Hi-Yield Turf & Ornamental Weed & Grass Stopper Containing Dimension, which is a preemergent herbicide. It kills weeds before they sprout from seed and even kills some weeds that have just started to grow. Spread the product on the yard between your first and third mowings in the spring. The company says a single application will last a full 120-day season. This is as close to a one-size-fits-all magic bullet as you'll find for eliminating annual weeds. No other product on the market will target both broadleaf and annual grassy weeds and stop them from growing. It's available at lawn and garden centers (call first to make sure). A 35-lb. bag that treats up to 15,000 sq. ft. costs about $30.

Park your broadcast spreader over a tarp or on the driveway (grains may leak out, and a heavy dose of herbicide on the yard can kill even healthy grass). Fill the spreader (**Photo 1**) and distribute the herbicide evenly over your lawn.

BROADCAST SPREADER

1 Spills will kill your grass. Park your spreader on a tarp or driveway when filling to avoid herbicide overdoses.

CREEPING CHARLIE

Late

If a few broadleaves pop up in the yard (you can always count on a few dandelions), spot-kill them with a post-emergence herbicide such as Ortho's Weed-B-Gon MAX ($9 for a 32-oz. concentrate that covers 16,000 sq. ft.). Look on the label for "broadleaf killer" then check to see which weeds it targets. Some broadleaf herbicides also kill crabgrass. There's no need to treat the entire lawn, just the weedy areas. Don't let them spread and create a bigger problem.

Premixed herbicides are OK if you have a small lawn and only a few weeds. Otherwise, buy concentrates to mix yourself—they're a better value. Wait until the temperature is between 60 and 85° F. (The herbicide vaporizes too soon in high temps, and weeds don't grow fast enough in low temps to absorb the chemicals.) Mix the herbicide with water (follow the directions) and pour it into a small pump sprayer ($7 to $15). Keep the nozzle 6 to 12 in. from the weed and spray until the leaves are slightly wet (**Photo 2**).

Too late

If your lawn has lots of weeds scattered over large areas, don't waste time spot-spraying individual weeds. Killing the weeds is as quick and easy as spraying the weedy area with a hose.

Pour a concentrated postemergence herbicide (the same kind you used for spot-spraying) into a dial sprayer ($11) and set the dial on the lid to the manufacturer's recommended mixture (such as 2 tablespoons per gallon of water). Attach the sprayer to a garden hose, turn on the water, and apply an even treatment to the weedy areas in the yard (**Photo 3**). Apply the herbicide when the weeds are actively growing in the late spring and early summer. You don't need to drench the weeds. A light misting will kill most weeds (if it doesn't, give them a second dose in a week). Spray only on a calm day. Even a slight breeze can carry vapors that can kill plants (anything that kills broadleaf weeds will also kill flowers or decorative plants and could harm trees, so watch for overspray).

2 Spot-kill broadleaf weeds using a trigger-controlled pump sprayer until a mist forms on the leaves.

Tip Only spray the weedy areas of the yard—not the entire lawn. You'll introduce less herbicide into the environment.

3 Cover large areas fast with a dial sprayer attached to a garden hose. Avoid spraying on a windy day so it won't drift onto (and kill) nearby plants.

CRABGRASS

KILL **ANNUAL** GRASSY WEEDS

Annual grassy weeds sprout from seed each year. The weed dies in the fall, leaving behind seeds that germinate the following spring. Crabgrass is the most notorious grassy weed, but there are others, like yellow foxtail and nutgrass.

How to restore bare spots

Killing large patches of weedy areas is going to leave bare spots in your yard that will need to be replanted with grass. The best times to reseed are the spring or fall when the temperature is 60 to 70° F. To start, water the bare spot until it's wet to a depth of at least 3-1/2 in. Water at intervals throughout the day (for about 15 minutes every two to three hours) rather than continuously. With constant soaking, the water just runs off. Check the depth of the water penetration by digging into the ground and lifting up the soil. You'll be able to see or feel how deep the water has seeped in.

Make a series of 3/8-in.-deep recesses in the ground, 1 in. apart, with a square-head shovel. Spread the grass seed over the bare spot. Then flip over a garden rake and use the "knuckles" to cover the seed with soil. Lightly water the area in the morning and evening until the grass starts to grow in.

If you want the seed to grow fast, plant Scotts PatchMaster ($21 for a 15-lb. bag), which is grass seed with fertilizer and mulch to keep the seed from drying. After making the recesses in the ground, spread PatchMaster seed over the bare spot. Water twice daily.

Early

Use a preemergent herbicide to kill annual grassy weed seeds in the spring before they germinate. Crabgrass preventer is the most common, but you might as well apply a herbicide containing Dimension in the spring because it also kills broadleaf weed seeds. Crabgrass often thrives along sidewalks and driveways because the ground is warmer there, so be sure to apply herbicide in those areas.

Late

The best way to handle a few scattered annual grassy weeds is to spot-kill them with a postemergence herbicide that's formulated for grassy weeds, such as Ortho's Grass-B-Gon ($6 for 24 ozs.). Look for Grass Weed Killer or Crabgrass Killer on the label (Crabgrass Killer kills other grassy weeds, too).

Mix the concentrated herbicide with water (per manufacturer's directions), then pour the mixture into a handheld sprayer ($20). Spray the individual patches of weeds (**Photo 1**). To ensure that there's plenty of plant material to absorb

the weed killer, don't mow the weeds just before applying the herbicide or for three days after. If you don't kill annual grassy weeds now, you can expect them to seed and produce even more weeds next year.

Too late

There's only one remedy for yards taken over by grassy weeds—spray the entire lawn with a postemergence herbicide (like the ones used in the "Late" stage). Mix the concentrate with water in a pump sprayer ($20; **Photo 2**).

Spray the yard with the herbicide in the late spring or summer. Apply just enough to get the weeds slightly wet. The weeds should start to die within five to seven days. Spot-kill any weeds that are still growing after seven days.

Tip
Always read the herbicide's label before applying to make sure it will kill the targeted weeds and not harm your lawn.

HANDHELD SPRAYER
CRABGRASS

1 Spray a second dose on weeds that survive the first spraying. Hunt for survivors seven days after spraying.

CONCENTRATED HERBICIDE

2 Save money by mixing concentrated herbicides rather than using pre-mixed versions. Concentrates give you about 60 percent more herbicide for your buck.

KILL **PERENNIAL** GRASSY WEEDS

Perennial grassy weeds come back every year, just like your lawn grass, and are the toughest weeds to deal with. That's because the herbicides that kill these weeds will also kill your grass. Perennial grassy weeds like Dallis grass and quack grass have deep, expansive root systems that make it impossible to kill them by pulling them out. Quack grass is easy to identify—three or four days after you've mowed your yard, quack grass will be noticeably taller than the surrounding grass.

Early

To spot-kill the weeds, apply a nonselective herbicide, such as Roundup ($22 for a 32-oz. bottle). Nonselective herbicides kill plants and weeds alike, so it has to be applied to the individual weeds by hand. Wearing cloth gloves over plastic gloves, wipe the herbicide directly onto the weed (**Photo 1**). Don't worry about covering every single blade. As long as you get most of them, the herbicide will absorb into the weed. It'll take seven to ten days before the weed starts to die. If it's not dead after two weeks, wipe on a second treatment.

Late

The solution is the same later in the year. But the longer you wait, the more work you'll have since these grasses continue to spread all spring and summer. The herbicide is most effective early in the season when grasses grow the fastest. As the weeds take root and become sturdier, they may require more applications to fully kill.

Too late

Once there are too many weeds to spot-treat by hand, it's time for draconian measures. Kill everything and start over. Spray a nonselective herbicide on the weedy area (**Photo 2**). Wait two weeks. If they're not dead, spray them again.

Once the weeds are dead, mow them as short as possible. After spraying the herbicide, wait 14 days to plant new grass so the herbicide won't kill it.

Buyer's Guide
- **BAYER: The product line includes herbicides.** bayer.com
- **FERTILOME: Includes Hi-Yield Turf & Ornamental Weed & Grass Stopper Containing Dimension.** fertilome.com
- **SCOTTS: Includes Ortho and Roundup. The product line includes grass seed, fertilizers and herbicides. (888) 270-3714. scotts.com**

1 Apply herbicide to perennial grasses without killing the surrounding grass. Wear a cloth glove over a rubber glove. Dip your gloved hand in the herbicide and wipe it on.

QUACK GRASS

2 Spray herbicide to kill patches of perennial grassy weeds. Mow the weeds after they are dead, then plant grass seed in the area.

OUTDOOR STRUCTURES & LANDSCAPING

GreatGoofs®

Outta-whack lawn mowing

While I was out of town, my wife decided to help out by mowing the lawn. That night, as we talked on the phone, she mentioned that the mower engine had died about a dozen times. I thought that was unusual since it's a new mower and I'd never had any trouble with it.

When I got home, I knew what the problem was as soon as I pulled into the driveway. An inspection of the mower confirmed it. I always kept the wheels at the highest setting. While my wife was mowing, she had hit a landscaping stone in the yard, knocking the left rear wheel down to its lowest setting. This caused the blade to drag through the dirt on one side, repeatedly killing the engine. Every pass of the mower gave the lawn a nice "cultivated" look.

Playhouse no child's play

I was nearly done with my kid's playhouse; all that was left was the vinyl flooring. I precut the vinyl to fit, rolled it up and leaned it against the rear wall. Working toward the door, I spread the glue and let it get tacky. Then, taking off my sandals, I jumped over the adhesive like a gazelle to where the roll of vinyl flooring was waiting. "This job is going to be done in no time," I thought.

My smile faded when I realized I had cut the vinyl to be rolled from the door. There was no space inside the playhouse for me to reroll it, and the roll was way too heavy for me to hold while I jumped back over the glue. I felt like a mouse facing a 7-ft. glue trap.

I hefted the roll, took a breath and boldly stepped into the glue with my bare feet. Immediately I was stuck to the particleboard beneath me. With each step I had to yank out my foot, covered with adhesive and bits of board, fighting the glue and the weight of the flooring I was carrying.

Afterward, I picked gluey wood chips off my feet for a good hour and decided that next time my kid should hire a pro.

A smash-in basement

We were getting ready to have a stamped concrete patio poured in our yard. I wanted to save some money and build my minimal DIY skills, so I decided to break up the old wood porch myself. When I cleared the debris, I was surprised to find a concrete pad under it.

I eagerly got out my never-used sledgehammer. Breaking up concrete was very cathartic for a keypad jockey like me, and I was beginning to think that DIY projects were kind of fun. That was, until the sledge head went through the pad and into a huge void, which happened to be my basement. I stared at the hole in disbelief.

Apparently the pad had been a cover for an unused and concealed well room. But the die was cast. We now had to replace the slab. But instead of a simple concrete pour, we had to spend a whole lot more money on a slab that was capable of spanning the open space.

Chop-chop

I was helping a friend put in a retaining wall and had spent most of the day digging the footing, which involved hacking through tree root after tree root. So it was nothing different when we came to a fat one that seemed a little tougher than the rest. After two or three swings, my friend had barely scratched it. Channeling his frustration, he took one final swing Paul Bunyan–style, which was met with a shrill "hiss."

The firefighters said we were lucky that nothing worse had happened when he sliced into the high-pressure gas line.

Now my friend goes by "Chopper."

Stop-and-go weed trimmer

My faithful weed trimmer started having problems. I plugged it into an extension cord only to have it run for a little bit and then stop. A good shake would bring it back to life, temporarily. I unplugged it, took the whole thing apart and reassembled it, only to have the same thing happen. Fed up, I threw it away and bought a new one. Guess what? The new one started and then stopped too. So I exchanged it for another one, which wouldn't stay running either. That's when I noticed an inconspicuous slice in my extension cord that left some of the wires barely touching. Yep, I spent $35 on a new weed trimmer and made two trips to the hardware store because of a bad extension cord.

You've got—ouch!—mail

Having just moved to a new rural residence, my friend needed to install a mailbox near the road. He bought a 6-ft.-tall post, and to make things easier, mounted the mailbox on one end before setting the unit into the ground. Then he dug a 2-ft.-deep hole, figuring his mailbox would be at the perfect height.

With everything ready, he lifted the post over his head and thrust it into the hole. In all his calculating, he forgot that as the post went into the hole, the 6 ft. would quickly become 4 ft. As a result, the protruding mailbox came down on his head, driving him to his knees. Even though the blow nearly knocked him out, his first instinct was to look around to see if anyone was watching.

How brown was my valley

Last spring, I'd had it with the weeds in my lawn, so I went to the local hardware store to get weed killer. I selected a product I thought might work really well because it was easy to apply and didn't require

a mechanical spreader. As soon as I got home I sprayed the entire lawn. I didn't bother to read the directions until a few days later when everything was dead: the weeds, the grass and even some flowers. I'd sprayed the lawn with Round-Up—formulated to kill almost all plants. Several weeks later I had my entire lawn replaced with new sod for $2,500!

I pushed and I pushed . . .

The previous owners of my new home left the yard looking like a hayfield, so I was anxious to get mowing. Not yet a proud lawn mower owner, I asked the clerk at the local hardware store to show me their mower selection. I quickly picked out the model I liked best but only half listened to his brief explanation of how it worked. "How hard can it be to run a mower?" I thought.

I hauled the mower home and got right to task. After about an hour of pushing, I was soaking wet and panting like a dog after a foxhunt. I stopped for a break to refill the tank. While pouring the fuel into the tank, I noticed a handle with three icons: a rabbit, a turtle and a stop sign. Suspecting these symbols to be more than decoration, I started the mower and pushed the lever toward the rabbit sign. The mower lurched forward. As I ran to catch the now-self-propelled mower, I vaguely remembered the sales clerk saying something like "It practically mows by itself!"

Dig, dig, dig . . .

Recently married and new homeowners, my wife and I wanted to get started on building a new deck. The first step was to dig the footings. My father (my chief consultant and laborer) and I went to the rental store to pick up a power auger. The auger made quick work of the first two holes, and we could see that we'd easily make it back and qualify for the half-day rental fee.

The guy at the rental store had warned us that the auger could get stuck and that we shouldn't try to remove too much soil without periodically clearing the hole. His warning faded when we neared the bottom of the third hole (about 3 ft. down) and the auger got stuck. We tried and tried but no amount of tugging would free it. And because we were close to the bay window, we couldn't turn the machine to free it. We each grabbed a shovel and dug. Three hours later, with a hole diameter of about 5 ft. and a full day's rental fee, we finally got the auger free.

7 Auto & Garage

IN THIS CHAPTER

Car&Garage

Replace a **broken taillight** and save $95

Use the Internet to find great prices on parts

Your teenage driver used the car and returned it washed and with a full tank of gas. Isn't it great that he's become a responsible adult? Oh, wait, you notice that the taillight is broken, and he has "no idea how that happened." Time to head off to the body shop? Nope—this is a job you can do with ordinary hand tools and the Internet.

Finding a replacement taillight assembly is easy. Simply enter "taillight" into your favorite search engine.

You'll be amazed at the number of hits you get. Most of the companies sell low-priced offshore "knockoffs" of the original equipment (OEM) parts. If you're OK with an "aftermarket" version, make sure the seller lists it as CAPA certified. A CAPA-certified part is guaranteed to fit and perform like the original. But don't end your search there. Many car dealers have set up consumer-friendly Web sites that sell OEM parts at discounted prices. Check out these dealer sites before you buy an aftermarket version. We

Threaded-stud style

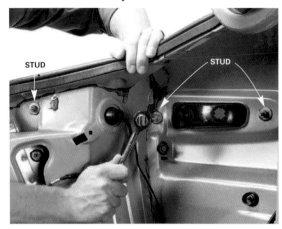

1 Locate the nuts and remove them from the threaded studs using a deep socket and ratchet.

2 Snap new lightbulbs into the sockets and install the new taillight.

Screws and stud/socket style

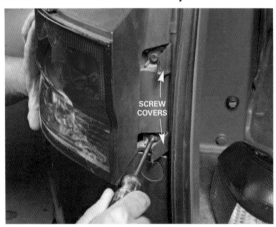

1 Remove the screws from the trunk or lift-gate side of the taillight. These were hidden under covers.

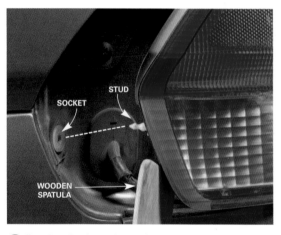

2 Pry the plastic stud out of the socket while pulling back on the taillight assembly.

actually bought a genuine Honda taillight for less than the aftermarket version cost.

Car manufacturers use two different techniques to attach taillights to the body. One method uses threaded studs embedded in the taillight. The studs are inserted into holes in the sheet metal and fastened with nuts (Photo 1, top). The second method uses screws to secure one end of the light, and captive stud/socket fasteners on the other end (Photo 1, bottom). If your vehicle has the captive stud/socket arrangement, use a wooden or plastic tool to pry the stud out of the socket. Metal screwdrivers will scratch the paint.

Once you have the taillight assembly disconnected, remove the lightbulb sockets by releasing the catch mechanism and twisting. If you haven't replaced the bulbs in the past two years, now is a good time to do that, since you already have everything apart. Then install the sockets in the new taillight and reassemble.

AUTO & GARAGE

Car&Garage

5 things to **lubricate before winter**

If you live in a northern region, here's what to lubricate on your vehicle before winter hits.

1 Spray window tracks with silicone spray or dry Teflon. Silicone stays slick even in cold weather, so windows slide smoothly, lessening the wear on your window motors.

2 Spray silicone on all weather stripping. Silicone will keep ice from bonding the rubber to the metal doors. That'll make doors open smoother and may even prevent tears in the weather stripping.

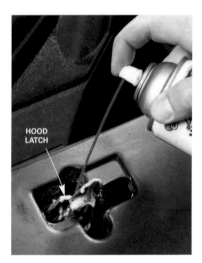

HOOD LATCH

DOOR HINGE

3 Spray aerosol lithium grease on the hood latch mechanism. You don't want to fight a balky hood latch when it's snowing and you're trying to add windshield fluid.

4 Keep your lock cylinders working smoothly by injecting dry Teflon lubricant spray. You never know when your remote keyless entry system might let you down.

5 Spray lithium grease on door hinges to keep them opening smoothly and prevent rust.

Switch to winter wiper blades

It's snowing hard and you turn on the wipers. The blade supports get packed with snow and the wiper blade either causes streaks or misses large swaths of your windshield. Winter wiper blades eliminate that problem. The entire blade is wrapped in a rubber boot that prevents ice and snow from sticking or packing. They make for much better visibility and safer winter driving.

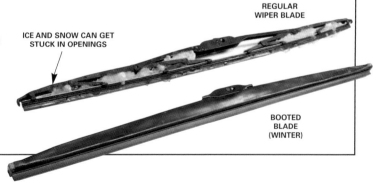

ICE AND SNOW CAN GET STUCK IN OPENINGS

REGULAR WIPER BLADE

BOOTED BLADE (WINTER)

Cool **LED lighting** keeps you safe and brightens your work

It's easy to burn yourself when you're using a metal caged incandescent drop light in tight places. But the bigger danger with these old-style lights is the possibility of blowing yourself sky-high by accidentally breaking the bulb near gasoline. It's time to start working safer with LED lighting. It provides just as much light as your old drop light but without any of the safety concerns. Here's what to look for:

LED light manufacturers promote their products by the LED count alone. That's important, but not nearly as important as the ability to focus all those LEDs on your work. There's no specification for that. If there are working display models at the store, compare how well each one casts its beam. You may find that the bargain LED lights aren't such a bargain after all.

While you're at it, check out the latest pocket-style LED lights. They're perfect for lighting your way in cramped areas like under a dashboard or around contorted hoses and wires in the engine compartment. Look for a pocket LED light with a long, flexible neck and a switch that allows you to lock it in the "on" position. Also, make sure it uses batteries that are readily available.

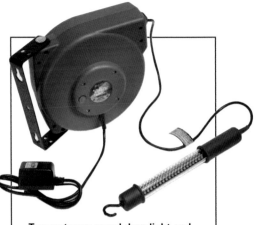

Toss out your caged drop light and work safer with a new retractable LED work light.

Retractable LED Light, Astro Pneumatic No. 6321. $86. tooldiscounter.com

Take this pocket LED light with you the next time you crawl under your dash. The flexible neck lets you put light right where you need it.

Pocket Light, Coast Lighting No. LL7582. $11. tooldiscounter.com

CHOOSE THE BEST BATTERY

The battery in my car is four years old. I checked my owner's manual and there's no replacement interval listed. When should I replace it, and what should I look for when buying a new one?

A battery functions somewhat like a water tower, but its job is to store and deliver power. But stop-and-go driving and power-hungry accessories like AC, electric defoggers and heated seats often draw more power than the charging system can provide. The deficit comes right out of the battery, taking a toll on battery life. Add freezing cold and searing engine compartment heat and it's no surprise that few batteries make it to the five-year mark. Since your battery is four years old, it's already on borrowed time. Replace it now, even if it appears to be working fine.

The storage capacity of a car battery is rated in either cold cranking amps (CCA) or cranking amps (CA). Shop for a battery with the largest CCA or CA rating that will fit into your car's battery tray. Then compare the terms of the warranties. Better batteries have a longer free-replacement period and then enter a prorating period. Less-expensive (lower quality) batteries start the prorating period much sooner. You'll typically find a $20 price difference between a standard battery and the premium battery with the best warranty. Our advice? Spend the extra $20—that's less than half the cost of a jump-start on a cold winter's night. Nobody ever regrets buying the best battery.

AUTO & GARAGE

Car&Garage

Power **window stuck**?

Spend $10 on the proper instructions and $115 on the part, and save $225 on labor!

So one of your power windows doesn't work. Check the fuse first. If that's good, the problem is either a bad switch or motor or a broken regulator (the device that actually lifts and lowers the glass). A shop will charge you upward of $350 to replace the motor/regulator, but you can do the job yourself in about four hours. The regulator for this Buick Century was $115 at rockauto.com.

You need a basic set of metric sockets, screwdrivers, a drill and most important, a subscription to an online service manual. That way, you can download instructions and diagrams that are specific to your car (see "Online Repair Manuals," p. 218). Use our instructions as a rough guide, and refer to your manual for specifics.

Start the repair by removing all the trim panel fasteners to access the switch for testing. Remove the trim panel and peel off the vapor barrier. A trim panel removal tool is cheap (about $5 at auto parts stores) and saves you a lot of time.

Reach into the door panel and disconnect the power connector to the window motor (wear leather gloves to protect against cuts). Connect the leads of your voltmeter to the two terminals on the connector. Turn the key to the "on" position and toggle the window switch up and down. If the switch is good, you'll see the voltage reading change from plus-12 volts to minus-12 volts. That means the problem is the motor/regulator. If your meter doesn't display those readings, you've got a bad switch or a broken power or ground wire. Download an electrical diagram and

MOTOR

REGULATOR

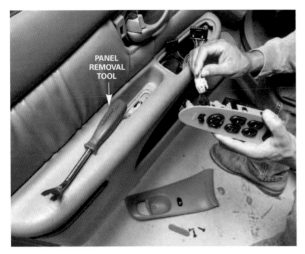

1 Pry out the switch panel and disconnect the electrical connectors. Then remove the door trim panel.

2 Reconnect the switch panel and attach the voltmeter test leads to the motor connector. Then toggle the window switch. If the switch is good, replace the regulator.

3 Remove the glass-to-regulator bolts (if needed, cut the mechanical cables to raise or lower the glass). Tilt the window up and out and set it in a safe place.

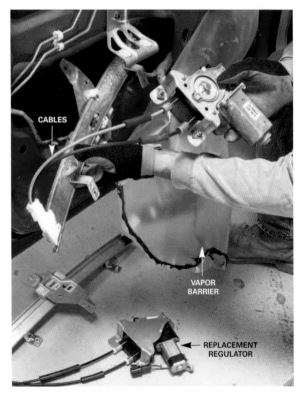

4 Remove regulator-to-door fasteners and snake the regulator out through one of the holes in the door. Install the new regulator.

check the power and ground wires leading to the switch to isolate the problem.

Replace the entire regulator assembly, not just the motor. Start by removing the window-to-regulator bolts (have someone hold the glass while you do this).

Then remove the glass by tilting it away from the door and lifting it out. Next, remove the regulator bolts or rivets (drill them out and snake the old regulator out through

one of the door panel openings. Reverse the procedure to install the new regulator. Bolt the regulator in place and then reinstall the motor and window switch electrical connectors and the window glass. Test the window for proper operation. If the glass binds, you may have to loosen the bolts and make minor adjustments to the regulator. Then tighten everything and replace the vapor barrier and trim panel.

Car&Garage

RUBBER-BAND BOLT HOLDER

Mechanics often use special magnetic inserts in sockets to prevent the bolt from falling out while they try to thread it into tight spots. You don't need to waste money on those gadgets. Simply cut a rubber band into strips and lay a strip across the opening of the socket. Then insert the bolt head. The rubber band will wedge the bolt head in the socket, allowing you to start threading without losing the bolt.

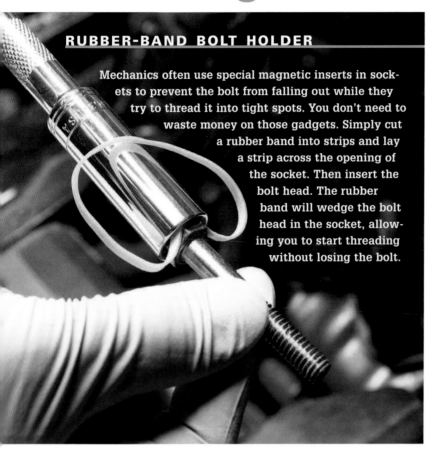

Online repair manuals

The inexpensive printed manuals that you find in bookstores and auto parts stores often cram many model years into the same book. To keep the price low, they often leave out exactly the kind of detailed repair instructions you may need—for example, to remove components like door trim panels, which have hidden fasteners.

But the Internet has revolutionized car manuals. Now you can download make, model and year-specific repair information for just about any repair job on any car. Simply find the pages that apply to your repair, print them out and haul them out to the garage.

In addition to full repair procedures, online services also provide the most up-to-date technical service bulletins and recalls for your vehicle. One site, eautorepair.net, allows you to save money by offering a one-week ($9.99) or one-month subscription ($14.99). A one-year subscription ($29.99) makes sense if you're a serious gearhead who does a lot of wrenching on the same vehicle.

Another of our favorite online services is alldatadiy.com, which also offers subscriptions.

POLISH ALLOY WHEELS WITHOUT DAMAGING THE COATING

Alloy wheels look pretty cool coming off the showroom floor. To keep them looking cool, carmakers apply a clear coating that prevents oxidation and repels road salt. But over time, that coating take a beating and you end up with dull-looking wheels.

The key to restoring the showroom look is to use the right polish on the clear coating. We get lots of samples of car polish. But no one had ever sent us a specification sheet that spelled out the size of the polishing particles in the product until the makers of Eagle One Nano Polish did. The particle size in its Nano Polish is about 1,600 times smaller than what you find in most other wheel polishes. That's 1/75,000th the size of a human hair. But since few of our editors have hair, we had to try it on a real car. The final finish was as smooth as glass.

Eagle One Nano Polish, $5.
Available at most auto parts stores and online.

Spruce up your car with **new carpet**

It's relatively inexpensive and you can do it yourself

YEP, WE CHOPPED OFF THE TOP OF THIS CAR. (THIS STEP IS OPTIONAL.)

1 Remove the four seat retaining nuts from the floor pan studs and disconnect the electrical connectors. Remove the seat and the console.

You got a great deal on a "preowned" vehicle, but the carpeting in the car is simply a disaster. It's too far gone for stain removers—new carpeting is the best solution. You can buy preformed carpet specifically for your car's make, model and color and install it yourself. In most cases, it'll only cost about $200 and take an afternoon to install.

Shop for carpet at an auto parts store or an auto carpet Web site. But make sure the carpet you buy is custom molded to fit your car's floor pan and hump. Better carpets include original factory features like a heel pad under the accelerator and brake pedal. Most manufacturers offer a "mass backing" that duplicates the padding and rigidity of the factory carpet, and an economy "poly" backing. Choose mass backing if you plan to keep the car, poly if you're going to sell it in the near future.

When the carpet arrives, unroll it and let it sit on a flat surface for at least two hours to lose its curl. While the carpet is "uncurling," start removing the trim and seats to expose the old carpet for removal.

Let the new carpet sit on a flat surface for at least two hours to lose its curl.

Car&Garage

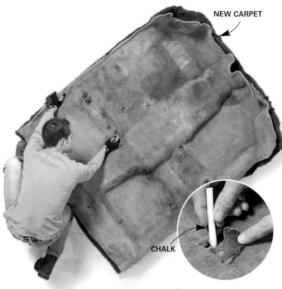

NEW CARPET

CHALK

2 Transfer the cutout openings onto the new carpet.

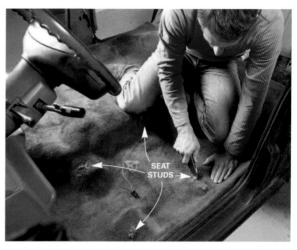

SEAT STUDS

3 Enlarge the openings once the carpet is fully in place and you're sure the fit is right.

4 Replace the seats, console, electrical connectors and trim.

CAUTION: If your car has side impact airbags located in the seat back bolster cushions, follow the airbag power-down instructions in the shop manual before disconnecting the seat electrical connectors.

Buy a shop manual that includes trim removal instructions and diagrams (sources below right). Detach the door sill covers and remove the kick panels from the bottom of the front pillars.

Unscrew/unsnap any trim pieces from the seat tracks so you can get to the four nuts that secure the seat to the floor pan studs. You may also have to remove the seat belt anchor bolts (you may need Torx bits for these bolts). Disconnect any electrical connectors under each seat and lift the seats up and out (call in a helper for this part). Then remove the rear seat cushion. If you have a console, remove the shifter knob and all the fasteners. Lift the console out of the vehicle and pull out the old carpet and pad. But don't throw out the old carpet just yet; you'll need it.

Vacuum the floor pan and check for rust. Treat rusted areas with a rust converter (such as Loctite Extend or naval jelly) and paint them with a rust-inhibiting paint.

Using the old carpet as a template, trace the cutouts onto the new carpet with chalk. Next, move the carpet into the vehicle and double-check your cutout marks with the actual stud and anchor points on the floor pan. When you're confident the marks are in the right places, cut X-shaped openings at each chalk mark. Fit the openings over the studs and feed the electrical cables through. Enlarge the openings to achieve a good fit.

Cut off excess carpet at the door sills and apply a light coating of spray adhesive such as 3M Spray 77 to the back of the carpet where it rides up onto the firewall. Then reinstall the seats and trim and reconnect the electrical connectors. Enjoy the look and feel of new carpet and buy a set of no-spill coffee mugs.

Buyer's Guide

ONLINE CARPET SOURCES:
- accmats.com
- automotivecarpet.com
- autotrimsupply.com
- stockinteriors.com

SHOP MANUAL SOURCES:
- alldatadiy.com
- chiltondiy.com (online and CD-ROMs)
- eautorepair.net

SPRAY ADHESIVE: $7
RUST CONVERTER: $7
- Both products available at home centers and hardware and auto parts stores

CHECK YOUR BRAKE FLUID CONDITION

As with every other fluid in your car, brake fluid contains a main ingredient along with protective additives. The main ingredient in brake fluid doesn't degrade, but the additives do. The most important additive is a corrosion inhibitor. The corrosion inhibitor prevents internal rusting of steel brake lines, calipers and ABS (antilock brake system) components. Once the inhibitors are exhausted, even minute amounts of moisture can cause dangerous and costly corrosion.

Most car manufacturers recommend a complete brake fluid flush every two years or 24,000 miles. Rather than rely on a general recommendation, you can test the actual condition of your brake fluid. Remove the cover of the master cylinder and dip a strip into the fluid. Shake off the excess fluid and wait 60 seconds before comparing the color of the strip with the guide on the package. The guide tells you when it's time to change the fluid. A package of 25 BrakeStrip test strips costs $24 at brakebleeder.com.

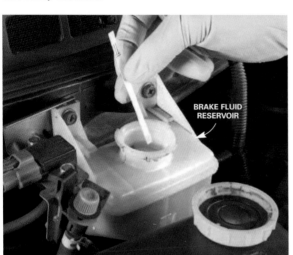

1 Dip the test strip into the brake fluid reservoir and wait for it to change color.

BRAKE FLUID RESERVOIR

2 Compare the test strip with the color chart to determine the condition of the fluid. Replace your brake fluid if the color of the strip falls in the "required service" category.

HASSLE-FREE TIRE DRESSING

Nothing beats the look of shiny wheels and dark glossy tires. But tire dressing can be a real pain to apply. Whether you spray it or wipe it on, you always have to clean up the wheel afterward. But not with this new product.

The Eagle One Tire Detailer comes with an applicator specifically designed for tires. Its curved foam pad fits the contour of your tire. Simply squeeze the bottle to saturate the foam pad and wipe it around your tire. There's nothing to clean up afterward. One bottle "dresses" up to 40 tires.

Eagle One Tire Detailer, $7, available at most auto parts stores.

Car&Garage

Top 5 **trailer problem solvers**

We informally canvassed about 30 trailer owners to find out what drives them nuts. Top of the list? Malfunctioning trailer lights! Followed by rusted-in-place nuts that make it impossible to change ball sizes, seized ball mounts and tough-to-tie-down trailer loads. And just about everyone wished there were an easier way to back up and line up a trailer coupler with the hitch on the first try, especially in the dark. So we did some sleuthing and came up with five cool new products that promise to eliminate these hassles.

Splice the new lights into your existing trailer harness or install the new harness from the kit. Test the brake lights and turn signals before you take the trailer on the road.

1. **LED** TAILLIGHTS

Taillights get bounced around, dunked in the lake and soaked with road salt. So it's no surprise that bulb filaments break and sockets corrode, causing a lot of lighting malfunctions. Sealed LED trailer lights are a brilliant solution.

This pair of submersible LED trailer lights, which come with a wiring harness and a license plate bracket, fit right into the existing mounting holes. Before you remove your old lights, write down the wiring scheme. Then swap in the new lights and follow our wiring tip on the next page for making watertight connections.

**Northern Tool, northerntool.com.
Blazer Trailer Light Kit, No. C7421, $49.99.**

Wiring new trailer lights

When you install your new lights, don't use the cheap crimp connectors to splice the wires. The crimp connectors will cause you plenty of aggravation when they start corroding a few years from now. Do the job right the first time—solder all electrical connections and seal each one with a piece of small-diameter heat-shrinkable tubing. Then seal the bundle of wires with a section of larger-diameter shrinkable tubing. Coat the ends of the larger tubes with liquid electrical tape to complete the watertight seal. Heat-shrinkable tubing assortments and liquid electrical tape are available at most auto parts stores.

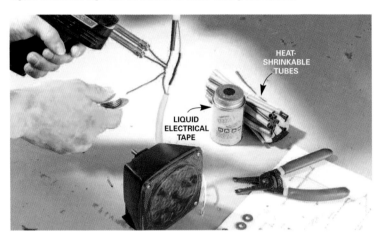

HEAT-SHRINKABLE TUBES

LIQUID ELECTRICAL TAPE

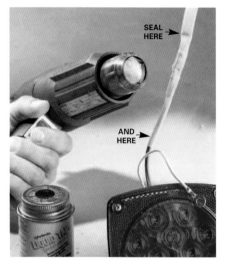

SEAL HERE

AND HERE

1 Thread the outer and inner tubes onto the wires and push them as far back from the splice area as they will go. Twist the wires to form a butt splice. Heat and apply rosin-core solder.

2 Slide the inner tubes over the splice and shrink with a heat gun. Repeat with the outer tubes. Coat the ends with liquid electrical tape.

2. BALL-MOUNT SOLUTION

If you own several trailers with different tongue heights or towing ball sizes, you know how hard it is to find a replacement for a rusted/seized ball or ball mount that will fit them all. Here's an aluminum ball mount that can tow up to 10,000 lbs. It's easy to adjust, never rusts and won't seize in the receiver hitch—ever! It's a bit pricey (about $200), but it'll last longer than your truck or trailer. The hitch comes in three "drop" sizes and several dual-ball combinations. To install, just remove the old ball mount and slide this one into its place. Buy the matching locking pin set to secure your investment.

hitchsolutions.com
Rapid Hitch, $200
Keyed locking pin set, $40
Greaseless Alumiball option, add $12

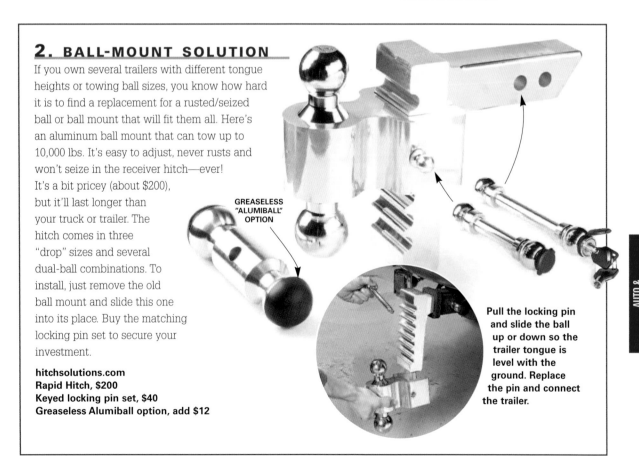

GREASELESS "ALUMIBALL" OPTION

Pull the locking pin and slide the ball up or down so the trailer tongue is level with the ground. Replace the pin and connect the trailer.

Car&Garage

3. TRAILER HITCH ACCESSORY LIGHT

It's a given—you never have a working flashlight when you need one. But if you have a newer truck (2000 and up), chances are it's equipped with a standard seven-blade trailer socket. If so, you can use that socket to power this cool accessory light. Simply plug it into the socket and switch on your running lights to get an additional 50 watts of light behind your truck.

Plug this accessory light directly into a seven-blade trailer socket or an adapter to light up your work area.

mototrixonline.com. (952) 476-2429. Light Buster Trailer Hitch Accessory Light, $25.

SEVEN-BLADE SOCKET

BOARD HOLDER

E-TRACK

2" x 16' RATCHET STRAP

TIE-OFF STRAP

ROPE RING

E-TRACK

4. TIE-DOWN SYSTEM

No matter what you load into your trailer, it seems you're always searching for secure spots to anchor your tie-down straps. The E-Track system eliminates that problem. Bolt the track to the trailer floor. Then snap in a variety of ratchet straps or rope anchor fittings. We especially liked the wood beam socket. Place the socket anywhere along the track and insert a board to prevent your cargo from shifting. E-Tracks are also available for mounting tie-downs to the sides of your trailer, but use them only if the sides of your trailer are metal reinforced and rock solid.

**Northern Tool, northerntool.com. (800) 221-0516
24-in. E-Track painted sections, $10.
Tie-off strap, $4.
Rope Ring, $5.
E-Track Board Holder, $5.
Ratchet strap with E-Track fitting, 2-in. x 16-ft., $20.**

Center your cargo over the axle and secure it with ratchet straps. Place a wood beam in the sockets as extra insurance against cargo movement.

5. QUICK COUPLER

Moving an empty trailer to the towing ball is a piece of cake. But heavy trailers require you to back the truck up to the trailer. You know how tricky it is to jockey the unseen hitch into the trailer's "capture zone." We found a new-style coupler that has "auto-capture jaws" and alignment rods that make it a lot easier to back your vehicle up to the trailer. Simply extend the collapsible alignment rods and sight them through your back window. If you're within 5 in. of the coupler, its jaws will automatically "capture" the ball and snap the latch mechanism closed. But make sure you get out and install the locking pin before you take the trailer out on the road.

Visit the Quickbite Web site to choose the right model for your trailer and to find a dealer near you.

Quickbitecouplers.com
No. 7000, $99.

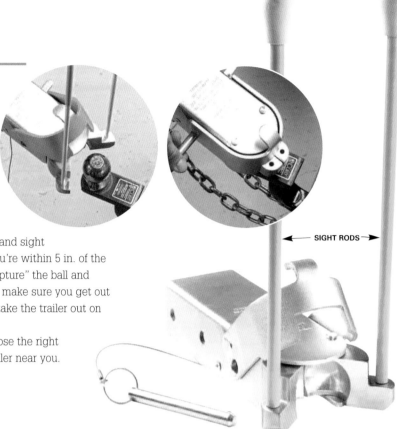

← SIGHT RODS →

Wheel cleaner blasts brake dust

You've got those really cool alloy wheels, but nobody can see them because they're covered with brake dust. Sure, you could get out the car wash gear and scrub the crevices with a toothbrush, but that's a real pain.

There are a lot of wild claims about automotive cleaners. The manufacturer of Eagle One All Wheel & Tire Cleaner claimed its product could remove that horrible brake dust and dirt without any elbow grease. Ever the skeptics, we sprayed the tires and the alloy wheels and stood back. The foam, dust and dirt melted away like the Wicked Witch of the West after a bucket of water. After hosing off the wheel, our work was done.

Eagle One All Wheel & Tire Cleaner, $6, available at most auto parts stores.

Car&Garage

Get your **car stereo** fixed

You own a high-end vehicle with a broken CD player. You could take it to a store where they offer free installation on a new player. But the thought of a 16-year-old "customizing" your dash gives you nightmares. Besides, you love the look and sound of your factory system. You would remove the factory radio yourself and send it in for repair, if only you could figure out how to do it.

Removing the radio itself is actually pretty easy. But to get to that point, you'll first have to remove some dash trim pieces. And there's usually a trick or two to getting those off without wrecking anything. We recommend investing in two things: a set of special tools for trim removal and an online set of instructions geared specifical-ly to your car. A set of the four most commonly used trim removal tools costs less than $16. It's worth every penny.

For help with the radio removal procedure for your vehicle, go to carstereohelp.com. This site sells complete radio and trim removal instructions (with photos) for over 4,000 different make/model combinations. The removal instructions cost less than $10. Some do-it-yourself repair instructions are also available (see the "DIY repairs" link on the Web site). After you pull the radio, you can send the unit directly to carstereohelp.com for repair. Repair rates run from $185 to $300, depending on the make and model. That may seem high, but new factory replacements can run almost twice that price.

Use nylon prying tools to prevent damage to the dash panel. Experiment to find which tool works best for each trim piece.

1 Slip the nylon prying tool between the heater control and the dash. Pop the control panel off.

RADIO BOLTS

REMOVAL INSTRUCTIONS

2 Pry out the radio trim panel to expose the radio fasteners. Then remove the retaining bolts.

3 Disconnect the electrical connectors and the antenna from the back of the radio. Then lift it out.

Buyer's Guide

■ Radio removal instructions and radio repair: carstereohelp.com

■ The nylon prying tools shown (item No. 95214-5VGA) are available at harborfreight.com. A similar set (item No. ATH-K-PP) is available at bojoinc.com.

THE FAMILYHANDYMAN'S BEST

TIPS FOR YOUR GARAGE

Organize it, outfit it and still park in it!

Some people think a garage is just a shelter for cars. But we at *The Family Handyman* know better. A garage is a warehouse, a toy shop, a workshop and—for many of us—our favorite place on earth. That's why we read everything written about garages, experiment with garage products and talk with garage consultants (yes, there really are such people). Sometimes we just sit in our own garages, dreaming up our own improvements. Here are the best ideas collected from all those sources.

Store more on walls

If you mount hooks, brackets and other hardware only on studs, you're wasting lots of opportunities. The best strategy is to add a layer of 3/4-in. plywood over the drywall or bare studs. That gives you a continuous fastening surface, so you can mount storage hardware easily, arrange items in a space-efficient way and cram more stuff onto the wall. To see how we doubled the storage capacity of this wall with plywood and inexpensive hardware, go to thefamilyhandyman.com and search for "storage wall."

PIPE FLANGE

Space-saving workbench

If your garage isn't big enough for your car and a workbench, you could get a smaller car. Or you could build a fold-down workbench. This one sets up in seconds and eats up zero floor space when not in use. The only things you'll need are a 2x4, a pair of beefy hinges, a couple of threaded pipes and flanges, and a handful of screws (about $30 altogether). For a work surface, we used a 30-in. solid-core door ($50), but you can use other materials such as two layers of 3/4-in. plywood glued together. To set up the workbench, just screw the pipes into the flanges.

Don't waste the high space

If all the stuff in your garage is within easy reach, you're probably wasting lots of storage space. The high spaces may not be prime real estate for often-used tools, but they're perfect for long-term storage. Deep shelving or cabinets near the ceiling can hold a ton of seasonal stuff like holiday decorations or camping gear. Another great way to make the most of high space is to install wall cabinets a foot or two from the ceiling and run a deep shelf across the tops of the cabinets.

Ceiling storage bonanza

This simple combination of plastic bins and homemade support carriages is perfect for holiday decorations and other rarely needed stuff. To make the carriages, just screw and glue 3/4-in. plywood flanges to 2x4s. Then screw the carriages to ceiling joists and slide in the bins. The heavy-duty bins we used cost about $20 each at www.simplastics.com (item snt-230-BL). For more details on building this system, go to thefamilyhandyman.com and search for "sliding storage."

SCREW HOOK

1x4

MENDING PLATE

Wheelbarrow hang-up

Don't waste floor space on your wheelbarrow—hang it on the wall. Special hardware is available at some home centers, but you can easily substitute a scrap of 1x4, a pair of mending plates and screw hooks that act as latches, locking the wheelbarrow against the wall.

Keep ladders out of the way

Hang ladders from the ceiling so they don't hog prime storage space. The rollers on this simple carriage let you easily slide in one end of the ladder, then the other. The materials you'll need cost about $20 at home centers. Fasten the corner braces to ceiling joists with 2-in. lag screws. Secure the ladder with an elastic cord so it can't roll out and fall.

2x4 x16"

5" CORNER BRACE

3/4" x 18" PVC CONDUIT

NUT

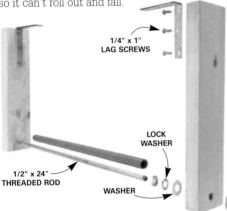

1/4" x 1" LAG SCREWS

LOCK WASHER

1/2" x 24" THREADED ROD

WASHER

Build big cabinets in place

You don't have to be a cabinetmaker to build big, sturdy cabinets—especially if you build them in place. All you have to do is screw 2x2s to the wall and ceiling and then screw plywood panels to the 2x2s to form the top, bottom and sides of cabinet boxes. In addition to its simplicity, this approach is fast and economical; it took us just one morning to build the huge bank of cabinets shown here, and the materials cost about $250. Our version has sliding doors, which are optional. For the complete story on building these cabinets, go to thefamilyhandyman.com and search for "super size cabinets."

Roll-around workshop

If your garage does double duty as parking space and work space, a rolling workbench is essential. It lets you convert your garage into a workshop quickly and rolls up against the wall to restore parking space. The version shown here began as a standard rolling bench made from 2x4s and plywood. Then we added a slick feature: heavy-duty shelf brackets that make it the Swiss army knife of workbenches. The four bracket-mounted wings can be installed at the height of the work surface to expand it or mounted lower to create instant tool stations. When not in service, the wings and tools stow away neatly for compact storage.

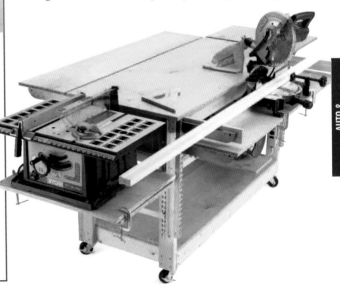

Add outlets

Most electrical codes require just one outlet in the garage. And that's just what most builders give you—one measly outlet for all your tools and toys. If you have open studs, you can easily run wire and add outlets as long as you follow a few basic rules (search for "garage wiring" at thefamilyhandyman.com). If your walls are covered, you don't have to cut into them to run wires. Instead, you can mount metal or plastic wiring channels and outlet boxes right on the wall. This approach is easy but not cheap; adding the five outlets shown here cost us about $50. If you're adding lots of outlets throughout a garage, consider using metal conduit. Running conduit takes a bit more time but cuts the materials bill in half. For articles covering channel systems and conduit installation, go to thefamilyhandyman.com and search for "surface wiring."

Add outdoor storage

Sometimes the best cure for garage chaos is to add storage space elsewhere. A small locker that holds garden gear, for example, provides big relief to a crowded garage.

Enlarge your garage

Whether you need more storage space or more work space, the ultimate solution for a too-small garage is an addition. In many cases, you can knock out a section of garage wall. Install a header to support the weight of the roof, and build a large "bump-out." It's easier than you might think. To see how you can build a 5 x 12-ft. bump-out without adding a concrete foundation, go to thefamilyhandyman.com and search for "bump-out."

HandyHints®

Rolling records

Write down important car information right where you need it—under your hood—with a paint pen ($2 at art stores). Mileage and dates for coolant, air filter and tire changes will never get lost again.

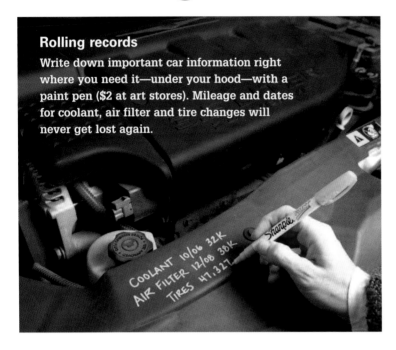

WOOD BLOCK

Garage storage

Cardboard concrete-forming tubes are inexpensive ($7 at any home center) and provide a great place to store baseball bats, long-handled tools and rolls of just about anything. Rest the tubes on a piece of 2x4 to keep them high and dry. Secure each tube to a garage stud with a plumbing strap.

Streak-free car

Your car will look like it rolled out of a professional car wash when you dry it with your leaf blower. Blow away the bulk of the water with the leaf blower and then finish up with a quick towel swipe. You'll get a streak-free finish without a pile of wet towels or waiting around to start waxing.

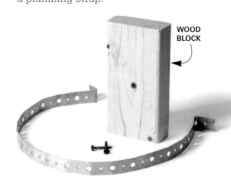

WOOD BLOCK

This&That

NO-PEEL **EPOXY GARAGE FLOORS**

CRACKING EPOXY

My neighbor painted epoxy on his garage floor and now it's peeling off in pancake-size patches. His floor passed the standard taped-on-the-floor plastic sheeting moisture test. I want to paint my floor too. How do I make sure mine will stay stuck?

Your friend's problem is most likely caused by too much slab moisture. Unfortunately, the widely used plastic sheeting test (taping a sheet of plastic film to the concrete and checking for condensation droplets after 24 hours) isn't reliable. A better method is to use calcium chloride–based testing kits (about $40 for the three kits you'll need).

For the most accurate results, conduct the test during the spring when the soil is damp and low humidity is forecast. Dry air draws moisture up through the concrete, so you'll be getting "worst case" results that time of year. Place two of the test kits at least 5 ft. away from walls, and the third test kit in the middle of the floor. Follow the surface preparation instructions to the letter. That means you'll have to grind off about 1/32 in. of concrete to remove any surface sealers or hardening agents (**Photo 1**). Once you've ground off the top layer, use the pH test liquid and strips included in the kit to determine the acidity (pH) level of the freshly exposed concrete. The pH level should be 6.5 to 7. If yours isn't, check with the paint manufacturer to see if its paint will stick.

If the pH level checks out, leave the test sections open to the garage air for 24 hours before starting the

1 Remove 1/32 in. of the top layer of concrete with an angle grinder and a masonry wheel. Let the area "breathe" for 24 hours before starting the test.

test. Place the calcium chloride dish in the test areas and apply the sealing dome (**Photo 2**). After the chemical absorbs moisture for 60 to 72 hours, cut openings in the domes and remove and seal the dishes. Then mail them off to the testing lab for analysis (included in the kit price).

The maximum amount of water vapor penetration is 3 lbs. per 1,000 sq. ft. If your results show more than that amount, don't even consider applying epoxy or any other paint-type coating to your floor. Instead, live with your old boring concrete or consider one of the "covering type" floors that lay over the top of the concrete.

However, if your tests hover around the 3-lb. mark, your results are borderline. Consider calling in a professional testing lab to conduct a more rigid (and accurate) test.

Buyer's Guide
- vaporgauge.com
- taylortools.com

2 Test for moisture with a calcium chloride dish covered by a plastic dome. When the test is done, cut a hole in the dome and lift the dish straight out so you don't spill the contents. Seal the dish and mail it back to the manufacturer for results.

IT'S A MONSTER, ALL RIGHT

My latest gearhead project was by far the most challenging: converting my stock Ford pickup to a manly mini monster truck. I had tricked it out with a lift package, giant struts, enormous tires—the whole bit! When it was done, I couldn't wait to take it out to show my friends and maybe even do a little "mudding."

But as I was getting ready to drive it out of the garage, I came to the ridiculously late realization that my truck was too darn high to get through the garage door! With my tail between my legs, I had to take off the wheels, rest the truck on dollies and have a tow truck pull it out like a beached whale. Nothing manly about that.

AUTO & GARAGE

EXPERT **AUTO CARE** ADVICE

Car mechanics are like doctors—wherever they go, people ask them for free advice. Bob and Rick, our ace mechanics, can barely remember their kids' birthdays, but they did manage to remember the best questions and answers from friends, relatives and customers. Here are their "Best of" fixes and tips and their most-avoidable "oopses."

MOST-IGNORED MAINTENANCE ITEMS

1 Cabin air filter. A clogged cabin air filter puts an added load on your car's A/C system and reduces heat in winter. Replace at least once a year.

2 Coolant change. Coolant doesn't last forever. Change it every 24,000 miles (green coolant) or 100,000 miles (extended-life coolant). If you keep driving on worn coolant, expect to replace the radiator, heater core and water pump.

Best quick tip

Test your coolant with a voltmeter. Set your digital voltmeter on the lowest DC setting reading and dip the positive probe right into the coolant. Touch the negative probe to the negative battery terminal and rev the engine to 2,000 rpm. If the reading is .4 volts or more, your coolant is toast.

Tip

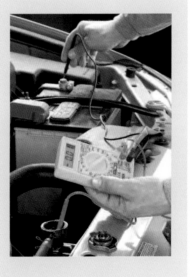

3 Transfer case fluid and differential oil changes. Replacing these components will cost you about $1,500 each—that's a high price to pay for neglect.

4 Shocks and struts. They're not just for comfort—they help stop your car! If you've already clocked 80,000 miles and want to keep driving on them, stay well behind other vehicles on the freeway. You'll need an additional 22 ft. of stopping distance.

10 BEST 10-MINUTE DIY FIXES

Save money or prevent future expenses with these 10-minute fixes you can do yourself.

1 Cloudy headlight lenses. You don't have to replace cloudy headlights. Buy a headlight restoration kit at any auto parts store and follow the sanding and buffing instructions.

2 Sticking or slow power windows. Give each window channel a shot of dry Teflon or silicone spray lubricant. Then run the window up and down a few times to spread the lubricant.

3 Avoid iced-up wipers. Install winter wiper blades. They're covered by a rubber boot that prevents ice from building up in the wiper and provides streak-free wiping (see p. 216).

4 Defroster grid out of action. Yes, you can fix this yourself. Pick up a Permatex Quick Grid repair kit ($13) at any auto parts store. Follow the instructions and you'll be defrosting in no time.

5 Clogged radiator fins. Disconnect the electrical connectors to your electric cooling fans and remove the fasteners. Lift out the entire fan assembly. Then use a garden hose and nozzle to spray the back of the radiator. That will dislodge the gunk stuck to the front side and provide better cooling. Reinstall the fan assembly.

6 Squeaky door hinges. Rusty hinges wear faster, causing the door to sag and not close properly. Replacing the hinges can be costly. A quick spray of white lithium grease is all you need to keep them from wearing out.

7 Prevent false ABS trouble codes. Anti-lock brake sensors contain a magnet that can pick up metallic road debris and set off a false "trouble code." Use a rag to wipe the debris off the sensor any time you have your wheels off.

8 Fix paint chips and scratches right away. Use these cool applicator tools and a can of touch-up paint to prevent rust.

9 Corroded battery terminals. Corrosion puts added strain on your charging system and can mess with computer-controlled systems. Cleaning is your cheapest insurance against electrical problems.

10 Rattling exhaust pipe. Replace exhaust clamps and brackets at the first sign of rust-through or rattling. They're cheap and easy to install, and they protect other exhaust components from vibration damage.

Best avoidable "oopses"

MIXING DIFFERENT TYPES OF COOLANT. Green, yellow, red, orange and blue coolants create cool "mud" when mixed. Cost of a new heater core: $400 to $1,000.

PUTTING E-85 IN A "NON-FLEX-FUEL" CAR. This little mistake will cost you the price of a tow, a fuel tank and fuel line flush, a new fuel filter and a new tank of gas. Expect to pay about $400 for this "oops."

AC OUTLET FOR YOUR VEHICLE

Need on-the-road power? Plug Black & Decker's new power inverter (No. PI100AB) into your vehicle's DC outlet (cigarette lighter). It's great for running a portable DVD player or video games when taking trips with the kids, or recharging a laptop on the way home from work—or using just about any other electrical device.

Besides 115-volt AC power, the inverter has a USB outlet for iPods. The inverter adjusts up to 45 degrees so the plugs aren't sticking up in the air and getting in your way. The inverter is available at home centers for $24.

Black & Decker, (800) 618-5178. blackanddecker.com

The power inverter gives you AC power in remote areas, so you can use your computer or charge your cell phone.

3-TON JACK KIT LIFTS VEHICLES FAST

if you're still using the jack from your trunk to lift your car, you know what a slow process it is. Check out the Kobalt 3 ton garage combo kit, which can safely jack up a vehicle in seconds. The kit consists of a heavy-duty floor jack and a pair of jack stands. Jack stands are crucial for safety if you're working under the car. But what really makes this combo kit special is the $125 price tag. A floor jack and jack stands of this quality typically cost a couple hundred bucks or more when bought separately. The only downside: The jack is super heavy and hard to carry, so it's only for your garage.

JACK STANDS

Voted the best value for the money by readers

New garage doors add curb appeal

If you're shopping for a new garage door, why not choose one that really jazzes up the place? Bumping up a home's curb appeal can bump up its value, too. And new garage door features make them more than just pretty. Higher insulating R-values offer a tighter seal for garages that double as workshops or playrooms, and heavy-gauge steel stands up better to kids' basketballs and skateboard crashes. Doors come with raised panels, carriage house styling or custom window inserts in aluminum, fiberglass, steel or traditional wood.

AUTO & GARAGE

New Tools&Gear

LONG-REACH GARAGE VAC

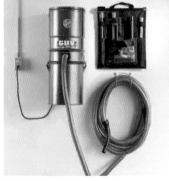

Included with the vacuum are a handy rack for storing the hose and an attachments caddy for the extra wands and brushes.

Mount the GUV ProGrade Garage Utility Vac from Hoover on the wall (saving valuable floor space!), and the 30-ft. hose will reach almost anywhere in your garage. It sure beats lugging a shop vacuum around and having it tip over every time you pull on it. Or hook it up to power tools and use it as a dust collector.

This heavy-duty hose is super flexible and "crush proof," so it can stand up to everyday use and abuse. (But "crush proof" doesn't mean you can run over it with the car!) The 12-amp motor is about the same as that found on larger shop vacuums, so it's no toy. It provides plenty of suction for cleaning your vehicle's upholstery or your workbench, yet it runs surprisingly quiet.

The vacuum handles wet or dry materials, just like traditional shop vacuums. At $180, it's not the cheapest vacuum on the block, but it might be the last shop vacuum you'll ever buy. You can order it online or find retailers on the company's Web site. **Hoover, (330) 499-9499. hoover.com**

BOOKCASE & SHELF TIPS

Our favorite ways to simplify building and get beautiful results

The editors at *The Family Handyman* have built nearly a hundred bookcases altogether—some for clients, some for magazine articles, some for our own homes. With all that experience, you might think we use a lot of complicated, for-pros-only building techniques. But just the opposite is true; our best building tricks are shortcuts that avoid complex steps. So whether you're a beginning builder or a veteran, these tips lead to beautiful results with less time and effort.

Save time with store-bought cabinets

Building and hanging cabinet doors is a fussy, time-consuming job. But there is a way to get enclosed space in your bookcase without all that hassle: Buy standard kitchen cabinets and build around them. The inexpensive cabinets we chose for the bookcase shown here cost about $150 more than building doors and boxes from scratch. Considering the huge time savings, that's a bargain. The main disadvantage of store-bought cabinets

is that almost all are prefinished. (Home centers carry unfinished cabinets in only one or two styles.) So before finishing the open shelves and other parts you've built from scratch, you'll have to select a stain and clear coating to match the cabinets. A perfect match is almost impossible. But after some experiments on scraps, you can get so close that you'll be the only one who notices the difference.

Dress it up with plastic trim

You probably don't associate plastic with elegance. But with trim made from polyurethane plastic, you can add curves and other fancy touches to your bookcase even if you lack the time or skill needed to make these complex parts yourself. Working with polyurethane trim is much like working with wood—you cut it with standard saw blades, nail it by hand or with a gun and paint it just like wood. Home centers carry a small selection of polyurethane trim. To browse through an endless variety of options and find dealers, search online for "polyurethane trim" (some products are listed as "urethane" rather than "polyurethane"). The polyurethane parts for the bookcases shown here cost about $130.

Protect against tipovers

Any bookcase you build should be anchored to the wall so it can't tip over and injure someone. Simply screwing it to wall studs is one good solution. If you choose that method, load up the bookcase with books so it fully compresses the carpet before you drive the screws. If you want to be able to move the bookcase without removing screws, pick up a couple of chain latches ($5 each). Fasten the chains to studs with 2-1/2-in. coarse-thread screws. Position the tracks so there will be just enough slack in the chains for you to detach them.

Cover plywood edges fast

Plywood is an essential material for bookcases. It's strong, affordable and good looking. There's just one problem: those ugly edges. You can hide edges behind solid wood or moldings, but the quickest, easiest edge solution is a thin strip of wood veneer called "edge banding" ($6 for 25 ft. at home centers). The process couldn't be simpler: You just iron on the adhesive-backed veneer and trim off the excess. You can trim with a utility knife, but that requires a steady hand, and any wrong move creates a wavy edge. An edge band trimmer ($20) eliminates mistakes and does the job much faster. To buy one online, search for "edge band trimmer." For complete edge-banding instructions, go to thefamilyhandyman.com and search for "edge banding."

EDGE BAND

TRIMMER

Adjustable shelves simplify building

Adjustable shelves beat fixed shelves in just about every way. They make storage and display space more versatile, of course, but the advantages don't stop there. Adjustable shelves are usually just slabs of plywood nosed with strips of wood or edge banding, so they're easy to make. Assembling the boxes that hold the shelves is a lot easier, too, since you don't have to simultaneously align and fasten a bunch of built-in shelves. And because you can remove them, adjustable shelves simplify staining and finishing.

Shelf standards are the easiest way to support adjustable shelves ($3 for 6 ft. at home centers). Just screw

PEGBOARD TEMPLATE

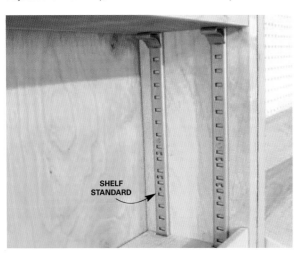

SHELF STANDARD

them into place and you're done. The only trouble with standards is their industrial look, which doesn't quite suit an elegant bookcase. To avoid that look, use peg-type shelf supports. Drilling dozens of holes takes a while, but a scrap of pegboard

CABINET BUMPER

makes positioning the holes easy. If you don't like the look of all those holes, drill only where you plan to place shelves. That way the holes will be hidden. If you want to move shelves later, you can drill new holes and hide the old ones with wood filler. Whether you choose standards or peg-type supports, stick rubber cabinet door bumpers on the supports to eliminate sliding or rocking shelves.

Perfect cuts every time with a sled

Before you start your bookcase, build a sled and turn your table saw into a crosscutting and mitering machine. You can build one, plus a miter-cutting attachment, in a couple of hours. To see how, go to thefamilyhandyman.com and search for "sled." If you already have a miter saw, you're probably wondering, "Why bother?" Here are three big reasons:

■ **Precision.** No miter saw can match the reliable accuracy of a sled. Because it has no finicky adjustable moving parts, a sled gives you consistent, exact cuts every time. That's why master woodworkers often prefer table saw sleds to miter saws.

■ **Capacity.** This sled crosscuts stock up to 19 in. wide—perfect for shelves and other wide parts.

■ **Clean cuts.** Whether you're cutting wide plywood or thin trim, a sled nearly eliminates splintering and tear-out.

SPECIAL SECTION

BEST OF THE FAMILY HANDYMAN

CARPENTRY
TRICKS & ADVICE

Most of us editors here at *The Family Handyman* weren't hired only for our rugged good looks. (Copy editor's note: Um, no comment.) No, it was because we all spent years and years pounding hundreds of thousands of nails into just about anything made from wood. We've built or worked on just about anything you can live in, park in, walk on, touch or see. The tricks and advice included here are some of the best of what we've learned on the job site.

From left, Spike Carlsen, Gary Wentz, Travis Larson and Jeff Gorton

Best way to perfect miters

"Fine-tuning a miter for a perfect fit is often a trial-and-error process. Practice on smaller test pieces until you get your miter saw set to exactly the right angle, then cut the actual parts."

— **Gary Wentz**

Forget strings and stakes

"You see it in print and on TV everywhere—some stake and board contraption set up to hold strings to help position postholes, or lay out footings or building footprints. But most of the time, there's a much better way. Tack together the construction lumber to outline the structure, square it up and use it as a giant template to do all your marking. Set it aside to do your digging and replace it to set the posts."

— **Gary Wentz**

Easy framing formula

You don't need a math degree to estimate framing materials for walls. Here's a formula that works every time, no matter how many doors, windows or corners your walls have:

- One stud per linear foot of wall.
- Five linear feet of plate material (bottoms, tops and ties) per linear foot of wall.

"It'll look like too much lumber when it arrives, but you'll need the extra stuff for corners, window and door frames, blocking and braces. Set aside the crooked stuff for short pieces."
— **Gary Wentz**

Buy a trim gun

"I haven't hand-nailed a piece of interior trim in 25 years. Why? Because air-powered trim guns make the results so much faster, better and neater. No splits, no predrilling, no knocking the piece out of place as you hammer, and only itty-bitty holes to fill. The gun I paid $300 for back then can now be had for $125—and it's better than the old one! If you're going to buy just one size, the most versatile choice is one that shoots 5/8- to 2-inch 18-gauge brads."
— **Travis Larson**

Memory (or lack thereof) trick

"Stick masking tape to your tape measure for jotting down shapes and numbers. That way you won't forget the length on the way to the saw."
— **Spike Carlsen**

Throw together a miter saw bench

"Whether you're working in your garage, out in the backyard building a shed or up at the in-laws' cabin building a deck, take a few minutes and cobble together a miter saw bench. With a little creativity, you can use just about any materials you have on hand. The only custom work you'll need to do is to rip some spacer boards to make the outfeed support the same height as the saw table. It sure beats kneeling on the grass or perching the miter saw on horses. And the bench does double duty as a super-convenient work surface, too."
— **Travis Larson**

BEST 12 QUICK TIPS

1. Use blue chalk in your chalk lines unless you want permanent marks, then use red.

2. Save a couple of old circular saw blades. They're great for demo work like cutting through shingles, dirty wood or wood that may have hidden nails.

3. Utility knife blades are cheap. Replace them often, especially when cutting drywall.

4. Don't skip the hearing protection. Even the occasional DIYer will lose some hearing from running loud power tools without it.

5. Don't waste all morning on extra lumber runs. Buy more than you need. You can always return the extra.

6. Only buy carbide-tipped saw blades and router bits. They stay sharp for ages.

7. Measure twice, cut once. Oldest one in the book, but still true!

8. Invest in a stout, 1-in.-wide, 20- to 25-ft.-long tape measure. Throw the cheap flimsy one in the junk drawer.

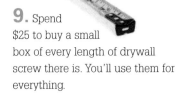

9. Spend $25 to buy a small box of every length of drywall screw there is. You'll use them for everything.

10. Circular saw blades are cheap. Change them at the first hint of dullness.

11. Don't leave cutoffs lying all over the ground. Every 19.5 days, you'll twist your ankle.

12. Stop fumbling through that jar of dull, disorganized drill bits. Buy new drill indexes of spade and twist bits and every time you use one, return it to its slot.

Harness the power of a toenail

"On my first job as a framing carpenter, I was beating on a stud to try to coax it into position. The stud just bounced back. A veteran framing carpenter walked over and drove a big nail at an angle through the edge of the stud. The last two hammer blows moved the stud into position, where it stayed. Now I use the toenail trick whenever I need to adjust stubborn lumber."

— Jeff Gorton

Need a third hand?

"It's surprising how inventive you can be when you have to work alone. One of the tricks I discovered is using a trim gun to tack up one end of the board while I go to the other end to mark the length or check the fit. If you have to take the board or trim piece down again, you'll only have one extra nail hole, which is easy to fill along with all the others."

— Jeff Gorton

Best all-purpose hammer

"Whether you're doing rough construction or fine finish work, the best all-around hammer is a smooth-faced 20-ounce with a straight claw. I use the claw to drive it under walls for lifting, to embed it in framing and even to do extremely crude chiseling. But best of all, it's a better shape for pulling nails than the curved claw style."

— **Spike Carlsen**

Mark, don't measure

"Early on in my carpentry career, I mismeasured an expensive baseboard and cut it too short. Instead of shouting, 'You're fired,' my boss just said, 'Don't use your tape measure unless you have to.' He was right. Holding trim in place and marking it is always more accurate than measuring, often faster and it eliminates mistakes. This is good advice for other types of carpentry work too, like siding, laying shingles and sometimes even framing."

— **Gary Wentz**

Nail safety

"There was one 'must-do' rule on my job sites. Don't ever let a board leave your hand if the sharp end of a nail is sticking out of it. They better be bent over or, better yet, pulled before that board hits the ground. Even with the edict, I still had to nurse foot punctures every few years."

— **Travis Larson**

Size does matter

"Don't bother with buying short, reciprocating saw blades. Just buy 8-inch bimetal blades. You can get the blade in where you need it and the tough metal will cut right through nails when you're doing demo work."

— **Gary Wentz**

Best investment

"It sounds crazy, but one of my best tool investments, and one of my favorite remodeling tools, is an 8-foot magnesium screed used to level concrete. I spent $80 for it about 20 years ago and it's still perfectly straight. I use it for a circular saw guide, checking walls for straightness, and for extending my 4-foot level. I've never used it as a screed, though."

— **Jeff Gorton**

Take a nip now and then

"Keep a pair of 'nippers' in your pouch whenever you're doing trim carpentry. When you pull trim from the wall, use them for pulling the nails through the back of the trim."

— **Spike Carlsen**

THE FAMILY HANDYMAN'S
BEST

THE HANDIEST
QUICK FIX
PRODUCTS

Sometimes the key to making a fix—even a big one—is just knowing the right product to use. We asked our team of professional carpenters, plumbers, painters, electricians and fix-it gurus what their favorite products were, and this is what they told us they never leave home without.

Incredibly versatile screws

No matter what you have to fasten, inside or outside the house, there's almost always a drywall-style screw that can handle it. With thin, hardened shanks, aggressive coarse threads (fine threads are just for metal studs), and deep Phillips or square-drive heads, these screws are tough enough to drive into most woods without stripping or breaking, and usually without predrilling. Most pros keep a selection of coated exterior deck screws on hand for dependable fastening even in treated wood, and black, coarse-thread interior screws for everything indoors—along with a few stainless steel and gold-colored screws for special repairs like replacing stripped-out brass hinge screws.

Screw-in drywall anchors

The first time you use one of these, you may just throw away all your other anchors. They drive in easily without predrilling and they hold firmly, just as they're supposed to. And you only need a screwdriver to put them in. The light-duty type shown above is perfect for hanging lighter shelving and artwork. Use the toggle bolt–type for heavier shelving, towel bars and curtain rods.

Stick-on bumpers

Bumpers do lots more than just stop cabinet doors from banging. Stick them under ceramic pots or hot plates to keep them from scratching tabletops; silence a rattling toilet tank lid by placing them at the corners of the tank; even stick them on a doorstop if you have a door that rattles because it's too loose. Note: Use felt bumpers on varnished wood surfaces. The plastic types can eventually leave marks.

Thread-locking compound

For mysterious, quantum-mechanical reasons, the screws that hold handles and doorknobs always eventually work loose. A few drops of thread-locking compound will permanently fix the problem, yet still allow you to remove the screw with ordinary tools if you need to later. A heavier-duty variety is also available for large bolts and machinery.

Appliance touch-up paint

A single scratch or chip can make a beautiful new appliance look like something you found out in the alley. Fortunately, you can make those eyesores, even up to 1/4-in. diameter, almost completely vanish with color-matched epoxy touch-up paint. The trick? Fill the chip with multiple thin coats instead of trying to cover it all at once. Use the porcelain-type version for stovetops and sinks.

Epoxy glue

Two-part epoxy glue is rock-hard, fills huge gaps, bonds to almost anything and dries very quickly. Some brands now come with an applicator tip that automatically mixes the two parts so you can spread it like a regular glue, without mixing. It's perfect for gluing irregular shapes and dissimilar materials to each other. Most epoxies set in five minutes, but you can buy quicker-setting types that allow you to just hold pieces in place for a minute, without any clamping.

Two-part filler

Two-part filler has to be mixed and it doesn't rinse off with water, so it's not as user friendly as other fillers. However, it's much tougher and a much better choice for any hole bigger than a nail head, especially outdoors. And it's not just for wood—you can patch metal, fiberglass—even concrete.

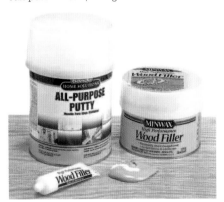

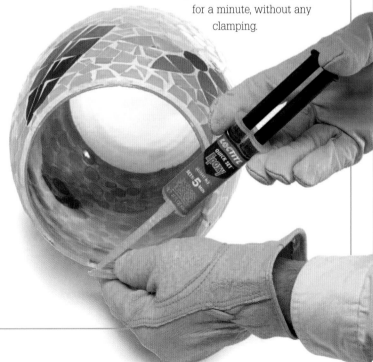

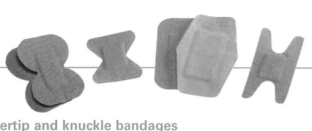

Fingertip and knuckle bandages

Sometimes the fixer needs a fix too. These specialized bandages stay in place and protect hands better than standard, one-size-fits-everything bandages, allowing you to finish your project without bleeding all over it.

Cleaning solvents

Remove stickers, tar, gum, dried paint drops, grease and a host of other unwanted substances quickly and without a lot of frustrating scrubbing by using a general-purpose cleaning solvent. They're a little stinky, but they make short work of nasty, gummy messes like price tag adhesive residue.

Fender washers

Keep a package of assorted fender washers in your toolbox and pretty soon you'll wonder how you got by without them. They're great for increasing the holding power of a small screw, but they also make indestructible shims for furniture, woodworking, and interior and exterior building projects.

Fast-setting drywall compound

Quick-setting drywall compound lets you finish small repairs and fill deep holes in minutes instead of waiting days for premixed joint compound to dry. The small boxes—available in most home centers and paint stores—are also easier to store and more likely to get used up than large bags or buckets.

Two lubricants that you need in your house

Silicone dries quickly and invisibly and doesn't attract dirt, making it a good lubricant for drawer rollers, window tracks, door locks, bike parts, and other plastic, metal and rubber surfaces. It also helps protect metal against rust. Lithium grease is a long-lasting, weather-resistant (though somewhat messy) lubricant for garage door tracks, car doors and latches, and other metal parts that get heavy use outside.

TOP TRICKS TO CUT REPAIR COSTS

Put away that checkbook! Our repair experts tell you how to save big by doing it yourself.

TEST BUTTON →

GFCI OUTLET →

Here at *The Family Handyman,* we have a group of pros that we call on for help with plumbing, electrical, heating and air conditioning, and major appliances. We asked them for examples of repairs they make that frankly are so simple that they feel bad charging for them. Many of the fixes they suggested are simple things that you may have just overlooked. Other solutions are less obvious. Of course, there are times when you must rely on the pros to get the job done. But if you follow the advice here, you may be able to save a big chunk of change the next time something goes wrong.

THE PROS

Al Hildenbrand

Al has a bachelor of science degree in electrical engineering and a master electrician's license. An electrical contractor for 30 years, he has his own company, Al's Electric Works.

Costas Stavrou

Costas graduated from technical college with a degree in refrigeration, air conditioning and major appliance repair. He has run his own company, CSG Repair, since 1982.

Les Zell

Les, the owner of Zell Plumbing and Heating, got his start in the U.S. Navy Construction Battalion. Then he went on to become a journeyman and finally a master plumber.

Bob Schmahl

Bob has 32 years' experience in the heating and air conditioning business. He worked as a journeyman until he got his Master Warm Air Venting & Heating license in 1987.

BEFORE YOU CALL THE PLUMBER

“ You'd be surprised how often we get calls complaining about no water or a lack of pressure, and then show up to discover something simple like a water valve that's shut off or a plugged faucet aerator. ”

— **Les Zell**

PACKING NUT

TIGHTEN SLIGHTLY

Got a leak?

Plumbers tell us that leaks are one of the most common complaints they get. Valves are one of the main culprits because they have moving parts and seals that can wear out. The next time you see a suspicious puddle of water, look for a leaky valve before you call the plumber. Look at the valve to see if water is leaking out around the valve stem. If it is, try turning the packing nut (**photo above**) about an eighth turn with a wrench. You'll know if you overtighten the nut because the valve will be hard to turn. If tightening the nut doesn't stop the leak, the fix is a little tougher. You'll have to shut off the main water valve, remove the handle and nut, and add to or replace the packing material—still a pretty easy fix.

"Your toilet's not a garbage can"

Les Zell got a call to unplug a toilet he had recently installed. He was surprised because he had put in a toilet that he knew was almost impossible to clog. After repeated attempts with a plunger and a toilet auger, he gave up and removed the toilet to look in from the bottom. The outlet was completely clogged with a tangled web of plastic dental floss holders, which had to be removed one at a time with a needle-nose pliers. Save yourself a service call. Use the wastebasket for garbage.

Low water pressure at the faucet?

Over time, aerators get clogged with minerals or other bits of stuff that break loose from the inside of the pipes. Remove the aerator by turning it clockwise when you're looking down on it. You may have to grip it with pliers to unscrew it. Once it's off, you can take the parts out of the aerator and clean them, but it's usually better to simply replace it. Take it along to the hardware store to find an exact thread match.

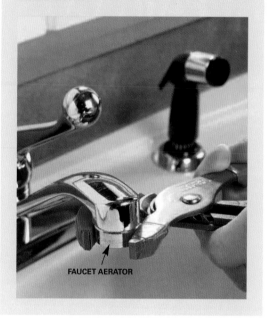

FAUCET AERATOR

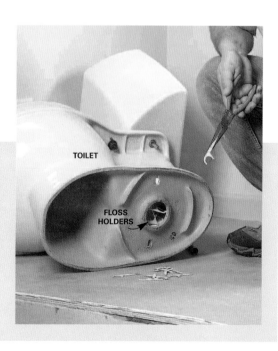

TOILET

FLOSS HOLDERS

BEFORE YOU CALL FOR AN APPLIANCE REPAIR

❝ The No. 1 thing for all appliances is to check the power first. In other words, is the breaker off, or did someone unplug the appliance to plug in a drill or something. Seriously, it's happened a million times. I'll go over there, plug in the appliance and say I'm really sorry, but I'll still have to charge you. ❞ — **Costas Stavrou**

Electric stove burner not heating?

The first thing Costas Stavrou asks is, "Did you clean the stove recently?" Usually the answer is yes, and the fix is easy. When you slid the burner back into the top, the terminal didn't engage with the receptacle under the stove top or the plastic terminal block got knocked out of its holder. Lift the stove top to see what the problem is. The fix usually involves reinstalling the terminal block. Also try spreading the terminals slightly to create a tighter connection.

Refrigerator not cooling?

It could be as simple as turning the dial to a cooler setting. Check the controls. Costas tells us it's not uncommon to find that the refrigerator controls are set wrong. Someone may have bumped the dial while putting away the milk or an inquisitive toddler may have twisted the knob.

Cooling coils completely caked with pet hair and dust are also incredibly common. Remove the front grille and vacuum the coils.

Is your freezer full of frost?

That's a sure sign that the freezer door is ajar. All it takes is one too many cartons of ice cream to hold the door open a crack. Rearrange the freezer contents so the door closes completely and you may save $60 on a service call.

No flame at the burners?

■ If you don't hear gas coming out when the burner is turned on, gas isn't getting to the stove. Check to make sure the gas is turned on.

■ If you hear gas coming out but the burner won't light, make sure the stove is plugged in. Even gas stoves need power.

■ If the stove is getting gas and has power, clean the igniter near the burner or clean out the pilot light hole.

❝ I can diagnose about 30 percent of electrical problems over the phone. I play a game of 'Twenty Questions' to see if I can avoid making a trip to the house. ❞

— **Al Hildenbrand**

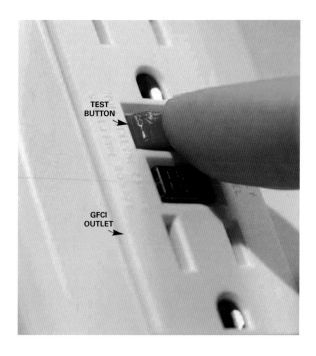

TEST BUTTON

GFCI OUTLET

Here are some of the most common complaints Al Hildenbrand gets, and the questions he asks.

"I screwed in a new fuse but I still don't have any power."
Are you sure you used the same amperage fuse as the one you replaced? Is the fuse good? Is it screwed in tight?

"I've checked the circuit breakers, but the outlet still doesn't work."
Some outlets are protected by upstream GFCIs or GFCI circuit breakers. Look in the circuit box for a GFCI circuit breaker and in bathrooms, kitchens and laundry rooms for GFCI outlets. Test and reset them. This may solve your problem.

"I replaced the lightbulb but the light fixture still doesn't work."
Are you sure the new bulb is good? Try it in another light fixture and make sure it's screwed all the way in.

"This outlet used to work. Now it's dead."
Check all the switches in the room. One of them might control the outlet.

❝ We always ask, is the furnace switch turned on? You'd be surprised how many times someone in the house accidentally switches the furnace off. ❞

— **Bob Schmahl**

Furnace quit?

If you live in an area with snow and have a furnace that vents out through the side wall, make sure the vent pipes aren't plugged with frost or snow. Plugged vents cause the furnace to shut off automatically. Once you've unplugged the vents, reset the furnace by switching off the power: Either turn off the switch located on or near the furnace, or flip the circuit breaker that controls the furnace. Wait a minute, then switch the power back on.

Not getting enough heat?

Check the furnace filter. Bob Schmahl says, "When I ask people when's the last time you changed the furnace filter and they give me that deer-in-the-headlights stare, I know what the problem is."

One of the most common causes of insufficient heat or cooled air is a plugged furnace filter. Change inexpensive woven fiberglass filters once a month or buy a better-quality pleated filter and change it every three months to avoid heating and cooling problems.

Another common cause of cold rooms during heating season is a blocked cold air return. Be sure your couch or an area rug isn't covering a cold air return vent because this can slow the entry of heated air into the room.

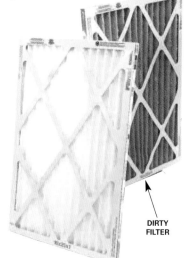

DIRTY FILTER

THE FAMILY HANDYMAN'S BEST

SPEED-CLEANING TIPS

Clean your house in minutes instead of hours

No one likes cleaning the house, but we can make the chore take a lot less time. We pulled some of our favorite cleaning tips from past issues, come up with the best cleaning products to keep your house sparkling and save you several hours of cleaning per week. You won't have to spend a lot of money either—some of these products that help you work smarter cost less than $5.

Use a HEPA vacuum filter

Stop blowing dust all over with an old vacuum. A HEPA vacuum filter (starting at $8) captures microscopic airborne particulates. Old-fashioned paper or conventional vacuum bags pick up only about 30 percent of dust and allergens, and blow the rest back into the air.

Use a Swiffer Duster

Lose the feather duster. Try a Swiffer Duster with Febreze ($23), which traps and locks dust in the duster's fibers. It doesn't just move the dust elsewhere like traditional feather dusters—it removes the dust.

Use a doormat

Eighty-five percent of the dirt that comes into the home is from shoes! So nag your family members to take them off. Place shoes on doormats to contain the dirt. A 20 x 30-in. mat costs about $20 at discount stores.

TOP
40 DIY
RULES

With 75-plus years of hard-core do-it-yourself experience under our belts, the editors here at The Family Handyman share our best rules for your next improvement project

1. Buy a tool belt

❝ When building or fixing something around the house, I sometimes get lazy and don't strap on the tool belt. And it automatically doubles or triples the amount of time it takes to do just about any carpentry work. Take my advice: Use a tool belt. ❞

— **Travis Larson**

2. Start with level, plumb and flat walls

Old walls are often crooked and out of plumb. One good method to fix the problem is to add new studs alongside the old ones, making sure the new ones are plumb and aligned. You'll be glad you did when it comes time to install cabinets and trim.

3. Start in the least conspicuous spot

Hone your carpentry skills where only you will see it. Start siding the back of the garage or trimming out the bedroom first. By the time you reach the more visible areas, you'll have all the bugs worked out.

4. Keep a job folder during remodeling

File away product info, colors, instruction manuals, and so on. You never know when you'll need this information, but you will.

5. Don't cut corners on the prep work

Rush painting prep, and you'll end up regretting it. Either the paint job will look bad or it won't last as long as it should. A little extra time spent filling dents and gouges, caulking gaps, and sanding and priming pays off in a much nicer job.

6. Be positive the power is off

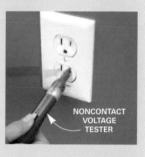

NONCONTACT VOLTAGE TESTER

When you're doing electrical work, don't assume that because you flicked a switch or flipped a circuit breaker the power is off—always double-check. Buy a noncontact voltage tester and check all the wires in the box before you do any work—or plan on some melted dental work!

7. Cut the longest parts first

If your project requires long and short parts, cut the long ones first. If you miscut a board, you'll still be able to use the leftovers for the short parts.

8. Prefinish and prepaint

When you're near the end of your project, the last thing you want to do is slow down to prefinish wood trim, but it's worth it. Painting or staining wood trim before you put it up will save you time and usually looks better in the end.

9. Get a building permit

You may save a few bucks sneaking by without a building permit, but it could come back to haunt you. Take advantage of the building inspector's expertise to ensure that your work is safe and complies with building codes.

10. Choose color in the room you're painting

The quality of light changes the way colors look. Always choose colors in the location where they'll be used.

11. Keep a beater chisel in your tool belt

❝ Aside from my hammer, my 'beater' chisel is the most useful tool I carry. It's a scraper, a pry bar and a putty knife. Sometimes I even use it as a chisel for crude work. ❞

— **Gary Wentz**

12. Finish each project before starting a new one

❝ I get bored with projects toward the end. If it weren't for my wife's gentle insistence that I finish, I'd just move on to the next thing and our home would be full of half-done projects. ❞

— **Jeff Gorton**

13. Buy extra plumbing parts

No matter how carefully you plan, it seems like you always need another elbow or extra length of pipe. Save yourself a trip to the store and buy extra the first time. Then return what you don't use.

14. Take a photo or old plumbing parts to the store

If you have to ask for help finding parts, it's easier if you have a photo or the original parts along.

15. Know when to call in a pro

Working on the main electrical service panel, adding gas piping and installing fireplaces are all projects that you should consider calling a pro to do if you're the least bit unsure of your ability to do them safely. It's not worth wrecking your house to save a few bucks.

16. Clean up every day

Make time at the end of each day to clean up and reorganize. It's a pleasure to start the day in a clean, orderly workplace. And you'll find all those missing tools, too.

17. Know your property lines

Don't build anything permanent close to the edge of your lot without first locating the property lines.

18. Beware of drywall dust

❝ I filled in a wall where a built-in entertainment center had been. It was such a small drywall job that I didn't bother to confine the dust. Sanding took me about 10 minutes, but cleaning the fine layer of dust from everything in sight took the rest of the afternoon. ❞

— **Brett Martin**

19. Protect your expensive floors

For painting projects, drop cloths are fine. But for heavy demolition or long-term projects, cover wood and tile floors with cardboard, thin plywood or some other durable material. Tape the seams to keep debris from sifting through.

20. Save leftovers for patching

Save leftover paint, carpet, tile, wood flooring, vinyl flooring, wallpaper, millwork and other stuff. If you have to patch or touch up later, you'll have the materials on hand to do it.

21. If in doubt, tear it out

If you're remodeling a kitchen or bath and debating about whether to keep or tear out old drywall or plaster, it's usually better to get rid of it. Getting down to bare studs makes electrical and plumbing work easier and simplifies drywalling.

22. Clear out the room

Working around furniture and other stuff is a drag. Take time to empty the room before you start a large project, or at least pile the furniture in an out-of-the-way spot and cover it with drop cloths or plastic.

23. Know where the pros shop

Home centers don't always carry unusual materials. Try a full-service lumberyard for moldings, a tile shop for the widest selection of adhesives and grout, or a plumbing retailer to find the largest selection of fixtures or that unique faucet part you need.

24. Know when to buy the cheapest

If you need a tool that you know you'll only use occasionally, buy a cheap one.

25. Have a backup plan for toilet repairs

If you don't have a second toilet in the house, you'd better let your family know your plan, start early in the day and have an extra wax ring and toilet bolts on hand to temporarily reinstall the toilet.

26. Plan jobs so you can have a temporary sink

Save the sink, base cabinet and a small section of the countertop if you demo your kitchen. Then jury-rig the sink. Trust us—your family will think you're a DIY superstar.

29. Leave "reveals" on windows and doors

Leave a space (reveal) alongside moldings. It'll give you a little fudge factor and looks better than trying to get trim flush with jambs.

REVEAL

27. Plan around the weather

❝ We poured a garage slab late one fall day. It was cool outside, and we didn't realize how long the concrete would take to set up. We finished troweling at about 2 a.m. ❞

— **Travis Larson**

28. Call 811 before digging

❝ I learned the hard way. The neighbors assured me there were no buried utilities in my backyard, so I ignored my own advice and dug fence-post holes without calling 811. I chopped halfway through what I thought was a tough root before reaching into the hole to discover a huge phone cable. Several weeks after the phone lines were spliced, I got a bill for $800 from the phone company. ❞

— **Jeff Gorton**

30. Don't underestimate concrete work

Miscut a board and it's no big deal, but mess up a concrete slab and you've got a big problem. If you're pouring more than a yard of concrete, make sure you have help. For really big jobs like garage slabs, see if you can round up a helper with concrete-finishing experience.

31. Time material deliveries carefully

You don't want to have to move a stack of drywall to install an outlet or, worse yet, a big pile of bricks in the way of a gravel delivery.

32. Rent scaffolding when you need it

Scaffolding is more stable and safer than any ladder could ever be. And your work will go easier and faster.

33. Get help when you need it

❝ I'm sort of stubborn about asking for help. I remember once attempting to install a 4- by 12-foot sheet of drywall on a ceiling by myself with a single stepladder in the middle of the room. A light fixture hole I'd cut in the center weakened the sheet so it broke in half over my head and nearly knocked me off the ladder. ❞   — **Jeff Gorton**

34. Order extra materials, just in case

Adding 10 percent to your materials order is a good rule of thumb, although for some items you may have to just pick up an extra piece or two.

35. Don't forget the little things for big jobs

It's easy to make a list of the big stuff you need. But it's worth the effort to visualize all the steps in your project and try to include every item, right down to the caulk, in your shopping list. It'll save you multiple trips to the home center.

36. Pick out nice lumber, trim or plywood

When quality matters, be choosy about your lumber purchases. But also be reasonable. If you're cutting boards into short lengths, for example, they don't have to be perfectly straight.

37. Plan switch and outlet placement carefully

This is especially true in kitchens and baths where exact placement of outlets and switches is critical. A bathroom light switch that's mounted an inch too high or low can end up straddling the tile wainscot or countertop. Then the fun really begins!

38. Have materials delivered close to the work site

It's a bummer to carry materials that could have been delivered close to the work site. For a few extra bucks, you can usually get shingles delivered onto the roof, drywall boomed up to the second floor or decking material moved to the back of the house.

39. Have a tarp for roof tear-offs

What will you do if you tear off the shingles and a storm pops up? At least if you have a plastic tarp that's large enough to cover the roof, you'll have a fighting chance of keeping your house dry.

40. Get it in writing

❝ I ordered 12 custom windows over the phone from an inexperienced salesperson once. The windows arrived and were all wrong, but I didn't have any way to prove it was the salesperson's mistake. ❞   — **Eric Smith**

SPECIAL SECTION
BEST OF THE FAMILY HANDYMAN

OUR FAVORITE
HANDY HINTS®

As our former executive editor Spike Carlsen said, a truly great Handy Hint has to meet three criteria: It has to solve a common problem quickly, make use of everyday stuff lying around and, last, draw the response, "Why didn't I think of that!" Based on these three important conditions, here are our editors' favorite Handy Hints of all time.

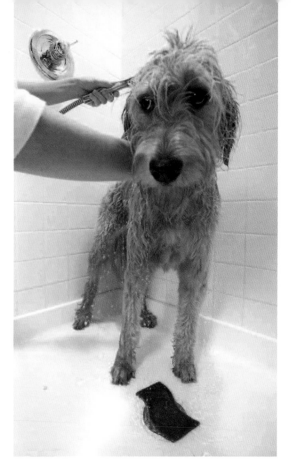

Fur filter for dog bathing

I used to pay to have my dog bathed because if I washed my dog in the bathtub or shower, I'd end up with a clogged drain. Not anymore. To keep fur out of the drain, use a mesh-type scrubbing pad. In a shower, clip the pad to the drain plate with a bobby pin. In a bathtub, wedge two pads under the stopper from two sides. The pads catch fur but let water flow through.

The classic tennis ball parking hint

Hanging a tennis ball from the garage ceiling so you know exactly where to stop your vehicle is the No. 1 most submitted hint of all time. There are high-tech electronic versions, but the low-budget setup of a tennis ball on a string has never lost its appeal—and probably never will.

Find lost parts with a light

I was talking with a friend of mine, telling him about our magazine, when a screw fell out of his glasses onto the floor. The timing was perfect. We had just run a Handy Hint on this. We turned off the lights and shone a flashlight on the floor. The light reflected off the screw, making it easy to find. The downside is that when you're on your hands and knees with a flashlight in the dark, you see everywhere you don't clean—and a lot of disgusting stuff suddenly comes to light!

Easy-release bumper stickers

Heat from a hair dryer softens adhesive, making bumper stickers, price tags and other labels easy to pull off. Start at one corner and pull slowly, allowing the heat to loosen the sticker.

See-through junk bag

A while back, I asked my wife where the "junk" coffee can was. You know, the one that's filled with a mishmash of screws, nails, fasteners, wire connectors—all the stuff you need for around-the-house projects and fixes. She said it was gone, replaced by a 1-gallon Ziploc bag.

I was impressed with the upgrade. I could see every single doodad right through the side of the bag, then reach right in and pluck out whatever I needed. No more dumping out the whole can on the countertop and pawing through everything to find the right size screw. Brilliant!

Caulking in tight spots

Ninety-five percent of the time, you can finagle a caulk nozzle into hard-to-reach spots—but for that other 5 percent, use this tip. Pull the wires out of a short piece of cable, then slip the plastic sheathing over the end of the caulk tube nozzle. You've just made a flexible extension that you can use to get caulk into all those tight spaces, like along the back edge of a sink.

Golf tee in the screw hole

I've used this tip dozens of times, especially when dealing with stripped-out latch and hinge holes on doors. Often the only problem with a sagging door or a door that won't latch is a loose hinge or strike plate. And that loose part is usually the result of a stripped screw hole.

The solution is to apply a dab of epoxy to a golf tee, then tap the tee into the screw hole. After an hour, chisel off the excess and you've got solid wood that will hold new screws. For tiny holes, use a few toothpicks instead of a tee.

GREATEST GOOFS
OF ALL TIME

We all love Great Goofs, maybe because they happen to all of us. These three goofs are the finest in three popular categories: wayward drilling, hitting something while digging, and building a project too big to fit through a door.

The best "you-drilled-into *what*?" goof

Our readers have drilled through all sorts of things—hidden pipes, furniture, even their own clothing. This, however, is our favorite:

I wanted to hook up the Internet for my wife's new laptop. My office is right below hers, so I decided to run a cable by drilling through the floor. I measured carefully, attached a long bit and started drilling—and then heard a scream. I had drilled through the ceiling into the shower below. As I pulled out the bit, I could see her wet, frightened face staring back at me. Luckily, I am really good at patching holes.

The best "built-it-too-big-to-get-out-the-door" goof

Nothing takes the joy out of a well-built project faster than discovering you can't get it out of the room. This has happened to more than a dozen readers with bookcases, seven with entertainment centers, four with desks and two with tables. We especially like this goof because we salute anyone who would rather take apart a doorway than dismantle a newly built project.

I was building a doghouse in my 8 x 12-ft. shop. Everything went fine—now I just needed to take it outside and paint it. I tried to get it out the door front-to-back, side-to-side, then top-to-bottom, but it was still too wide. After all my work, I wasn't about to dismantle this fabulous project. Two hours later, I finally got it out— after I'd removed the trim, the door and the door frame!

The best "hit-something-while-digging" goof

No matter how many times we're cautioned to call 811 before digging, people still don't do it. It can be an expensive (even fatal!) mistake. Readers have hit everything from phone lines to old foundations to sprinkler systems (but no buried treasure that we know of). We like this goof because it illustrates how one tiny little mistake can turn an entire neighborhood against you.

One morning, I decided to start digging for my new garden. Because the site was 40 yards from the house, I figured I didn't have to worry about underground electrical wires. Wiring, no, but I cut right through the main cable feed for the whole neighborhood. No one had TV reception for the rest of the day. Talk about upset neighbors—it was Super Bowl Sunday!

QUICK & CLEVER
KITCHEN STORAGE
SOLUTIONS

THYME SAVER

Does your stew boil over every time you're distracted for five minutes looking for the right spice? If your spices are jammed into a drawer with only the tops visible, take an hour to make this nifty rack that slips neatly into the drawer. Make it with leftover scraps of 1/4-in. and 1/2-in. plywood. Now you can spend less time cleaning the burners and more time stirring the pot!

COOKWARE ORGANIZER

Most kitchen base cabinets lack vertical storage space for big, flat cookware like cookie sheets and pizza pans. To provide it, just remove the lower shelf, cut a vertical panel of plywood and fasten it at the cabinet bottom with furniture braces and at the top with a strip of wood. Drill holes for the adjusting pins to match the original locations and trim the shelf to length.

MEASURING CUP HANG-UP

Free up drawer space by hanging measuring cups inside a kitchen cabinet. Position and mount a wood strip so that the cups will hang between the shelves and allow the door to close completely. Mount a second strip for your measuring spoons, then screw in cup hooks on both strips.

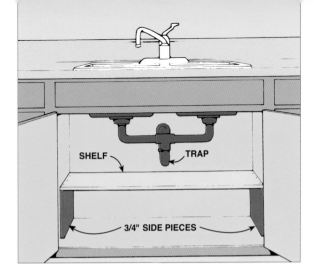

SHELF

TRAP

3/4" SIDE PIECES

EASY CABINET SHELF

Here's a fast and easy way to add a shelf to a kitchen cabinet under the sink, or to a bathroom vanity. Cut side supports from 3/4-in. plywood to the height you want, allowing the shelf to fit under the sink trap. Cut the shelf from either 1/2-in. or 3/4-in. plywood, about 1/4 in. shorter than the inside cabinet width. Nail the shelf to the side supports with 6d finishing nails, prime and paint the shelf and sides, and slide the unit in place.

PLASTIC BAG HOLDER

An empty rectangular tissue box makes a convenient holder for small garbage bags, plastic grocery bags and small rags. Simply thumbtack it to the inside of a cabinet door.

WINE GLASS MOLDING

T-molding designed for wood floor transitions makes a perfect rack for stemware. Just cut it to length, predrill screw holes and screw it to the underside of a shelf. For a neater look, use brass screws and finish washers. Prefinished T-molding is available wherever wood flooring is sold. A 4-ft. section costs about $28.

T-MOLDING

FINISH WASHER

CONCEALED MESSAGE CENTER

Don't let shopping lists, phone messages and to-do notes clutter up counter space. Mount a dry-erase board and a plastic bin on the inside of a cabinet door with double-sided foam mounting tape. The bin will protrude into the cabinet, so be sure to position it where it won't collide with shelves or the stuff inside. Get the board, bin and tape at a discount or office supply store for about $15 altogether.

TIDY FILE CENTER

Countertops are a landing pad for paper—mail, news clippings and other assorted notes. Get that mess off the counter with folders and a file holder. The one shown here ($8 at an office supply store) mounts with screws or double-sided foam tape. If there's not a suitable vertical surface, get a file holder that sits on the countertop. It will take up less space (and look neater) than a stack of loose papers.

BAG DISPENSER

Plastic grocery bags turn up everywhere these days, so you might as well corral them for reuse. Simply cut the top and bottom off a two-liter plastic soft drink bottle with a utility knife. Make the hole in the top about 3 in. in diameter. Using small screws and washers, mount the bottle on the back of a cabinet or closet door with the 3-in. opening down. Stuff the bags into the bottle and pull them out as needed.

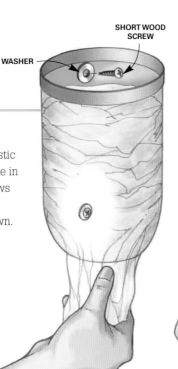

SHORT WOOD SCREW

WASHER

SPECIAL BONUS SECTION

EASY-TO-BUILD KNIFE BLOCK

Store your kitchen cutlery in style with this handsome knife block. It's fast, easy and fun to build, and includes a 6-in.-wide storage box for a knife sharpener. The Accusharp knife sharpener ($11, product No. 001, accusharp.com) tucks neatly inside.

To build one, you only need a 3/4-in. x 8-in. x 4-ft. hardwood board and a 6-in. x 6-1/2-in. piece of 1/4-in. hardwood plywood to match.

Begin by cutting off a 10-in. length of the board and setting it aside. Rip the remaining 38-in. board to 6 in. wide and cut five evenly spaced saw kerfs 5/8 in. deep along one face. Crosscut the slotted board into four 9-in. pieces and glue them into a block, being careful not to slop glue into the saw kerfs (you can clean them out with a knife before the glue dries). Saw a 15-degree angle on one end and screw the plywood piece under the angled end of the block.

Cut the 6-1/2-in. x 3-in. lid from the leftover board, and slice the remaining piece into 1/4-in.-thick pieces for the sides and end of the box. Glue them around the plywood floor. Cut a rabbet on three sides of the lid so it fits snugly on the box and drill a 5/8-in. hole for a finger pull. Then just add a finish and you're set for years of happy carving!

SPICE STORAGE

Small spice containers use shelf space inefficiently and are difficult to find when surrounded by taller bottles and items. Use a small spring-tension curtain rod ($3) as a simple shelf. It's easy to install and strong enough to support the spices.

RACKS FOR CANNED GOODS

Use those leftover closet racks as cabinet organizers. Trim the racks to length with a hacksaw and then mount screws to the back side of the face frame to hold the racks in place. The back side of the rack simply rests against the back of the cabinet. Now you can easily find your soup and check the rest of your inventory at a glance.

SIMPLE GIFT PROJECTS

MAGAZINE STORAGE BINS

Finally got the time to build that project in *The Family Handyman* from three years ago? Great … if you can find the right issue! Here's a handsome solution. Build these bins and stock them with an orderly archive, and you'll have instant access to years of projects and plans. You can build four bins from one 2 x 4-ft. sheet of 1/4-in. plywood and two 6-ft.-long 1x4s. Here's how:

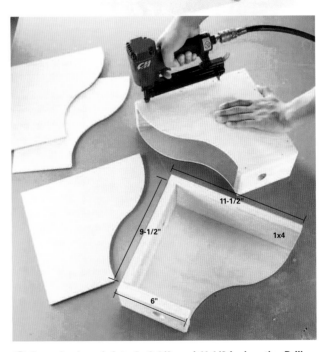

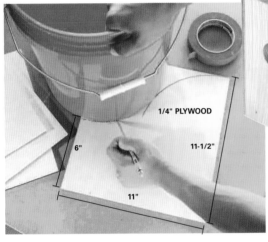

1/4" PLYWOOD

6" 11-1/2"

11"

1 Cut the 1/4-in. plywood into eight 11-1/2-in. x 11-in. pieces. Use a 5-gallon bucket to trace a graceful S-curve from the 11-1/2-in.-high corner across the plywood to a 6-in. mark on the opposite side. Simply establish a smooth curve.

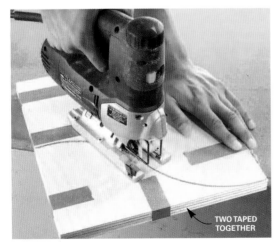

TWO TAPED TOGETHER

2 Stack pairs so the best sides face each other and tape all the sheets together flush at the edges. "Gang cut" the curve with a jigsaw or a band saw.

11-1/2"

9-1/2" 1x4

6"

3 Saw pine boards into 6-, 9-1/2- and 11-1/2-in. lengths. Drill 1-in.-diameter finger pulls in the 6-in. pieces, then nail the frames together. Nail the sides to the frames with 1-in. finish nails, sand as needed and apply a finish.

PORTABLE BOOKSHELF

Here's a cool knockdown shelf for a dorm room or den. You just slide the shelves between the dowels, and they pinch the shelves to stiffen the bookshelf. It works great if you're careful about two things: Make the space between the dowel holes exactly 1/16 in. wider than the thickness of the shelf board. And be sure the shelf thickness is the same from end to end and side to side.

After test-fitting a dowel in a trial hole (you want a tight fit), drill holes in a jig board so the space between the holes is your shelf thickness plus 1/16 in. Clamp the

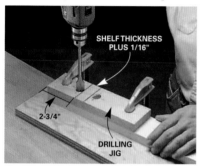

jig board on the ends of the legs and drill the holes. Cut the dowels 1-3/4 in. longer than the shelf width, then dry-assemble (no glue). Mark

the angled ends of the legs parallel to the shelves and cut off the tips to make the legs sit flat. Disassemble and glue the dowels in the leg holes. When the glue dries, slide the shelves in and load them up.

Cutting list

Perfectly flat 1x12 lumber or plywood
2 shelves: 11-1/4" wide x 3' long
4 risers: 2-1/4" wide x 24" long
8 dowels: 3/4" dia. x 13" long

SIMPLE STEPSTOOL

Here's a great gift idea that will draw raves. The joints are accurately made in seconds with a plate jointer, but don't tell your admirers. You'll also need a miter saw to crosscut

the boards and a jigsaw to cut the half-circles in the risers. The lumber you'll need:

- One 8-ft. 1x8 clear hardwood board (actual width is 7-1/4 in. and actual thickness is 3/4 in.). Oak is a good choice because it's readily available at home centers.

- One 3-ft. 1x3 hardwood board (actual width is 2-1/2 in. and actual thickness is 3/4 in.).

Cut the 8-ft. board into:
- Two 22-in. riser boards
- Two 11-in. riser boards
- One 14-in. step board
- One 14-in. seat board

You'll use 94 in. of the 96-in. board, so make practice cuts on a scrap board first to check the angle and length of cut. Don't cut the 3-ft. 1x3 board until you've dry-assembled the step, seat and risers and measured for a perfect fit.

To create two risers, join the 11-in. boards to the 22-in. boards with No. 20 biscuits and glue. Let dry 30 minutes, then lay the step and seat across and mark for two No. 20 biscuits at each joint. Dry-assemble the step, seat and risers with biscuits, then cut and snugly fit the

crosspieces. Mark the riser-to-crosspiece joint and cut slots for No. 0 biscuits. Glue and firmly clamp the step, seat and crosspieces to the risers. Check for square and let dry 30 minutes, then cut out the 4-1/2-in.-diameter arc on the bottom of the risers to create the legs. Finish-sand and apply your favorite finish. This project is designed for use on hard-surface flooring only—not carpeting.

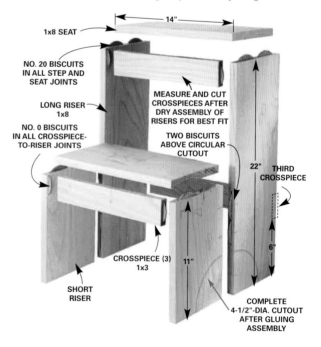

BETTER BAGEL SLICER

This bagel slicer is as easy to build as it is to use. Making it requires only a few simple tools, two dowels and a scrap of hardwood. When your stomach growls, drop the bagel in the cage, squeeze the dowel tops so the side dowels bend and pinch the bagel, then slice away. It keeps your fingers out of harm's way (and the crumbs and knife blade off your counter).

Dowel diameters vary slightly. To ensure you get a good fit, drill a sample hole with your 3/16-in. brad point bit and take that scrap with you to test-fit the 3/16-in. dowels you buy.

Use mineral oil (available at drug stores) to finish your bagel slicer. It's nontoxic dry or wet. (If you decide to use a different finish, be sure it's nontoxic when dry.)

Build the bagel slicer

Cut the dowels and hardwood base to the dimensions in the Cutting list on p. 268.

Lay out the holes in the base (**Figure A**). Make a drill guide by cutting a 5-degree angle on the end of a piece of scrap wood, then use it to guide your bit as you drill (**Photo 1**). Use a 2-in.-high guide and let the bit protrude 2-3/8 in. beyond the chuck. With this setup, when the chuck meets the top of the guide you'll get uniform 3/8-in.-deep holes.

Lay out the holes in the handles. Hold each in a vise or clamp while drilling the holes. Wrap a piece of masking tape 3/8 in. from the tip of your bit to act as a depth guide.

Glue and tap the uprights into the handles. Be careful not to damage the ends of the uprights that fit into the base. Then glue and tap the uprights into the base (**Photo 2**).

Let the glue dry, ease all the sharp edges with sandpaper, then apply a coat of mineral oil for the finish (**Photo 3**). Let the finish dry overnight and you're ready for breakfast.

Figure A: Bagel slicer details

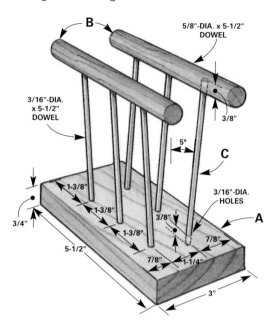

5/8"-DIA. x 5-1/2" DOWEL

3/16"-DIA. x 5-1/2" DOWEL

3/8"

5°

C

3/16"-DIA. HOLES

B

A

1-3/8"

1-3/8"

1-3/8"

3/8"

3/4"

5-1/2"

7/8"

7/8"

1-1/4"

3"

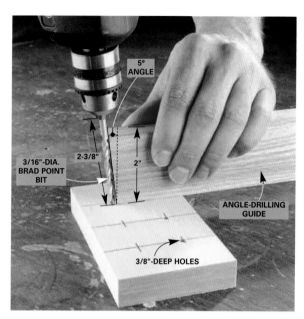

5° ANGLE

3/16"-DIA. BRAD POINT BIT

2-3/8"

2"

ANGLE-DRILLING GUIDE

3/8"-DEEP HOLES

1 Drill the angled holes in the base. Guide the bit against the end of a 2-in.-wide piece of scrap wood with a 5-degree angle cut on the end. Set the bit in the chuck at a depth so that when the chuck hits the guide block, the hole is 3/8 in. deep.

WOOD GLUE

RUBBER MALLET

2 Tap the preassembled dowel sides into the base using a rubber mallet. Start by inserting one of the end dowels, then work your way down to the other end. Glue all joints.

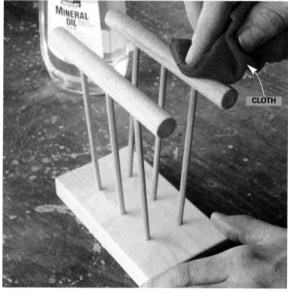

MINERAL OIL

CLOTH

3 Wipe on a coat of mineral oil to finish the wood, or choose your own nontoxic finish.

MATERIALS LIST

ITEM
3/4" x 3" x 5-1/2" birch
5/8"-dia. x 12" hardwood dowel
3/16"-dia. x 36" hardwood dowel
Small bottle of mineral oil

CUTTING LIST

KEY	PCS.	SIZE & DESCRIPTION
A	1	3/4" x 3" x 5-1/2" birch (base)
B	2	5/8"-dia. x 5-1/2" hardwood dowel (handles)
C	6	3/16"-dia. x 5-1/2" hardwood dowel (uprights)

BUTTERFLY HOUSE

Butterflies like the protection of dark, sheltered areas—whether it's for months at a time (during long, cold winters), or for just a few moments (when dodging hungry predators). Here's a simple refuge you can build for them for under $20.

Use smooth or rough-sawn cedar; it's rot-resistant and weathers to a mellow gray. For durability, assemble the house using moisture-proof glue and galvanized nails. Make sure to hinge and latch one side so you can insert and maintain the long twigs and tree bark the butterflies roost on (**Figure A**, p. 270).

A jigsaw, drill and common hand tools are all you need, although a table saw (to cut angles and the wood to size) speeds up the work greatly.

To attract butterflies, locate the house in an area with lots of flowering plants, and mount it 2 to 3 ft. off the ground.

Build the butterfly house

Cut the parts to the sizes and angles listed in the Cutting list, p. 270, and shown in the photos.

Lay out the entry slots on the front (**Figure A**), drill the ends with a 3/8-in.-dia. bit, then cut the slots the rest of the way with a jigsaw (**Photo 1**). Smooth the sides of the slots with sandpaper.

Use a 7/8-in. spade bit to drill the holes for the support pipe in the bottom, and one of the pipe stops.

Glue and nail the back to the side. Glue and clamp the two support pipe stops together, then glue and clamp them to the back. Glue and nail the bottom to the assembled back and side.

Glue and nail the false front roof pieces to the front, then glue and nail the front in place, and attach the roof boards. Use the door as a spacer between the front and back when you attach the roof.

Trim the door, if necessary, so it fits loosely between the front and back. Align the door, and hammer in the two hinge pivot nails (**Photo 2**).

Use two pliers to bend a nail in half. Drill a pilot hole, then tap in this latch.

Insert the support pipe through the bottom and into the pipe stop. Drill pilot holes for the pipe strap screws, attach the strap (**Photo 3**), then loosen it and remove the support pipe.

Determine the best location and height for the house (keep it low). Hammer the pipe into the ground (protect the end of the pipe with a scrap piece of wood), then slide the house on the pipe, tighten the pipe strap, and watch for your first fluttering houseguests.

1 Create the entry slots. Drill 3/8-in. holes for the top and bottom of each slot, then connect the holes using a jigsaw.

To attract butterflies, locate the house in an area with lots of flowering plants

MATERIALS LIST

ITEM	QTY.
1x6 x 10' cedar	1
4d galvanized casing nails	25
3/4"-dia. type L copper pipe*	1
3/4" copper pipe strap*	1
No. 8 x 1/2" pan head screws	2
Titebond II moisture-proof glue	small bottle

*Available at home centers

CUTTING LIST

KEY	PCS.	SIZE & DESCRIPTION
A	2	3/4" x 5" x 24" cedar (front and back)
B	2	3/4" x 5" x 6-1/4" cedar (roof boards)
C	2	3/4" x 3-3/4" x 22-1/4" cedar (side and door)
D	1	3/4" x 3-3/4" x 3-1/2" cedar (bottom)
E	2	3/4" x 1-1/4" x 3-1/2" cedar (support pipe stop)
F	2	1/2" x 3/4" x 3-1/2" cedar (false front roof)

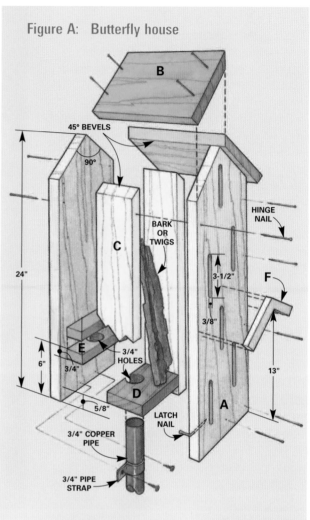

Figure A: Butterfly house

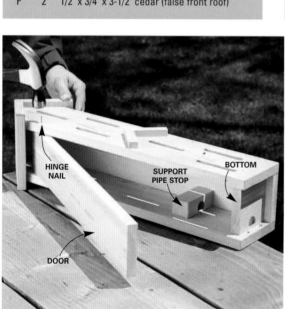

2 Assemble the house. Use straight nails for the door hinges and a bent one for the latch. (Note: Here the door is open so you can see the inside, but it's easier to align everything with the door closed.)

3 Loosely screw the pipe strap to the back, using the support pipe as a guide. Remove the pipe, pound it into the ground, then permanently tighten the strap around the pipe to prevent the house from spinning.

HINTS & TIPS FOR
PET OWNERS

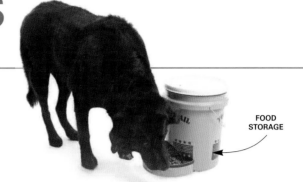

QUICK CLEANUP CAT LITTER

Cut your litter cleanup time in half with this nifty trick! Line your litter pan with a plastic kitchen garbage bag before adding the litter. When it's time to change the litter, simply lift out the bag, tie it off and throw it all away.

FOOD STORAGE

5-GALLON DOG FEEDER

Make a tough, self-filling dog feeder from a couple of 5-gal. buckets. With a saber saw, cut the bottom off one bucket to create a serving tray, and cut a food dispensing hole in the food storage bucket (as shown). Cut part of the lip off the bottom of the food storage bucket to flatten it, then use silicone to glue the two pieces together.

NOTE: Don't build this dog feeder unless your pooch can exercise some self-control.

FOOD DISPENSER HOLE

BOTTOM LIP REMOVED

FEEDING TRAY

SILICONE

GLUE AREA

TINFOIL COUCH-SAVER

Keep your cats off the couch with tinfoil. Tear off a piece of tinfoil long enough to cover the top of your couch, and set it on the cushions. The feel and sound of tinfoil drives cats nuts and they'll immediately jump off.

SPECIAL BONUS SECTION

MOVING WITH **PETS**

Tips for a smooth move with Spot and Miss Kitty

Be it cross-country or across town, a move can be hard on your pets. A little preparation and a consult with your vet before shipping, driving or flying Fido or Fifi to your new home will ease the adjustment.

Underwater

Air shipping fish takes special planning, but it can be done. Your aquarium needs to be emptied and packed, so your fish need interim boarding before traveling. Ask your fish dealer to help; your fish will need to be packed in individual plastic bags, half air, half water, and boxed to offset too much heat or cold. Talk to your airline five to six weeks before your move for guidance regarding your aquatic airlift. For more help with fish moving tips, visit aquariumfish.net.

In the air

If your move is across state lines, consult a vet near your new home to be sure your pet meets your new state's health and vaccination requirements. Before flying with or shipping a pet, check with your airline regarding what proof of health is required. Consider before air shipping: Can your pet withstand extreme heat or cold in the cargo hold and on the tarmac? And never sedate an animal traveling by air—it can be fatal.

On the wing

Moving Petey over the road may be noisy, but should be safe—keep the ambient temperature inside the car moderate, cover the cage if that's what he likes, and never let him out, even in your motel room. If flying with a feathered friend, check with your airline. Most will not let birds travel in the cargo hold due to extreme temperatures and many will allow your bird to fly with you in the cabin.

On the road

Acclimate Fido to car travel with short trips around the neighborhood. Take time for toileting and exercise. Don't let your dog off-leash and don't give your cat a chance to bolt. Pack a clean cat box with litter and familiar food, and bring an emergency photo of your pet in case the unthinkable happens and she's lost en route.

PEA GRAVEL

STONE
COBBLES

PET FOOD DISPENSER

Build this bin and you can fill the
dog dish with the flick of a finger.
For complete how-to instructions, go
to thefamilyhandyman.com and search
"pet food dispenser." Scroll to the bottom
of "Three Garage Storage Projects."

DOG-SPOT SOLUTIONS

Growing a neat lawn in an area frequented by dogs is difficult
but not impossible. Acidic dog urine discolors and kills the grass,
leaving a patchwork of brown spots. Here are a few tricks for
keeping the grass green.

1. Apply lime or gypsum regularly to neutralize the acid in the soil
   and restore the balance that grass prefers.
2. Add 1 tablespoon of tomato juice each day to your dog's food to
   help neutralize the urine.
3. Water the area heavily each week to dilute the urine.
4. Don't fight it! Replace the grass with small round gravel (pea
   gravel) bordered with stone cobbles or brick. Place landscape
   fabric beneath the rock to prevent weeds from popping up and
   your problem is solved, permanently. And another plus—less
   grass to mow!

DON'T BRUSH THE DOG—
USE A VACUUM INSTEAD!

If your dog has a heavy coat that requires a lot of brushing, use
your vacuum cleaner with an upholstery attachment! Your dog
may be a little apprehensive at first, but he or she may learn to love
it. The vacuum sucks up all the loose hair so you don't spend any
time cleaning it up.

CAT REPELLENT

Tired of the cat jumping up onto the kitchen table while
you're eating? Fill a clean spray
bottle with water. Whenever the cat
hops up there, give him a quick
squirt. Eventually, the mere sight of
the bottle in your hand will
send your cat
running.

**HOOK-AND-LOOP
FASTENER**

PRIVATE DINING

To stop your dog from eating the cat's food,
move the cat's dish into a different room. Then
attach adhesive-backed hook-and-loop fasteners to
the back of the room's door and to the front of the
trim. After filling the dish, hook up the fasteners so
the door only opens 5 in. Now your cat can come
and go and eat his meal in peace.

PET FOOD CUSHION

Save your back when you reach under the sink to
fix that leaky P-trap. Lie on top of a 40-lb. bag of pet
food. It will lift you over that sharp cabinet edge.

PLASTIC SHEET

SEE-THROUGH DOOR PROTECTOR

Protect your doors from your dog's claws with a sheet of plastic. Buy
1/8-in. or thinner Plexiglas or plastic at any home center. Cut the
Plexiglas so it fits just inside the door jambs and is 1 ft. higher than
the reach of your dog. Most home centers will cut the Plexiglas for
you, but you can also cut it with a utility knife and a straightedge. (If
you have a large dog and need plastic above the doorknob, use a 3-in.
hole saw to make a cutout for the knob.) Mount the Plexiglas to the
door with 3/4-in. roundhead wood screws.

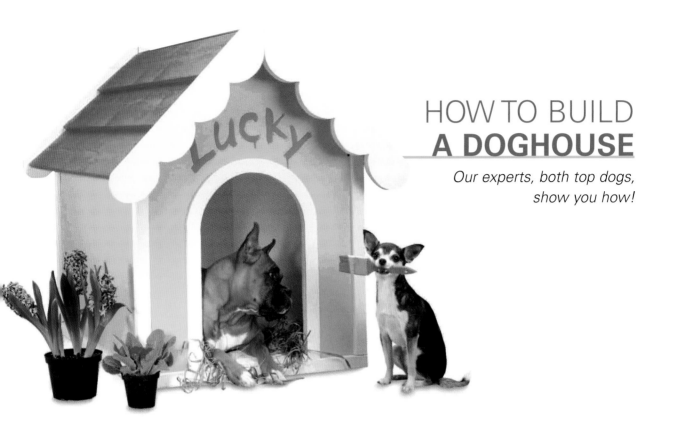

HOW TO BUILD
A DOGHOUSE

*Our experts, both top dogs,
show you how!*

Best friends deserve the best. So give your pal the finest doghouse around—this one. What makes this house so doggone good? First, it's sized right for comfort (see "Sizing Your Doghouse"). Second, you can build it from readily available 2x2s, plywood and siding. Third, it's easy to build—you should be able to finish it in an afternoon—unless of course, you're all paws.

Following are some tips to keep in mind:

■ Insulate the floor (as we did) with rigid, extruded polyurethane; it resists moisture and has a high R-value.

■ Secure the back wall in place using easy-to-remove drywall screws. This allows easy access for changing bedding or airing out the house.

■ If you're building a house more than 40 in. long, add an extra pair of roof rafters (**Photo 3**) in the middle to support the roof boards.

■ Build your house from nontoxic materials, especially if a chewing pup is the occupant. We used standard plywood rather than pressure-treated.

■ Bend over any nails or screws that protrude into the doghouse.

■ Paint the exterior for protection and appearance. Add fascia, corner boards and door trim as desired.

■ Provide bedding—hay, straw, cedar shavings or blankets—to help ward off cold, dampness and wind.

■ Face the door away from prevailing winds. A door flap (required in some states) also helps keep the place cozy. Locate the house in the shade to help your dog stay cool.

Sizing your doghouse

Bigger isn't better when it comes to doghouses. You want to provide a shelter large enough so your pet can easily enter it and turn around, but small enough so your dog's own body heat can warm the place. There's no need to make room for a hot tub or overnight guests.

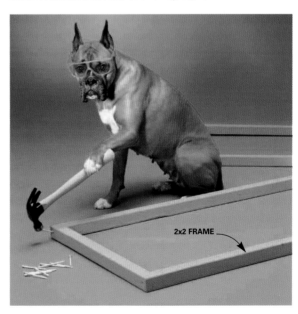

2x2 FRAME

1 Nail together the 2x2s that make up the floor and roof support frames. The corners can be mitered (as we show) or square-cut.

Figure A: Doghouse overview

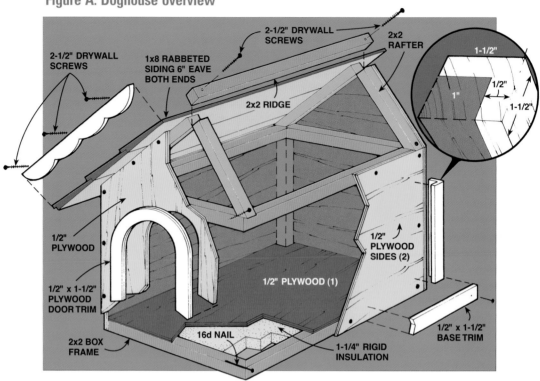

- 2-1/2" DRYWALL SCREWS
- 1x8 RABBETED SIDING 6" EAVE BOTH ENDS
- 2-1/2" DRYWALL SCREWS
- 2x2 RAFTER
- 2x2 RIDGE
- 1-1/2"
- 1/2"
- 1"
- 1-1/2"
- 2-1/2" DRYWALL SCREWS
- 1/2" PLYWOOD
- 1/2" PLYWOOD SIDES (2)
- 1/2" x 1-1/2" PLYWOOD DOOR TRIM
- 1/2" PLYWOOD (1)
- 2x2 BOX FRAME
- 16d NAIL
- 1-1/4" RIGID INSULATION
- 1/2" x 1-1/2" BASE TRIM

Following are rules of thumb to take into account when designing your doghouse:

- **Length:** 1-1/2 times the length of your dog (not including tail).
- **Width:** 3/4 to 2/3 the length of your dog (not including tail).
- **Height:** About 1/4 taller than dog (from top of head to paws while standing).
- **Door opening:** 2 to 3 in. taller and wider than the dog's measurements at the shoulder.

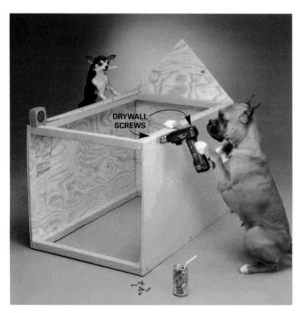

2 Secure the plywood walls to the 2x2 frames and to one another using drywall screws. Add optional 2x2 uprights at the corners for strength and weathertightness (see Figure A).

DRYWALL SCREWS

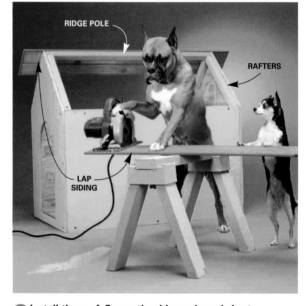

RIDGE POLE

RAFTERS

LAP SIDING

3 Install the roof. Screw the ridge pole and short rafters to the gable ends first. Install the rabbeted lap siding, starting at the top and working down for a tight-fitting ridge.

Fire&Ice
GreatGoofs®

Hot pants!

Working down a list of weekend chores, I found myself on a stepladder changing the 9-volt in a smoke detector. After I stuck the new battery into the unit, I slipped the old one into my pants pocket and headed off to the hardware store for my next task.

On the drive, I felt a strange warmth on my thigh. It quickly escalated to dang hot and then there was a worrisome burning smell. I screeched to a stop on the side of the road and hopped out of my truck and my pants.

Pocket change had shorted out the not-so-dead battery terminals, making the coins hot enough to char clear through the lining of my pants and singe a few leg hairs.

Now I know where the Energizer Bunny gets the spring in its step.

Turn down the heat

After trimming an overgrown tree in my yard, I piled the limbs into the backyard about 20 ft. from my garage. On a calm day a couple of weeks later, I decided to burn the pile. To be safe, I had the garden hose ready. The fire started just fine but soon it was so hot that I had to step back a bit. This hot fire didn't last long and when it was nearly out, I turned around toward the garage. Yikes! The vinyl siding on the whole side near the fire was curled and melted from the heat. I'm now doing a project that wasn't on my list.

Light my fire

Many years ago, my wife and I lived in a very small house with only one electrical circuit. We decided to add a receptacle in the ceiling so she could iron in the laundry room. I turned off the power, lit a candle for light and got right to work.

Soon my wife and boys were complaining about the smell of something burning. But I assured them the power was off and there was nothing to worry about. As I spoke, they all said in unison, "Your pants are on fire." I'd backed into the candle and the seat of my corduroys started smoldering. For my next project, my wife volunteered to hold a flashlight!

Those helpful neighbors

We used to live in a friendly Ohio neighborhood where people socialized and were quick to lend a helping hand. For a winter celebration, we once all lined our driveways and sidewalks with candle-lit paper bag luminaries. The white bags were carefully packed with candles in baby food jars and ballasted with cat litter so they wouldn't blow over.

Overnight we had an 8-in. snowfall and awoke to a winter wonderland—and the growl of my neighbor's snow blower accompanied by the tinkle of glass. He had forgotten all about the festivities as he kindly blew the snow from our drive—and spewed shredded bags, cat litter and broken jars all over our yard.

We enjoy our new home in Florida, but the neighbors aren't nearly as helpful.

Commode flambeau

A part from my young son's plastic potty had somehow gotten stuck in the toilet trap. I couldn't snake it out, nor could the plumber, who left saying, "Buy a new toilet." But I had a brilliant idea: I'd burn it out! I pulled the toilet and dragged it outside. There I poured charcoal lighter fluid down the trap and lit it up. Standing back, I basked in the glory of the geyser flames and my phenomenal ingenuity... until the bang. The commode literally cracked from the heat.

I bought a new toilet.

Frozen thinking

Not long ago, we decided to get a freezer for the basement. To get electricity to it, I tapped into an existing circuit and installed a new electrical box and receptacle. After plugging in the new freezer, we loaded it with food and it seemed to work fine. A couple of hours later, we checked it and discovered that the food was no colder than when we'd put it in. Disappointed, I called the appliance store and angrily told them the freezer didn't work. Later that night, it dawned on me that I'd wired the new receptacle from a basement light switch box. I got out of bed and checked out my theory. Sure enough, when I turned the light switch on, the freezer worked. The next morning I sheepishly called the dealer and told him that it was not his freezer that was awry but my own electrical skills!

Fire water

My 84-year-old mother decided to clear brush behind her house and burn it. She built a good, hot fire and was watching with satisfaction when a fountain of water sprang up in the middle of the flames. She thought she was seeing a miracle, a wonder of wonders—water and fire living together!

Then she remembered the plastic water pipe running right under that spot to the garden spigot.

No wonder.

Insulation conflagration

While paneling his basement, my neighbor drove a nail into a copper water pipe. No big deal. He just turned off the water, cut the pipe and slipped on a repair coupling. But while soldering, he set the insulation's paper facing on fire. As the small fire grew, he ran for the garden hose and his wife called 911. Only after dragging the hose into the basement did he remember that the water supply was off. Luckily, there was a fire extinguisher handy and he finished off the flames just as a fire truck arrived.

Pants aflame

As I was installing a basement water softener, my family started to complain about the water being shut off. Well, I tried to hurry.

I was holding a propane torch with one hand while trying to join the pipes with the other. No go—I needed both hands, so I tucked the flaming torch between my knees to free up my other one.

As I reached upward, the torch flipped downward and set my pants on fire! I swatted the fire out and did a fancy two-step to get my pants off. I spent the next hour in the tub soaking off the melted polyester that had stuck fast to my skin.

Luckily, I didn't have a serious burn. I have learned not to rush jobs—or at least to wear flame-retardant work duds when I do.

Great balls of fire

Last spring we found our house being invaded by mice. My husband went into the crawlspace below to see where the critters were getting in and found a hole under the pantry and near the water heater. Using an aerosol can of spray foam, he got to work filling the hole. The pilot light on the water heater suddenly ignited the foam and flames shot across the kitchen floor. I grabbed my son and flew out the door yelling to my husband. Luckily he was able to put out the small fire and no one was hurt. I later noticed the warning label on the can. Now we're a bit more careful about pilot lights and spraying foam just anywhere!

Crackpot idea

On a cold morning, my uncle's car was iced over. He had turned on the engine and defroster and started scraping, but the whole thing was taking too long. Then he had the brilliant idea of melting the ice by throwing a bucketful of hot water over the windshield. With a loud snap, the windshield cracked from end to end. After he had a new windshield installed, my uncle went back to scraping like the rest of us.

Broken toy box

The toys at my northern Michigan cabin were multiplying in the garage, so I decided it was time for an addition. I doubled the length of the garage, making it an end-to-end, two-car structure. To save money, I hand-framed the roof rather than use factory-built trusses. With all this extra garage space, I'd be able to buy even more toys!

After several snow and ice storms up north, I received a call from my neighbor, who asked the dreadful question, "Remember the garage you used to have?" The weight of the snow had caused the roof to cave in, crushing my speedboat, trailer, snow-mobiles and dirt bike inside. After careful forensic study, I figured the over-loaded rafters had pushed out the walls until the roof collapsed. Probably, I hadn't used enough crossties, leaving me with the lesson that a sturdy toy box is worth spending more for.

Great Goofs Special

Ladder launch

After a near hit by Hurricane Floyd, I decided to trim the deadwood from our live oak tree. One particular 15-ft. limb was just within reach of my extension ladder, so up I went. I decided to cut off about 8 ft. on my first cut. As that portion hit the ground, the remaining portion, on which my ladder rested, suddenly rose up, relieved of the weight of the end of the branch. My ladder was no longer "just within reach." On my way to the ground (without injury, thank goodness), I knew I had just experienced Great Goof material!

— Howard Creech

Bonus bun warmer

After living with reversed hot and cold faucets on our bathtub for years, I decided to fix them. As the tub has no plumbing access, I devised a plan that didn't require breaking into any walls. I would switch the hot and cold water lines to the bathroom in the basement where I had easy access. And I would then switch the lines under the vanity so the sink faucet still worked properly. Great plan. I completed the job in less than an hour. Later that day, my wife mentioned a vague warm sensation during her last visit to the bathroom. A quick investigation uncovered the reason—hot water in the toilet!

— Michael McGroary

Going down, anyone?

Because I use my unfinished attic space for storage, I laid boards across the joists in places to keep from stepping through the fragile drywall below. Last year, I went up there to grab a big box of Christmas lights and carry it down. As luck would have it, I stepped exactly where I shouldn't have. The board teetered and before I knew it I was headed straight through the drywall ceiling and into my daughter's bedroom. She let out a blood-curdling scream as I felt my pride disappear into the dust and debris surrounding me.

— Gilbert Casillas

INDEX

Visit thefamilyhandyman.com to search five years of article archives.

ACKNOWLEDGMENTS

FOR THE FAMILY HANDYMAN

Editor in Chief	Ken Collier
Senior Editors	Travis Larson
	Gary Wentz
Associate Editors	Elisa Bernick
	Mary Flanagan
	Jeff Gorton
	Brett Martin
	Eric Smith
Senior Copy Editor	Donna Bierbach
Design Director	Sara Koehler
Senior Art Director	Bob Ungar
Art Directors	Becky Pfluger
	Marcia Roepke
Photographer	Tom Fenenga
Office Administrative Manager	Alice Garrett
Financial Assistant	Steven Charbonneau
Reader Service Specialist	Roxie Filipkowski
Production Manager	Judy Rodriguez
Production Artist	Mary Schwender

CONTRIBUTING EDITORS

Bob Lacivita	Jeff Timm
Rick Muscoplat	Bruce Wiebe

CONTRIBUTING ART DIRECTORS

Kristi Anderson	David Simpson
Roberta Peters	

PHOTOGRAPHERS

Mike Krivit, Krivit Photography
Ramon Moreno
Bill Zuehlke

ILLUSTRATORS

Steve Björkman	Bruce Kieffer
Gabe De Matteis	Don Mannes
Roy Doty	Paul Perreault
Mario Ferro	Frank Rohrbach III
John Hartman	

OTHER CONSULTANTS

Charles Avoles, plumbing
Al Hildenbrand, electrical
Jon Jensen, carpentry
Bruce Kieffer, woodworking
Bob Lacivita, automotive
Dave MacDonald, structural engineer
Costas Stavrou, appliance repair
John Williamson, electrical
Butch Zang, painting and wallpapering
Les Zell, plumbing

To subscribe to *The Family Handyman* magazine:
- By phone: (800) 285-4961
- By Internet: FHMservice@rd.com
- By mail: The Family Handyman
  Subscriber Service Dept.
  P.O. Box 8174
  Red Oak, IA 51591-1174

Also Available from Reader's Digest

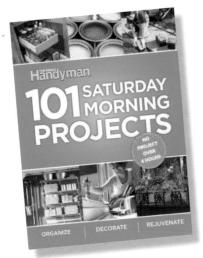

101 Saturday Morning Projects

From the experts at *The Family Handyman*—the #1 home improvement magazine—here are more than 100 do-it-yourself projects ideal for every homeowner or apartment dweller. Each project can be completed in a half day or less.

ISBN 978-1-60652-018-5
$14.95 USA

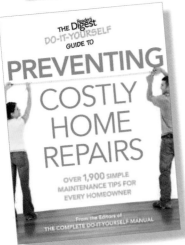

The Reader's Digest Do-It-Yourself Guide to Preventing Costly Home Repairs

Easy fix-its, touch-ups, and make-rights for the most common trouble spots in your home, condo, or co-op—perfect solutions to correcting problems confidently, efficiently, and economically. You'll save thousands of dollars in preventable damage with more than 1,900 practical tips.

ISBN 978-1-60652-022-2
$16.95 USA

Save Energy, Save Money!

Based on the latest ideas and newest technology in energy-efficient home-management, this essential guide from the experts at *The Family Handyman* will show you how to save money based on the condition and location of your home, your budget, and your skill level.

ISBN 13: 978-0-7621-0902-9
$17.95 USA

Reader's Digest books can be purchased through retail and online bookstores.
In the United States books are distributed by Penguin Group (USA), Inc.
For more information or to order books, call 1-800-788-6262.